Shielding the Poor

Social Protection in the Developing World

Nora Lustig
Editor

Brookings Institution Press

Inter-American Development Bank

Washington, D.C.
2001

Copyright © 2001
INTER-AMERICAN DEVELOPMENT BANK
All rights reserved. No part of this publication may be reproduced or transmitted in any form or by any means without permission in writing from the Brookings Institution Press.
e-mail: permissions@brook.edu; fax: (202) 797-6195

To order this book, contact:

IDB Bookstore
1300 New York Avenue, N.W.
Washington, D.C. 20577
Tel: 1-877-PUBS IDB/(202) 623-1753
Fax: (202) 623-1709
E-mail: idb-books@iadb.org
www.iadb.org/pub

Brookings Institution Press
1775 Massachusetts Avenue, N.W.
Washington, D.C. 20036
Tel: 1-800-275-1447 / (202) 797-6258
Fax (202) 797-2960
www.brookings.edu
e-mail: bibooks@brookings.edu

Library of Congress Cataloging-in-Publication data

Shielding the poor: social protection in the developing world / Nora
Lustig, editor.
    p. cm.
Includes bibliographical references and index.
  ISBN 0-8157-5321-7 (pbk. : alk. paper)
 1. Poor—Developing countries. 2. Public welfare—Developing
countries. 3. Poverty—Developing countries. 4. Human
services—Developing countries. 5. Structural adjustment (Economic
policy)—Social aspects—Developing countries. I. Lustig, Nora.
  HV525 .S54 2000   00-010531
  362.5'8'091724Cdc21   CIP

The paper used in this publication meets minimum requirements of the American National Standard for Information Sciences—Permanence of Paper for Printed Library Materials— ANSI.48-1992

Printed by R. R. Donnelley and Sons
Harrisonburg, Virginia

Contents

Preface   v

1. Introduction   1
   Nora Lustig

2. Has Aggregate Income Growth Been Effective in Reducing
   Poverty and Inequality in Latin America?   21
   Alain de Janvry and Elisabeth Sadoulet

3. Social Protection for the Unemployed: Programs in Latin America   41
   Gustavo Márquez

4. Heterogeneity and Optimal Unemployment Insurance   63
   Hugo A. Hopenhayn and Juan Pablo Nicolini

5. Helping the Poor Manage Risk Better: The Role of Social Funds   91
   Steen Lau Jørgensen and Julie Van Domelen

6. Insuring the Economic Costs of Illness   109
   Paul Gertler

7. Coverage under Old Age Security Programs and Protection
   for the Uninsured: What Are the Issues?   149
   Estelle James

8. Social Assistance on Pensions and Health Care for the Poor
   in Latin America and the Caribbean   175
   Carmelo Mesa-Lago

9. The Safety Net Role of Microfinance for Income
   and Consumption Smoothing   217
   Manfred Zeller

10. Consumption Smoothing and Extended Families:
    The Role of Government-Sponsored Insurance   239
    Orazio Attanasio and José-Víctor Ríos-Rull

11. Social Protection for the Poor in the Developed World   267
    Timothy M. Smeeding and Katherin Ross Phillips

Authors   309

Index   311

Preface

Most countries in the developing world do not have effective mechanisms in place for softening the impact of adverse shocks on the poor. The contributions presented in *Shielding the Poor: Social Protection in the Developing World* explain why the poor are particularly vulnerable to adverse shocks and discuss appropriate policy responses for minimizing the impact of shocks on poverty and how to exploit the growth-enhancing elements of safety nets and social protection more generally. The volume covers a broad range of issues in the social protection agenda, including an analysis of the empirical evidence of the impact of shocks on poverty and inequality in Latin America, unemployment insurance and employment programs, the safety net role of microfinance, the role of social investment funds in helping the poor manage risk, old age security for the poor, the impact of health shocks on the poor, and lessons learned from social protection programs in the developed world.

The articles included in this book were presented at the conference, "Social Protection and Poverty," held at the Inter-American Development Bank (IDB) in February 1999 in Washington, D.C. The authors benefited greatly from comments by the discussants who participated in the conference, including Marguerite Berger, Gary Burtless, Gaurav Datt, Ruthanne Deutsch, Christiaan Grootaert, Carmen Pagés, Inder Ruprah, William Savedoff, Miguel Székely, and Andras Uthoff, as well as from anonymous reviewers.

Many people collaborated in the preparation of this volume. In particular, Alexander Kazan coordinated the logistics of the editorial process with the support of Gustavo Yamada and Daniel Myers. Celine Charveriat—with the collaboration of Ellen Connors and Heather McPhail—was the logistics coordinator of the conference and was supported by Miguel Almeyda, Soledad Bustos, César Cantú, Laura Sotomayor, and Luis Tejerina. We would like to thank Sandra Gain from the Publications Section of the IDB for her editorial input. We extend our warm appreciation to the Brookings Institution Press, especially Christopher Kelaher, acquisitions editor, and Janet Walker, managing editor. Theresa Walker edited the manuscript, Tanjam Jacobson proofread it, and Shirley Kessel prepared the index.

CHAPTER ONE

Introduction

Nora Lustig

Social protection consists of the set of public initiatives that can lessen the impact of adverse shocks on the income of the population. In more technical terms, social protection is the set of public interventions designed to assist individuals and households in better managing economic risks. These interventions typically include labor market interventions, social safety nets, and pensions. They also include public actions aimed at reducing risk such as prudent fiscal policy to prevent macroeconomic crises, large-scale reforestation to prevent natural disasters, or public health campaigns to reduce the incidence of illness. Measures designed to better equip the population to protect itself such as building a more solid asset base (through land distribution and titling, for example) and access to credit and insurance markets belong to the social protection agenda as well.

The primary focus of this book is not social protection in general but social protection for the poor in the context of a developing country. That is, we are concerned with providing social protection to the segment of the population that has little or no access to state-sponsored social insurance schemes (because it does not participate in a contributory system because of legal or de facto restrictions) or private market insurance or credit mechanisms (because of "cream skimming" practices and moral hazard issues); cannot save in adequate amounts precisely because it is poor; and has little or no voice to demand the protection of pro-poor programs and the implementation of safety nets in times of fiscal retrenchment. The mechanisms considered are those that serve to smooth downward risks, that is, adverse shocks.

The key objectives of social protection for the poor can be summarized as follows:

- To lessen the vulnerability of the poor through ex ante measures that reduce the occurrence of adverse shocks or mitigate their impact, and through ex post measures that help the poor to maintain adequate consumption and access to basic services once the shock occurs.

• To allow for better consumption smoothing over the life cycle of poor families through market and nonmarket mechanisms.

• To enhance equity by ensuring that the poor are not disproportionately exposed or hurt by adverse shocks.[1]

Why may social protection for the poor be an important concern for policymakers? One obvious reason is because policy interventions can improve the well-being of the poor simply by preventing sharp downfalls in income or consumption. Poor people in the developing world give high priority to economic security.[2] Empirical studies show that large fluctuations in income are common for the poor and that a large proportion of people fall into poverty at one point or another in their lives.[3] Large aggregate shocks such as economywide crises result in sharp increases in poverty (table 1–1). As seen in table 1–2, panel data indicate that the share of households that are "sometimes poor" is considerable and almost always exceeds the proportion of households that are "always poor." Because the poor are less equipped to smooth consumption, income downfalls will translate into large consumption downfalls.[4]

However, an equally compelling reason is that social protection can be growth enhancing as well. If the poor have access to mechanisms that protect them from sharp downfalls in income, they will be more likely to undertake riskier initiatives in the production and labor market spheres, and these initiatives could result in a higher return for the poor and for the economy overall. Similarly, if social protection helps prevent or at least mitigates irreversible damage to the accumulation of human capital (such as a rise in abusive child labor, malnutrition, or school dropouts), it will also be beneficial for overall growth and contribute to poverty reduction on a more permanent basis and not just during the period of the shock. In table 1–3 we present examples of the impact of economic crises on education and health and nutrition indicators.[5] Christiaan Grootaert finds that in Côte d'Ivoire, in re-

---

[1] See World Bank (1999a, p. 14).

[2] World Bank (1999b, 2000a).

[3] World Bank (2000b, chap. 8). At the more microeconomic level, Townsend (1994) finds that the coefficients of variation of income from the main crops in two Indian villages are between .37 and 1.01.

[4] Jalan and Ravallion (1997), for example, show that 40 percent of an income shock is passed on as lower consumption for the poorest 10 percent of households in China, while for the richest third only 10 percent is passed on.

[5] See also Lustig (1995, 1999).

Table 1–1. Poverty Headcount Ratio Before, During, and After Crisis

Country	Year of crisis	Before crisis Ratio	Before crisis Year	During crisis Ratio	During crisis Change	After crisis Ratio	After crisis Year	After crisis Change	Change in GDP per capita relative to year Of crisis	Change in GDP per capita relative to year Before crisis
Argentina (Greater Buenos Aires)	1985	10.1	1980	20.6	+	25.2	1987	+	+	−
Argentina (Greater Buenos Aires)	1989	25.2	1987	47.3	+	33.7	1990	+	+	−
Argentina (Greater Buenos Aires)	1995	16.8	1993	24.8	+	26.0	1997	+	+	+
Brazil (all metropolitan areas)	1990	27.9	1989	28.9	+					
Chile (metropolitan areas) §	1982	40.3	1980			48.6	1987	+	+	−
Costa Rica *	1982	29.6	1981	32.3	+	29.7	1983	+	+	−
Dominican Republic *	1985	37.3	1984			38.2	1986	+	+	+
Dominican Republic *	1990	35.7	1989			39.5	1992	+	+	−
Guatemala §	1982	65.0	1980	18.9		68.0	1986	+	−	−
Indonesia *	1998	11.3	1996	16.7	+	11.7	1999			
Jordan *	1989	3.0	1987			14.9	1992	+	+	+
Korea (urban) *	1998	8.6	1997	19.2	+					
Mexico	1986	28.5	1984			32.6	1989	+	+	+
Mexico §	1995	36.0	1994			43.0	1996	+	+	−
Panama *	1983	40.6	1980			44.0	1986	+	−	−
Panama *	1988	44.0	1986			50.0	1989	+	−	−
Peru §	1983	46.0	1979			52.0	1986	+	+	−
Peru (urban) *	1988	32.2	1985			50.0	1991	+	−	−
Russia **	1998	21.9	1996	32.7	+					
Thailand	1998	11.4	1996	12.9	+			+		
Uruguay §	1982	11.0	1981			15.0	1986	+	−	−
Venezuela §	1983	25.7	1982	32.7	+	34.8	1985	+	−	−
Venezuela §	1989	40.0	1988	44.4	+	41.5	1990	+	+	−
Venezuela §	1994	41.4	1993	53.6	+	48.2	1996	+	−	−

+ Increase.
− Decrease.
§ Based on household income.
* Based on per capita expenditure.
** Based on household expenditure.
Note: Headcount based on individual per capita household income and national poverty lines unless otherwise noted. For Argentina, Brazil, Chile, Korea, and Peru there was no information at the national level.
Source: World Bank (2000a); real GDP per capita data from World Bank (2000b); for Argentina, Ministerio de Economía de Argentina (1998) and Morley and Alvarez (1992); for Brazil, Barros, Mendonça, and Rocha (1995); for Chile, Lustig (1995, table 1–1); for Costa Rica, the Dominican Republic, and Panama, Londoño and Székely (1997); for Guatemala, Peru (1983), and Uruguay, ECLAC (1996); for Indonesia, Korea, and Thailand, World Bank (1999a); for Jordan, World Bank (1994); for Mexico (1986), Lustig and Székely (1998); for Mexico (1995), ECLAC (1999); for Peru (1988), Escobal, Saavedra, and Torero (1998); for Russia, Lokshin and Ravallion (2000); and for Venezuela, Ruprah and Marcano (1998).

Table 1–2. Households by Poverty Status in Selected Developing Countries, Various Years

Percent

Country	Period	Always poor	Sometimes poor	Never poor
China	1985–90	6.2	47.8	46.0
Côte d'Ivoire	1987–88	25.0	22.0	53.0
Ethiopia	1994–97	24.8	30.1	45.1
Pakistan	1986–91	3.0	55.3	41.7
Russian Federation	1992–93	12.6	30.2	57.2
South Africa	1993–98	22.7	31.5	45.8
Zimbabwe	1992/93–1995/96	10.6	59.6	29.8

Source: Baulch and Hoddinott (forthcoming).

sponse to a severe economic recession, the poorest households increased the labor force participation of children the most. Hanan Jacoby and Emmanuel Skoufias find that in rural India households used child labor as a way to respond to seasonal income fluctuations. In Zimbabwe, John Hoddinott and Bill Kinsey find that the 1994–95 droughts reduced annual growth rates of the height of small children.[6] These responses show how transient shocks can affect the ability of the children of poor families to grow out of poverty when they reach adulthood.

Finally, if the poor are protected from the income variability associated with openness and flexible labor markets, they are more likely to support stabilization programs and growth-enhancing reforms. Recent work has shown that the combination of weak institutions—including among them the lack of adequate social safety nets—and divided societies lies at the bottom of the growth collapses experienced in the past twenty-five years.[7]

A TYPOLOGY OF ADVERSE SHOCKS

Although adverse shocks are accompanied by a downturn in income or consumption, they are not all economic in origin. Economic shocks are those resulting from macroeconomic mismanagement, terms-of-trade shocks, volatility in capital flows,

---

[6] Grootaert (1998); Jacoby and Skoufias (1997); Hoddinott and Kinsey (1998).

[7] Rodrik (1997).

Table 1–3. Health and Educational Impact of Economic Crisis

	Argentina, 1995	Mexico, 1995	Indonesia, 1998
Main crisis indicators	Per capita GDP fell 4.1 percent. Per capita private consumption fell 5.6 percent.	Per capita GDP fell 7.8 percent. Per capita private consumption fell 11.1 percent.	Per capita GDP fell 14.6 percent. Per capita private consumption fell 5.1 percent.
Health	Per capita daily protein intake fell 3.8 percent in 1995 but increased 1.9 percent in 1996.	Among children under age 1, mortality from anemia increased from 6.3 deaths per 100,000 live births in 1993 to 7.9 in 1995. Among children age 1–4, the rate rose from 1.7 to 2.2.	The share of women whose body mass index is below the level at which morbidity and mortality risks increase was 25 percent. Most indicators of child nutritional status remained constant. The exception may be the weight (conditional on height) of children under age 3, suggesting that families may be investing in some members at the expense of others.
Education	Growth in gross primary enrollment declined from 2.2 percent in 1993 to 0.8 percent in 1996.	Gross primary school enrollment increased 0.44 percent in 1994 but fell 0.09 percent in 1995.	The dropout rates for children age 7–12 in the poorest quartile rose from 1.3 percent in 1997 to 7.5 percent in 1998. For children age 13–19, the rate rose from 14.2 percent to 25.5 percent. In both cohorts, the poorest quartile experienced the largest increase in dropout rates. The share of children age 7–12 in the poorest quartile not enrolled in school rose from 4.9 percent in 1997 to 10.7 percent in 1998. For children age 13–19, the rate rose from 42.5 to 58.4 percent. In both cohorts, the poorest quartile experienced the largest increase.

Source: World Bank (2000b).

and so on. Physical shocks include ill health, disability, and death in the family as well as large-scale epidemics. Natural shocks include droughts, pests, hurricanes, floods, and earthquakes. Social or political shocks include wars, conflicts, massive strikes, upheavals, and violence in various forms (domestic or otherwise). Environmental shocks include pollution, deforestation, and nuclear disasters. Table 1–4 summarizes the types of shocks that people may face.

Depending on the number of individuals or households that are simultaneously affected, shocks are either idiosyncratic or covariate (aggregate) (table 1–4). Idiosyncratic shocks are those that occur when only one or a few individuals or households in a community suffer losses. Typical idiosyncratic shocks are noncommunicative illness or frictional unemployment. Covariate shocks occur when large numbers of households are hit at the same time. Covariate shocks can affect entire villages, communities, or regions within a country as occurs, for example, with climatic events, downsizing of the public sector, and sharp capital outflows or terms-of-trade shocks. Entire countries are affected by economywide crises such as financial meltdowns and large-scale natural disasters such as El Niño; and groups of countries experienced the debt crisis of the 1980s. The global economy felt the impact of the Great Depression and the two world wars.

Some types of shocks are few and far between, such as the death of the breadwinner of a household, and others occur with frequency, such as a bad crop because of weather conditions. Some shocks are serially correlated. For example, natural disasters can be followed by sickness and death, compounding the initial impact of the environmental event.

Some shocks, even if they are infrequent, have a long-lasting effect, such as death or disability of the breadwinner or technological redundancy of skills. Such *catastrophic* adverse shocks may require permanent transfers to the affected households. There are other shocks that might be of high frequency but whose effects are not very severe, such as transient illness or temporary unemployment. In such cases the required relief is temporary.

STRATEGIES FOR MANAGING ADVERSE SHOCKS

The strategies for managing adverse shocks can be classified into three categories: nonmarket, market-based, and publicly mandated or provided (table 1–5). *Nonmarket* arrangements include the safety nets provided by social networks such as marriage, the extended family, and mutual community support, as well as the self-insurance mechanisms used by individuals and households, such as saving in

Table 1–4. Main Sources of Risk

Type of risk	At the household or individual level (idiosyncratic)	At the community level (covariate)	At the nationwide level (covariate)
Natural	Rainfall	Earthquakes Landslides Volcanic eruption	Floods Drought High winds
Health	Illness Injury Disability Old age Death	Epidemic	
Social	Crime Domestic violence	Terrorism Gangs	Civil strife War Social upheaval
Economic	Frictional unemployment	Resettlement Harvest failure	Growth collapse Balance-of-payments, financial, or currency crisis Technology- or trade- induced terms-of-trade shocks
Political		Riots	Political default on social programs Coup d'état
Environmental	Pollution	Pollution Deforestation Nuclear disaster	

Source: Adapted from World Bank (2000); Holzmann and Jørgensen (2000); Sinha and Lipton (1999).

the form of goods and real assets (food, farm animals, land), crop and field diversification, the use of safer technology, labor market decisions (migration, occupational choice, labor force participation), schooling decisions, and so on. *Market-based* arrangements include financial intermediaries and insurance companies. *Publicly mandated* or provided arrangements include the rules and regulations that mandate or provide insurance for unemployment, old age, disability, survivorship, accident and sickness. They also include the array of safety nets and social assistance programs designed to ameliorate the impact of adverse shocks on the poor regardless of their origin.

By their very nature the poor in developing countries are more likely to rely on nonmarket and self-insurance arrangements. Because of market failures arising from asymmetric information, moral hazard, and "cream skimming" practices, the poor are less likely to have access to formal credit and insurance markets. But while some informal and self-insurance arrangements might be effective for coping with idiosyncratic shocks, their effectiveness against covariate shocks is limited. Informal or self-insurance arrangements may be suboptimal even in the case of idiosyncratic shocks because they could result in lower potential incomes such as would be the case with safer but less productive technologies, inefficient crop and field diversification, or the decision to discontinue school attendance. In all such cases public intervention is warranted to improve the access of the poor to market-based arrangements and to reduce the use of self-destructive informal and self-insurance schemes to cope with adverse shocks.[8]

Government action is also fundamental in the prevention of adverse shocks. Reducing the likelihood of adverse shocks includes, for example, measures in the international financial architecture and economic policy realm for preventing economywide crises; environmental and population measures to reduce the likelihood that an environmental-climatic event results in a calamity; and public health policy to reduce the occurrence of preventable health shocks.

The purpose of this book is to discuss alternative interventions that can reduce and mitigate the impact of adverse shocks on the poor as well as allow for better consumption smoothing over the life cycle of poor families in the most efficient way. The latter implies paying particular attention in designing the interventions so as to exploit the growth-enhancing elements of safety nets, minimize leakage of the benefits to the nonpoor (targeting issues), and avoid perverse incentives. Essentially, the book will concentrate on the italicized concepts in table 1–5, that is, publicly provided risk-coping measures, such as employment programs and social assistance for health shocks and old age; and risk reduction and mitigation instruments, such as microfinance and social investment funds. It will also include a discussion of social protection programs in the developed world and the

---

[8] Extreme cases of self-destructive behavior in coping with shocks exist throughout the world. In India, for instance, it was discovered that poor women were forfeiting a kidney to pay back money they had borrowed to feed their families (University of California, 1999).

Table 1–5. Mechanisms for Managing Risk

	Informal mechanisms		Formal mechanisms	
	Individual and household	Group based	Market-based	Publicly provided
Risk reduction	Preventive health practices Migration Less risky income sources	Collective action for infrastructure, dikes, terraces Common property resource management		Sound macro-economic policy Environmental policy Education and training policy Public health policy Infrastructure (dams, roads) Labor market policies
Risk mitigation				
Portfolio diversification	Crop and plot diversification Income source diversification Investment in physical and human capital	Occupational associations Rotating savings and credit associations	Savings accounts in financial institutions *Microfinance*	Agricultural extension Open up trade opportunities Protection of property rights
Insurance	Marriage and extended family Sharecrop tenancy Buffer stocks	Investment in social capital (networks, associations, rituals, reciprocal gift giving)	Old age annuities Accident and disability insurance	*Pension systems Unemployment insurance* Health and disability insurance
Risk coping	Sale of assets Loans from moneylenders Child labor Reduced food consumption	Transfers from networks of mutual support	Sale of financial assets Loans from financial institutions	*Social assistance Workfare* Subsidies *Social funds* Cash transfers

Source: World Bank (2000a, chap. 8); adapted from Holzmann and Jørgensen (2000).

role of informal safety nets. Although the topics covered are by no means exhaustive, the chapters provide lessons from experience and a good overview of the issues that policymakers will have to face in designing appropriate ways of shielding the poor from adverse shocks.[9] While a few of the chapters are very technical in nature, others are primarily descriptive and accessible to a wide audience. The more technical chapters show the elements that have to be considered when attempting to strike a balance between social protection and efficiency.

Because of its focus on the uninsured poor, this book has great relevance for developing countries and a very limited one, if any, for the industrial world. As development proceeds in the less developed world, one would expect to see a transition away from self-insurance and social assistance to market-based risk management strategies and publicly provided social risk management instruments such as sick pay, health care, disability and old-age insurance, and unemployment insurance. One key question is what set of policies can accelerate the process of formalizing the informal labor market. A common view is that many of the labor market regulations designed to protect the labor force from abuse are major impediments to the latter because their costs and design make it rational to evade and avoid those regulations. Although of utmost importance, this discussion has been dealt with elsewhere and will not be a topic of this book.[10] Two other areas are not addressed: weak institutions and weak public finances. Although the latter are usually cited as a reason for not implementing more aggressive publicly funded consumption smoothing mechanisms, evidence shows that this factor has been exaggerated.

A ROAD MAP

The chapters in this book address various topics: the impact of economic crises on poverty and inequality and the importance of a safety net to shield poor people from their impact; mechanisms to address unemployment; health shocks and old age among the poor; the role of social funds as safety nets; microfinance to smooth consumption; and lessons from the developed world.

---

[9] For a broader discussion of risks and social protection, see Inter-American Development Bank (2000) and World Bank (2000a, chaps. 8, 9).

[10] See, for example, Edwards and Lustig (1997).

The Costs of Economic Crises

Chapter two, by Alain de Janvry and Elisabeth Sadoulet, shows how economywide crises in Latin America can result not only in sharp increases in poverty but also in inequality, making it harder to reduce poverty in the future even if growth at previous levels is resumed.[11] Using data for 48 growth and recession spells for 12 countries in Latin America between 1970 and 1994, the authors find that "there are strong asymmetries in the relation between income and poverty/inequality according to growth episode: recession is systematically devastating on poverty and inequality." They find that a 1-percent decline in per capita gross domestic product during the 1980s eliminated the gains in urban (rural) poverty reduction achieved by 3.7 (2) percent growth in the 1970s. Recession episodes in the 1980s were found to have a strong ratchet effect on inequality, since the higher level of inequality is not reversed with subsequent growth.

These results, together with those shown in table 1–1, should suffice to demonstrate how important it is for countries to reduce the likelihood of economic crises. They also indicate the importance of *countering* with the appropriate countercyclical safety nets to help the poor cope with the impact of economic crises. Pro-poor programs must be protected from budget cuts when a nation is introducing fiscal austerity measures to restore macroeconomic balance.[12]

Unemployment Insurance and Employment Programs

In chapter three Gustavo Márquez succinctly describes existing programs and their limitations in the region. During the 1990s Latin America experienced very high unemployment rates in general. According to data from the Economic Commission for Latin America and the Caribbean, the open unemployment rate in Latin America (excluding the Caribbean) reached 8.4 percent in 1998, up from 5.8 percent in 1992.[13] Furthermore, 12 out of 22 countries in the region with regular data

[11] That crises result in increases in inequality is not always the case. Economic downturns in the recent East Asian crises, for example, have not been accompanied by a rise in inequality. Sometimes inequality falls during a crisis.

[12] For more on this subject, see Lustig (1995, 2000); Inter-American Development Bank (2000, chaps. 1, 5); World Bank (2000a, chap. 9).

[13] ECLAC (1999).

had an unemployment rate close to or above 10 percent in 1997.[14] What is striking from this overview is how limited is the protection awarded for unemployment hazards in a region that has been facing major structural changes resulting from the introduction of market-oriented reforms and recurrent economic downturns. Although part of the unemployment problem would be solved if hiring and firing become less restrictive and costly, some of the available evidence does not indicate that the gains from reforming the labor market regulations would be large.[15]

In chapter four Hugo A. Hopenhayn and Juan Pablo Nicolini use modern optimal contract theory to discuss what the effects of heterogeneity are on the design of an optimal unemployment insurance scheme. Heterogeneity is understood in two senses: systematic differences in workers' reemployment rates and cyclical variations in reemployment probabilities. The authors find that for workers whose reemployment rates differ because of age and skill differences—but not in search effort—unemployment benefits should have a steeper profile: that is, they should be reduced more quickly. Overall, higher-risk workers—that is, those with lower reemployment probabilities—should have more lifetime coverage than low-risk workers. The authors also find that it is optimal to fully insure all aggregate risk and that the reemployment tax should be lowered during recessions. When recessions mostly affect baseline reemployment probabilities, the benefits should be decreased more slowly.

Hopenhayn and Nicolini's analysis allows us to interpret the advantages of workfare and training programs in a new light. It is very hard to monitor the employment status of workers in the informal sector. A very strong incentive problem occurs because an unemployed worker receiving benefits would not have incentives to report having found a job. One way to cope with this problem is to require that beneficiaries of the program follow a schedule, for instance, do public works. Examples are workfare programs such as the Maharashtra employment program in India, *Trabajar* in Argentina, and the minimum employment program in Chile in the past.[16] Furthermore, if the nonlabor costs are decentralized to the operating unit of the program, the monitoring of the employment status of the beneficiary is done in an incentive-compatible way. The operating unit finds it in its best interest to enforce the participation of the worker. In other words, workfare

---

[14] The countries are Argentina, Barbados, Colombia, Dominican Republic, Ecuador, Jamaica, Nicaragua, Panama, Peru, Trinidad and Tobago, Uruguay, and Venezuela.

[15] See Kugler (1999).

[16] See Lipton (1996); Ravallion (1998); Subbarao and others (1997).

programs can be interpreted as an unemployment insurance contract with a technology to monitor the employment status of the beneficiary. An alternative way of monitoring would be to require workers to attend training programs. The main objective of such programs may not be the productivity-enhancing effects but the monitoring services they supply.

Social Investment Funds

Chapter five by Steen Lau Jørgensen and Julie Van Domelen shows how to help the poor better manage risks by building up their social capital and physical infrastructure. Social funds are agencies that finance demand-driven projects in several sectors targeted to benefit a country's poor and vulnerable; these projects must meet a set of eligibility criteria. The first fund was established in Bolivia in 1987. At present there are social funds in almost all countries in Latin America and the Caribbean, Africa, the Middle East, Eastern Europe, Central Asia, and a few in Asia. Most of the funds have focused on building or refurbishing social infrastructure, particularly health posts, schools, and water supply and sanitation. Originally, the social funds were set up to provide temporary employment and relief from a crisis situation through labor-based income transfers and subsidization of social services and infrastructure. Although social funds continue to respond to emergency situations, such as Hurricane Mitch in Central America, fall-out from the wars in Cambodia and Angola, an earthquake in Armenia, or a drought in Zambia, they are evolving into permanent structures with multiple objectives. Nevertheless, for social funds to fulfill their emergency and nonemergency roles a number of institutional changes will have to be introduced. Systematic impact evaluation studies are also needed to identify what works best in the implementation of social funds.

The authors argue in favor of rethinking the use of social funds in the broader context of a social risk management framework. Community development funds, decentralization funds, and infrastructure funds can be used to reduce and mitigate risks by, for example, building earthquake proof buildings and dams, introducing reforestation programs, helping households relocate to safer areas, and so on to reduce the risk of natural disasters. Social funds can strengthen the informal networks and support risk-mitigating strategies of informal insurance. Employment generation and social assistance funds can provide sources of livelihood to communities hit by an adverse situation and protect the human capital (nutrition, health, and education) of the children of communities hit by a shock.

Coping with Health Shocks

In chapter six Paul Gertler compares the welfare gains from providing social insurance for major illness versus small health shocks.

Major or catastrophic illness has two important economic costs for households: the cost of medical care used to diagnose and treat the illness and the loss in income associated with reduced labor supply and productivity. Given the high cost and unpredictability of major illness, poor families in developing countries may not be able to smooth their consumption. Drawing on panel data for China and Indonesia, Gertler shows that while households are able to insure (through the mechanisms mentioned above) the economic costs of small health shocks, they are not able to insure against the costs of major or catastrophic illness. The results of the empirical exercise show that reducing the variation in income associated with major illness can have large welfare gains. Since poor families in developing countries do not have access to formal insurance owing to market failures (or, even if they could have access, they may not be able to afford it), there is a role for social insurance for income loss because of disability and medical care expenses. However, the fact that households are able to insure against the costs of small health shocks suggests that relying on user fees to expand publicly delivered health care services will have little impact on welfare.

Averting an Old-Age Crisis for the Poor

Estelle James points out in chapter seven that the majority of workers and old people in developing countries are not covered by formal social security programs. Coverage rates range from less that 10 percent in Sub-Saharan Africa and South Asia and less than 30 percent in most of East Asia, to 50 to 60 percent in middle-income countries in South America, and 70 to 80 percent in Eastern European transition economies. The uninsured fall into two categories: workers who have jobs that are not covered by contributory programs (self-employed rural workers and workers in small firms, for example); and women who have worked in the household rather than in the labor market for most of their lives.

As development proceeds, coverage will rise, but to achieve near full coverage will take quite some time. Until that happens, a large portion of the population will remain uninsured or partially so. While recent pension reforms tying benefits more closely to contributions are desirable from the point of view of incentives and fiscal soundness of the contributory systems, they may reduce coverage among the poor. In particular, benefits are reduced substantially for those who contribute for only part of their working lives, hence they may not be eligible for the redistributive pillar of the new pension systems. Because the minimum amount of years that workers must have contributed is rather large, workers who do not anticipate such a long participation in a contributory system or in the labor market will have an incentive to stay out of the system.

James proposes the implementation of the requirement to purchase survivors' benefits and joint annuities to cover the spouses who worked in the home as part of the household division of labor. For workers who participated in noncovered jobs and were too poor to save for old age, social assistance is essential. To reduce moral hazard problems, social assistance should be financed out of general revenues and should offer less than the redistribution given to the low-income groups who participate in contributory systems.

In chapter eight Carmelo Mesa-Lago provides an overview of the characteristics of social protection programs for health and old age. While some countries have very developed national health systems, a recurrent problem is that coverage in the rural areas is lower and poorer in quality than in urban areas (the incidence of poverty is higher in rural areas and most of the poor live in rural areas in the poorest countries of the region). The author advocates establishing national health care systems that cover all the population and argues in favor of using government resources in the prevention of health hazards by such means as vaccination campaigns, health education, potable water, and sewerage systems. The latter would bring expenses required in curative care down and free up resources for the inevitable cases. Mesa-Lago suggests establishing mandatory programs for the incorporation of low-income groups such as the self-employed, domestic servants, and employees of microenterprises, and creating schemes with lower financing burdens and benefits.

Improving the Poor's Ability to Mitigate Risks: The Role of Microfinance Programs

In chapter nine Manfred Zeller explores the role of microfinance in reducing the downward risk of falling below some minimum threshold levels of consumption for poor households. The author argues that the role of microfinance to smooth income is limited. However, "access to financial services can have a far greater role for smoothing consumption, and thereby increasing the risk-bearing capacity of households for increasing future income." In particular, the largest potential for microfinance is seen for helping the poor address idiosyncratic risks such as ill health, disability, old age, and divorce. Viewed this way microfinance goes beyond the traditional role of assisting the poor in earning income from microenterprises to a safety net role.

The author discusses several of the innovative microfinance institutions that offer financial products to respond to the above-mentioned idiosyncratic risks. The most common ones are precautionary savings services. Some microfinance institutions offer explicit lines of consumption credit. This is true of many village banks in Latin America and Sub-Saharan Africa. In addition, some microfinance institutions have developed insurance products such as life insurance. Broadening the outreach of financial services will carry higher risks. That is why microfinance institutions should circumscribe themselves—at least at first—to offer the new services to areas with low covariate risks such as illness, death, divorce, or disability.

Microfinance used for consumption smoothing purposes is likely to crowd out informal schemes. Given that microfinance services are likely to be indirectly subsidized by the government, for example, by grants for product innovation, staff training, and institutional expansion, formal financial services can have social costs that exceed their benefits. But Zeller argues, "evidence from recent research suggests that the informal responses are far from adequate, and that publicly supported institutional innovations in microfinance can offer in many circumstances a viable policy instrument that generates net social benefits."

How to Avoid Crowding Out Informal Insurance

Orazio Attanasio and José-Víctor Ríos-Rull develop an analytical model in chapter ten to explore the impact of the provision of a safety net on informal insurance arrangements. They find that the provision of a safety net from some external agency such as an international organization or the central government could, under certain assumptions, reduce the amount of idiosyncratic insurance achieved by a private contract such as that provided by what the authors call the "extended family." In other words, "the simple provision of aggregate insurance that just shrinks the variance of aggregate shocks without considering the possible crowding out of private insurance is not necessarily optimum." Moreover, such crowding out could, in certain circumstances, lead to an overall welfare decrease.

Regardless of whether the introduction of aggregate insurance leads to a welfare decrease, the authors stress that their results imply that it is worth thinking of insurance schemes that avoid these problems, though designing aggregate insurance schemes that do not crowd out private insurance arrangements is difficult. Attanasio and Ríos-Rull propose some possible mechanisms to avoid the crowding-out effect. For example, when the government can identify the "extended families" in the village, they can make the payment of aggregate insurance to each of the two members conditional on the agreement of the other partner. Therefore, a reversion to autarky would imply not only losing the benefit of the informal insurance agreement but also the access to the aggregate safety net. This would give members of the extended family a powerful mechanism to punish the individuals who renege on the informal insurance agreement. As the crowding out is generated by increasing the value of autarky, this kind of scheme would avoid it.

Whether an aggregate insurance scheme crowds out private informal arrangements depends on the specific functioning of these arrangements as well as the characteristics of the shocks that households face. As a result, the authors end their chapter by making a series of recommendations on how the relevant information could be collected by longitudinal household surveys.

Lessons from the Developed World

The first lesson one can learn from reading chapter eleven by Timothy M. Smeeding and Katherin Ross Phillips is that spending on social protection in the developed world makes a difference in terms of poverty reduction. A second lesson is that the developed world makes an effort to measure the impact of its social insurance and social assistance programs on household income. In contrast, most surveys in developing countries do not collect reliable information on these components of income.

In terms of specific programs, the authors argue that social insurance has the greatest impact on poverty reduction for working age adults (including the unemployed and those who do not participate in the labor market) and for the elderly. Social assistance plays a significant role in some countries (for example, Australia and the United Kingdom) and for some specific groups such as single parents and the elderly. All in all, while most of the countries have responded well to the more traditional risks such as extended unemployment, old age, and disability, not all have done so. Furthermore, only Sweden and to a lesser extent France, Spain, and the Netherlands appear to have dealt well with the new risk of single parenthood.

While social insurance schemes have a strong impact on reducing poverty without stigma, they have two problems: their large cost and their disincentive effects on the labor market. In addition, social insurance schemes for the aged in the current pay-as-you-go pension systems are not financially sustainable under current demographic trends. The authors conclude that tax-transfer systems in the style of a developed country are not likely to be fiscally affordable for developing countries, and they are liable to generate large economic costs because of their impact on work effort. The developing world will have to rely more heavily on targeted and self-targeted social assistance programs for the poor and on less expensive social insurance schemes.

References

Barros, Ricardo, Rosane Mendonça, and Sonia Rocha. 1995. "Brazil: Welfare, Inequality, Poverty, Social Indicators, and Social Programs in the 1980s." In Nora Lustig, ed., *Coping with Austerity*. Washington, D.C.: Brookings Institution.

Baulch, Bob, and John Hoddinott. Forthcoming. "Economic Mobility and Poverty Dynamics in Developing Countries." *Journal of Development Studies*.

Economic Commission for Latin America and the Caribbean (ECLAC). 1999. *Social Panorama of Latin America*. United Nations: Santiago de Chile.

Edwards, Sebastian, and Nora Lustig, eds. 1997. *Labor Markets in Latin America: Combining Market Flexibility with Social Protection*. Washington, D.C.: Brookings Institution.

Escobal, Javier, Jaime Saavedra, and Máximo Torero. 1998. *Los activos de los pobres en el Perú*. Documento de trabajo no. 26. Grupo de Análisis para el Desarrollo, Lima, Peru.

Grootaert, Christiaan. 1998. *Child Labor in Côte d'Ivoire—Incidence and Determinants*. Policy Research Working Paper no. 1905. World Bank, Washington, D.C.

Hoddinott, John, and Bill Kinsey. 1998. "Child Growth in the Time of Drought." International Food Policy Research Institute, Washington, D.C. Unpublished.

Holzmann, Robert, and Steen Jørgensen. 2000. *Social Risk Management: A New Conceptual Framework for Social Protection and Beyond*. Discussion Paper no. 0006. World Bank, Washington, D.C.

Inter-American Development Bank. 2000. *Social Protection for Equity and Growth*. Washington, D.C.: IDB.

Jacoby, Hanan, and Emmanuel Skoufias. 1997. "Risk, Financial Markets and Human Capital in a Developing Country." *Review of Economic Studies* 64 (3): 311–35.

Jalan, Jyotsna, and Martin Ravallion. 1997. *Are the Poor Less Well-Insured? Evidence on Vulnerability to Income Risk in Rural China*. Policy Research Working Paper no. 1863. World Bank, Washington, D.C.

Kugler, Adriana. 1999. *The Impact of Firing Costs on Turnover and Unemployment: Evidence from the Colombian Labour Market Reform*. Economics Working Papers. Department of Economics and Business, Universitat Pompeu Fabra, Barcelona, Spain.

Lipton, Michael. 1996. *Successes in Anti-poverty*. Discussion Paper no. 8. International Labor Office, Geneva.

Lokshin, Michael, and Martin Ravallion. 2000. "Welfare Impact of Russia's 1998 Financial Crisis and the Response of the Public Safety Net." World Bank, Washington, D.C. Unpublished.

Londoño, Juan Luis, and Miguel Székely. 1997. *Persistent Poverty and Excess Inequality: Latin America, 1970–1995*. Washington, D.C.: Inter-American Development Bank.

Lustig, Nora, ed. 1995. *Coping with Austerity: Poverty and Inequality in Latin America*. Washington, D.C.: Brookings Institution.

Lustig, Nora. 2000. "Crises and the Poor: Socially Responsible Macroeconomics." *Economía, Journal of the Latin American and Caribbean Economic Association*. Washington, D.C.: Brookings Institution.

Lustig, Nora, and Miguel Székely. 1998. *Economic Trends, Poverty and Inequality in Mexico*. Washington, D.C.: Inter-American Development Bank.

Ministerio de Economía de Argentina. 1998. "Informe Económico 28." Buenos Aires, Argentina.

Morley, Samuel, and Carola Alvarez. 1992. *Recession and the Growth of Poverty in Argentina.* Working Paper no. 92. Vanderbilt University, Nashville, TN.

Ravallion, Martin. 1998. *Appraising Workfare Programs.* Technical Study. SDS/POV, Inter-American Development Bank, Washington, D.C.

Rodrik, Dani. 1997. "Where Did All the Growth Go? External Shocks, Social Conflict, and Growth Collapses." Harvard University, Cambridge, MA. Unpublished.

Ruprah, Inder, and Luis Marcano. 1998. "Work in Progress." Inter-American Development Bank, Washington, D.C. Unpublished.

Sinha, Saurabh, and Michael Lipton. 1999. "Damaging Fluctuations, Risk and Poverty: A Review." In *World Development Report* 2000/2001. Commissioned Paper. Brighton and Washington, D.C.: Sussex University and World Bank.

Subbarao, Kalanidhi, and others. 1997. *Safety Net Programs and Poverty Reduction: Lessons from Cross-Country Experience.* Washington, D.C.: World Bank.

Townsend, Robert M. 1994. "Risk and Insurance in Village India." *Econometrica* 62 (May): 539–91.

University of California. 1999. *Berkeley Magazine.* Summer, p. 19.

World Bank. 1994. *Hashemite Kingdom of Jordan Poverty Assessment.* Report 12675-JO. Washington, D.C.

———. 1999a. "Social Protection Sector Strategy Paper." First Draft (February 15).

———. 1999b. *Poverty Trends and the Voices of the Poor.* Poverty Reduction and Economic Management. Washington, D.C.

———. 2000a. *World Development Report 2000/1: Attacking Poverty.* Washington, D.C.

———. 2000b. *World Development Indicators.* Washington, D.C.

CHAPTER TWO

Has Aggregate Income Growth Been Effective in Reducing Poverty and Inequality in Latin America?

Alain de Janvry and Elisabeth Sadoulet

Compared with other regions of the world, Latin America is characterized by high levels of poverty and inequality given the prevailing levels of per capita income. This has been referred to as "excess" poverty and inequality.[1] Latin American populations have also been subjected to unusually high income variations, most particularly during the past 30 years with rapid debt-led growth, the debt crisis, implementation of stabilization and adjustment policies, economic recoveries, and more recently the peso crisis and repercussions of shocks in Asia and Russia. Again, compared with other regions of the world, there has been "excess" instability. Poverty, inequality, and instability are thus issues of concern as they have high social costs. They reduce long-term economic growth (as demonstrated by sustained growth and lower levels of poverty, inequality, and instability in Asia for more than three decades), and they can create political backlashes on economic reforms.[2] They are sources of social breakdown with symptoms like crime, violence, and deterioration of social norms.

It is common knowledge that aggregate income growth, as measured by GDP per capita (GDPpc), is the main source of poverty reduction and potentially of inequality reduction.[3] Yet Latin America has not been short of successful growth over the long run. This suggests some features of Latin American growth and its context

---

We are indebted to Miguel Székely for useful suggestions.

[1] Londoño and Székely (1997).

[2] See Aghion and Howitt (1998) and *The Economist* (1996).

[3] World Bank (1990).

may be limiting the capacity of growth to make a dent in poverty and inequality. These features are clearly unequally present across countries. Indeed, while there are general features of Latin America as a region, poverty and inequality vary widely across countries, implying that, over the long run, growth has been differentially successful in affecting poverty and inequality.[4] If there is a concern with poverty and inequality, it is important to identify these features, so they can be modified through policy interventions that may render aggregate income growth more effective for reduction of poverty and inequality.

Based on these considerations, we address three questions in this chapter:

- How effective has aggregate income growth been in reducing poverty and inequality, and under what conditions has it been more or less effective?
- Given the continuing history of economic instability, what are the relative gains and costs in poverty and inequality of growth versus recession? Are they symmetrical in the sense that the elasticity of poverty and inequality with respect to income is the same whether income rises or falls?
- Latin America has gone through different "styles" of growth, shifting from import substitution industrialization before the debt crisis ("early" growth) to more open economy growth after structural adjustment ("late" growth). Is aggregate income growth under these two models differentially effective in reducing poverty and inequality?

We address these issues using econometric analysis to isolate the relationships among income and poverty and inequality from other determining factors. Surprisingly, virtually no econometric analysis of this relationship has been made. The growth-welfare relation has typically instead been analyzed by simple correlation or by constructing two-way tables with income growth/income recession crossed with increases/decreases in poverty and inequality.[5] This leaves uncontrolled a host of spurious correlations, which we attempt to control for in this chapter. It also does not allow us to identify how the context in which growth occurred affected poverty and inequality outcomes, a conditional analysis needed for the design of policy reforms.

---

[4] IDB (1998).
[5] Morley (1995); Psacharopoulos and others (1995).

DATA AND METHODOLOGY

It is clearly difficult to develop a consistent database on poverty and inequality across a sufficient number of countries and for a sufficient number of years to allow econometric identification of the determinants of poverty/inequality. Yet, a sustained effort at developing such data has been done, principally by Oscar Altimir at CEPAL, offering information from 1970 to 1994 for 12 countries for the years when household income and expenditure surveys were conducted.[6]

The timing of episodes of early growth, recession, and late growth varies sharply across countries. For this reason, distinguishing episodes of early growth, recession, and late growth by fixed dates—for instance, by decades, associating the 1970s with early growth, the 1980s with recession, and the 1990s with late growth, as is commonly done—is inadequate to capture "styles" of growth.[7] In addition, the way these episodes are captured by the available data varies across countries owing to the timing of the household surveys in relation to these episodes. Some countries do not have observed episodes of recession (Chile, Colombia, Costa Rica), others do not have data for early growth (Venezuela), some do not escape from recession (Brazil), and yet others fall back into recession after experiencing recoveries from recession (Honduras and Venezuela). As shown in table 2–1, we have organized the data in 53 spells of early growth (spells with positive GDPpc growth starting in 1970 and extending up to the debt crisis), recession (negative GDPpc), and late growth (spells with positive GDPpc growth originating after the 1970s), with dates that are idiosyncratic to each country. There is of course some arbitrariness in classifying spells by episodes of early growth, recession, and late growth, since the spells observed between data points may hide subperiods of growth or recession.[8] The data characterize urban poverty, rural poverty, and national-level inequality.

The variables to be explained are the rate of growth in the number of urban poor over a spell, the rate of growth in the number of rural poor, and the rate of growth in the Gini coefficient as a measure of inequality. We use a specification of a

---

[6] Altimir (1995). Most of these data are reported by CEPAL in *Social Panorama for Latin America* (1994, 1995, 1996). Details on data construction are given in de Janvry and Sadoulet (1998).

[7] See, for example, Londoño and Székely (1997).

[8] This correct observation was made by Miguel Székely. There is, however, no way out of this dilemma since we do not have annual survey data. By chance, there is a relatively good correspondence between the years of the surveys and the economic turning points in most countries.

Table 2–1. Growth Spells and GDP Per Capita Annual Growth Rates, Latin America, 1970–94

Average annual growth rates in percent

Country	Early growth Period	Rate	Recession Period	Rate	Late growth Period	Rate
Argentina	1970–80	0.84	1980–86	–1.99	1990–92	7.31
			1986–90	–3.29	1992–94	5.44
Brazil	1970–79	5.85	1987–90	–1.92		
	1979–87	0.61	1990–93	–0.53		
Chile	1970–80	0.19			1980–87	0.43
					1987–90	5.34
					1990–92	7.37
					1992–94	3.73
Colombia	1970–80	2.89			1980–86	0.80
					1986–90	2.29
					1990–92	1.18
					1992–94	3.59
Costa Rica	1970–81	2.38			1981–88	0.33
					1988–90	1.87
					1990–92	2.87
					1992–94	3.14
Guatemala			1980–86	–3.86	1986–90	0.73
Honduras	1970–86	0.76	1992–94	–0.72	1986–90	0.72
					1990–92	1.30
Mexico	1970–84	2.96	1984–89	–1.47	1989–92	1.65
					1992–94	0.21
Panama	1970–79	1.25	1986–89	–7.93	1989–91	4.96
	1979–86	1.52			1991–94	4.56
Peru	1970–79	0.85	1979–86	–1.85	1991–94	3.33
			1986–91	–5.88		
Uruguay	1970–81	2.80	1981–86	–3.28	1986–90	1.53
					1990–92	4.80
					1992–94	3.92
Venezuela			1970–81	–0.33	1990–92	5.40
			1981–86	–2.55		
			1986–90	–1.48		
			1992–94	–3.44		
Number of spells	12		15		26	

Source: World Bank (1997).

poverty equation where the rate of change in poverty is explained by aggregate income growth, characteristics of the macroeconomic performance during the growth spell, and characteristics of the structural context in which growth occurred, measured at the beginning of the corresponding spell. This specification is similar to those used by Martin Ravallion and Gaurav Datt.[9] The equation explaining inequality is similarly specified. Hence, we are assuming that aggregate income growth is a determinant of household income poverty and inequality as opposed to jointness. In making this assumption, we note that GDPpc contains many elements beyond household income, and that there is consequently no simple relation that relates income growth to poverty and inequality indicators. However, the qualitative nature of growth (early, recession, and late) and the macroeconomic and structural contexts in which growth occurs are determinants of poverty and inequality outcomes. We also give importance to analyzing how a given growth rate affects poverty and inequality differentially according to the macroeconomic and the structural conditions where growth occurs. This is done by specifying selected interactions between GDPpc growth and macro and structural characteristics. Most important among these are the initial levels of poverty and inequality, the initial level of education, and the length of the episodes of growth or recession.

By specifying the regression equations in rates of change, we control for country-idiosyncratic characteristics that would explain levels of poverty. To control for residual country fixed effects, we ran regressions with country dummies, but these were globally not significant and are consequently not reported here.

The explanatory variables used in the poverty and inequality equations are:

- the rate of growth in GDPpc over the corresponding spell classified in three episodes
- GDPpc growth during early growth episodes
- GDPpc growth during recession episodes
- GDPpc growth during late growth episodes.

The following are characteristics of macroeconomic performance:

- the rate of growth in the real exchange rate over the spell
- the incidence of hyperinflation, defined as a rate of growth in the CPI that exceeds 100 percent a year

---

[9] Ravallion and Datt (1996, 1999).

- instability of growth during the spell measured by the coefficient of variation of GDPpc around its trend
- length of the regime of growth or recession, defined as the total number of successive years of growth or recession during and before the spell
- sectoral composition of growth measured by the growth differential between agriculture and nonagriculture, and growth of the services sector.

The following are characteristics of the structural context in which growth occurred:

- the level of GDPpc at the beginning of the spell
- the share of agriculture in GDP at the beginning of the spell
- the natural growth rate of population during the spell
- the share of urban population at the beginning of the spell
- the predicted level of rural-urban migration during the spell
- the level of secondary education at the beginning of the spell
- the level of inequality at the beginning of the spell
- the incidence of poverty at the beginning of the spell.

URBAN POVERTY

Analysis of the determinants of growth on urban poverty in table 2–2 shows that no significant decline in poverty took place owing to aggregate income growth under early growth. The elasticity of urban poverty with respect to GDPpc is –0.32, and it is not significantly different from zero. Recession, however, severely increased urban poverty, with an elasticity of –1.11, meaning that for every 1 percent decline in GDPpc there was an increase in the number of urban poor of 1.11 percent. There consequently was a strong asymmetry between the role of growth under import substitution industrialization and the role of recession: the 1 percent decline in GDPpc under recession eliminated the gain in urban poverty reduction achieved by as much as a 3.7 percent increase in GDPpc under early growth.

Contrast in the roles of early growth and recession in urban poverty illustrates the fallacy of analyzing the relationship between income and poverty without separating periods: pooling together years of early growth and recession would have yielded a negative relation between aggregate income growth and poverty, an encouraging result. However, this relation comes from recession, not from growth. Hence, while existence of a negative relation is correct, the policy implication that

Table 2–2. Determinants of Change in Urban Poverty

Variable	Coefficient	Student t
Aggregate GDP per capita growth		
Early growth episode	–0.32	–0.5
Recession episode	–1.11	–2.2
Late growth episode	–1.25	–2.1
Macroeconomic performance		
Real exchange rate growth	0.31	2.5
Hyperinflation dummy	3.94	2.4
Structural context		
GDP per capita (thousands of 1987 dollars)	–1.96	–1.0
Share of agriculture in GDP	0.09	0.6
Population growth	1.75	0.4
Urban population share	0.0004	0.0
Rural-urban migration (predicted rate)	1.10	0.3
Secondary education	0.001	0.0
Initial inequality	–4.45	–0.5
Initial incidence of urban poverty	–0.10	–0.9
Intercept	4.18	0.2
Number of observations	48	
R^2	0.73	

Note: The endogenous variable is the annual growth rate in the number of urban poor by spell.
Source: Authors' calculations.

growth reduces poverty is totally misleading, a mistake that permeates much of the quantitative analysis on poverty.

While early growth was not effective for urban poverty reduction, this is not the case for late growth. Results show that the income elasticity of poverty for late growth is –1.25. This is not unexpected if we believe that removal of distortions on the price of capital allowed for a more labor-intensive growth path, resulting in greater ability for growth to reduce poverty than under import substitution. This is indeed an encouraging result that deserves further attention. Among other determinants of change in urban poverty, structural variables have no role, while what matters is the macroeconomic performance. Both real exchange rate depreciation (associated with stabilization policies) and the occurrence of bouts of hyperinflation have strong nefarious contemporaneous effects on urban poverty.

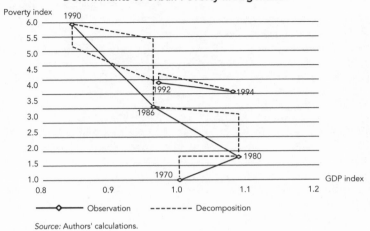

FIGURE 2–1.

Determinants of Urban Poverty in Argentina

Source: Authors' calculations.

The ratchet effect of instability in GDPpc on urban poverty is illustrated for Argentina in figure 2–1 using the estimated equation in table 2–2. The solid line represents the observed relation between GDPpc growth and urban poverty growth. The data for Argentina cover one period of early growth, two periods of recession, and two periods of late growth. The dotted line is the predicted role of income using the equation estimated in table 2–2. The vertical line from each point is the change in poverty explained by exogenous variables other than GDPpc and by the error term in the equation. These vertical shifts show that factors other than GDPpc, both explained and unexplained, are important in predicting changes in poverty. The graph also clearly shows that recession was devastating for the rural poor, with declining aggregate income leading to a sharp increase in poverty.

The context in which growth occurs is a determinant of the effect that income growth can have on poverty reduction. We analyze the role of these contextual variables on growth by introducing interaction terms between context and GDPpc growth. In table 2–3, we report only the coefficients of the direct and interaction terms and only of the episodes when significant, not the full corresponding regression. There are four important results.

Role of initial level of inequality. When GDPpc is interacted with the initial level of inequality in the corresponding spell, the poverty reduction effect of aggregate income growth is diminished by high inequality. Ravallion observes that "the higher

Table 2–3. Effect of Initial Level in Determinants of Change in Urban Poverty

Variable	Coefficient	Overall effect of growth	
		Lowest	Highest
Effect of initial level of inequality on			
GDPpc growth: early growth episode		(Costa Rica)	(Colombia)
GDPpc growth	–4.44*	–2.29*	0.48
GDPpc growth*initial inequality	7.39*		
Effect of initial level of inequality on			
GDPpc growth: late growth episode		(Uruguay)	(Guatemala)
GDPpc growth	–9.26**	–3.84**	0.29
GDPpc growth*initial inequality	18.02**		
Effect of initial level of poverty on			
GDPpc growth: late growth episode		(Uruguay)	(Honduras)
GDPpc growth	–2.66**	–2.23**	0.82
GDPpc growth*initial level of poverty	0.053°		
Effect of initial level of education (percent			
secondary enrollment) on GDPpc			
growth: late growth episode		(Honduras)	(Uruguay)
GDPpc growth	2.60°	–0.63	–2.50**
GDPpc growth*initial level of education	-0.06**		
Effect of sectoral composition of growth and			
initial inequality on GDPpc growth:			
late growth episode		(Uruguay)	(Guatemala)
Services growth	–5.64**	–2.28**	0.27
Services growth*initial inequality	11.15*		

° Significant at the 85 percent level.
* Significant at the 90 percent level.
** Significant at the 95 percent level.
Note: The endogenous variable is the annual growth rate in the number of urban poor by spell.
Source: Authors' calculations.

the initial level of inequality, the less effective aggregate income growth is in reducing poverty."[10] With high inequality, the tails of the distribution of income are thick, and a change in the mean income level has little effect on frequency in the tails. Recall that, across all countries, the elasticity of urban poverty with respect to GDPpc is –0.3 in early growth. We can illustrate how this overall effect changes by using

---

[10] Ravallion (1997).

the level of inequality prevailing in countries at the extremes of the distribution of inequality. If we use the level of inequality prevailing in Costa Rica (0.29, the lowest in the region for early growth observations), growth was effective in reducing poverty, with a significant elasticity of –2.3. By contrast, in Colombia with the higher Gini among early growth observations (0.67 in 1970), the elasticity is an insignificant 0.48. For late growth, the elasticity across all countries is –1.3. For Uruguay, with the lowest observed level of inequality among late growth observations (0.30), this elasticity is a large –3.84, while in Guatemala, which has the highest level of inequality (0.53), the poverty reduction effect is completely erased, resulting in an elasticity of 0.29. The results hence support Ravallion's contention that inequality can erase the beneficial poverty-reducing effects of growth, even under late growth. High-inequality countries cannot consequently rely on growth to reduce inequality.

Role of initial level of poverty. Growth is similarly found to be effective for poverty reduction if the initial level of poverty is not too high. Under late growth, the income elasticity of poverty is a significant –2.2 at the poverty incidence level prevailing in Uruguay (0.08, lowest in the sample), while it is an insignificant 0.8 at the poverty incidence level prevailing in Honduras (0.66, highest in the sample). This suggests that scale is significant in poverty reduction, at least within the range observed in Latin America: it is easier to reduce urban poverty if there is less urban poverty to start with.

Role of secondary education. Results show that late growth is only effective in reducing poverty if the initial levels of secondary school enrollment are sufficiently high. Thus, in Uruguay, with the highest level of secondary school enrollment, the income elasticity of poverty is –2.5 with a secondary school enrollment of 81 percent, while it falls to –0.6 with the enrollment levels prevailing in Honduras (32 percent). Education is thus key if growth is to serve as an effective instrument for poverty reduction.

Sectoral composition of growth. Interacting growth in services and initial level of inequality shows that, in late growth episodes, service sector growth combined with low initial levels of inequality is effective for urban poverty reduction. Indeed, PREALC observes that the informal sector (with a large service component) has been the most effective at employment creation since the debt crisis.[11]

We thus conclude that growth is only effective as an instrument for poverty reduction if the initial levels of inequality and poverty are not too high, if secondary education is sufficiently prevalent, and if it is accompanied by high service

---

[11] PREALC (1992).

Table 2–4. Determinants of Change in Rural Poverty

Variable	Twelve countries		Nine countries[a]	
	Coefficient	Student t	Coefficient	Student t
Aggregate GDP per capita growth				
Early growth episode	−0.27	−0.8	−0.23	−0.6
Recession episode	−0.60	−2.0	−0.60	−1.9
Late growth episode	−0.99	−2.9	−0.97	−2.4
Macroeconomic performance				
Real exchange rate growth	0.07	1.1	0.08	1.0
Hyperinflation dummy	0.30	0.3	0.51	0.3
Structural context				
GDP per capita (thousands of 1987 dollars)	−2.11	−2.3	−1.67	−0.9
Share of agriculture in GDP	−0.15	−1.4	−0.09	−0.6
Rural population natural growth	1.13	1.0	0.57	0.3
Rural-urban migration (predicted rate)	−0.75	−1.4	−0.57	−0.9
Secondary education	−0.003	−0.1	−0.02	−0.3
Initial inequality	−1.67	−0.3	−4.00	−0.5
Initial incidence of rural poverty	−0.06	−1.8	−0.05	−1.1
Intercept	8.39	1.6	9.00	1.4
Number of observations	40		35	
R^2	0.61		0.61	

a. Data for Argentina, Colombia, and Uruguay are omitted.
Note: The endogenous variable is the annual growth rate in the number of rural poor by spell.
Source: Authors' calculations.

sector growth in a context of low inequality. These are all contextual characteristics that can be molded by policy interventions to make growth more effective for poverty reduction.

RURAL POVERTY

Data for rural poverty are not as solid as for urban poverty, and the explanatory power of a poverty equation is consequently lower. Some observations are dubious (Argentina, Colombia, and Uruguay) and the analysis is consequently repeated deleting them, reducing the number of countries to nine.[12] Results in table

---

[12] Personal communication from Nora Lustig.

FIGURE 2–2.

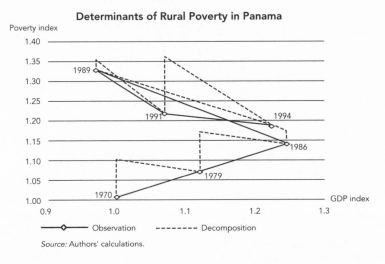

Determinants of Rural Poverty in Panama

Source: Authors' calculations.

2–4 show similar patterns to those for urban poverty, although muted, as agricultural incomes do not respond to the economic cycle as strongly as urban incomes, in part because the migration buffer exists unilaterally from rural to urban sectors, and in part because production for home consumption reduces the impact of price shocks. Early growth is not effective at reducing poverty. Recession has a strongly significant negative elasticity of –0.6 (meaning an increase in poverty as income is falling). There is consequently again a strong asymmetry between early growth and recession. A 1-percent decline in income erases the poverty reduction effect of 2 percent of early growth. Late growth is, however, quite effective at poverty reduction, with an elasticity of –0.99, although lower than the effect of growth in the urban sector.

The other determinants of change in rural poverty are structural, as opposed to derived from macroeconomic performance in the case of urban poverty. The initial level of GDPpc lowers the growth rate in poverty reduction, indicating that there is convergence as GDPpc rises. The initial incidence of rural poverty also lowers the growth rate of rural poverty, showing again that scale is relevant in poverty reduction.

When suspicious data for Argentina, Colombia, and Uruguay are removed, the sample is reduced to nine countries and 35 observations. The results are reported in table 2–4. We see that eliminating these data makes no difference in the results, stressing the robustness of the findings.

The asymmetrical effects of growth and recession are illustrated with data for Panama in figure 2–2. The data for Panama cover two spells of early growth, one

Table 2–5. Effect of Length of Regime in Determinants of Change in Rural Poverty

Variable	Elasticity	Overall effect of growth	
		Lowest	Highest
Estimation with 12 countries		(1 year)	(4 years)
GDP per capita growth	−1.35**	−1.13**	−0.50*
Length of regime*GDP per capita growth	0.21*		
Estimation with 9 countries		(1 year)	(4 years)
GDP per capita growth	−1.43**	−1.18**	−0.45
Length of regime*GDP per capita growth	0.24*		

* Significant at the 90 percent level.
** Significant at the 95 percent level.
Note: Values show the effect of length of regime on GDPpc growth. The endogenous variable is the annual growth rate in the number of rural poor by spell.
Source: Authors' calculations.

spell of recession, and two spells of late growth. The large vertical segments show that GDPpc is not a strong predictor of observed changes in rural poverty, except during recession and the first period of economic recovery, where GDPpc growth explains most of the observed changes in poverty. Recession has a strong ratchet effect on poverty. Yet, the encouraging observation is the strong poverty reduction effect of late growth that outperforms (in a positive direction) the impact of recession per percentage point of change in income.

The length of the recession period affects the income elasticity of rural poverty. As shown in table 2–5, a 1-percent decline in GDPpc in the context of a one-year recession is more devastating than a 1-percent decline in a longer recession. Thus, the elasticity is −1.18 with a one-year recession, while it is −0.45 with a four-year recession. These results stay the same when countries with suspicious rural poverty data are removed. Longer recessions allow the poor to engage in risk management. This shows that the poor lack access to risk-coping instruments and can reduce the costs of declining income through risk management over the longer run. Giving access to risk-coping instruments such as social funds should thus be important in helping the poor reduce the cost of short-term income fluctuations.

INEQUALITY

Inequality, as measured by the Gini coefficient, is even harder to explain than rural poverty. The results in table 2–6 are quite disturbing for the potential of growth to

Table 2–6. Determinants of Change in Inequality

Variable	Coefficient	Student t
Aggregate GDP per capita growth		
Early growth episode	0.32	0.9
Recession episode	–0.44	–2.2
Late growth episode	–0.05	–0.2
Qualitative features of growth		
Differential growth agriculture-nonagriculture		
Early growth episode	–0.26	–0.6
Recession episode	0.04	0.1
Late growth episode	–0.24	–1.0
Coefficient of variation of GDP per capita	–0.43	–1.8
Macroeconomic performance		
Real exchange rate growth	0.06	1.0
Hyperinflation dummy	1.16	1.4
Structural context		
GDP per capita (thousands of 1987 dollars)	–0.69	–1.1
Share of agriculture in GDP	–0.12	–1.6
Population growth	–0.72	–0.5
Urban population share	–0.08	–0.7
Rural-urban migration (predicted rate)	0.45	0.4
Secondary education	0.002	0.1
Initial inequality	–10.12	–2.0
Intercept	13.71	1.2
Number of observations	49	
R^2	0.50	

Note: The endogenous variable is the annual growth rate of the Gini coefficient by spell.
Source: Authors' calculations.

reduce inequality: neither early nor late growth has significant effects on inequality. Recession, by contrast, has a powerful effect, but evidently in the unfortunate direction: every 1-percentage point of decline in GDPpc increases inequality by 0.44 percent. Structural factors affect inequality, particularly the share of agriculture in GDP and the initial level of inequality, which both help reduce the growth in inequality.

Using Panama again as an illustration, figure 2–3 shows the devastating effect of recession on inequality, with a 1-percent decline in income eliminating the gains from 9 percent in late income growth. The figure again illustrates how wrong

FIGURE 2–3.

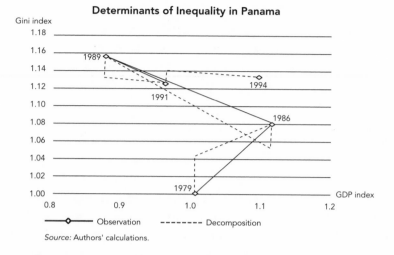

Determinants of Inequality in Panama

Source: Authors' calculations.

an analysis of the relationship between income growth and inequality could be if it did not decompose the relation by periods. In this case, with nonsignificant effects of early and late growth, the negative relation between income and inequality would wholly come from recession. The policy implication that growth reduces inequality would thus be totally unfounded.

The length of the regime of growth under early growth shows that growth was neutral on inequality only if the number of years of sustained growth was large enough. Thus, with the shortest period of early growth observed in Panama

Table 2–7. Effect of Length of Regime on Determinants of Change in Inequality

Variable	Coefficient	Overall effect of growth	
		Lowest	Highest
		(Panama, 4 years)	(Panama, 21 years)
GDP per capita growth	2.11**	1.59**	−0.60
Length of regime*GDP per capita growth	−0.13*		

* Significant at the 90 percent level.
** Significant at the 95 percent level.
Note: Values show the effect of length of regime on GDPpc growth for early growth episodes. The endogenous variable is the annual growth rate of the Gini coefficient by spell.
Source: Authors' calculations.

(four years), growth increased inequality with an elasticity of 1.59 (table 2–7). By contrast, sustained growth over 21 years, the longest sequence of years of sustained growth, also observed in Panama, eliminates the recessive effect of growth, with a nonsignificant elasticity of –0.6 (table 2–7). Short bouts of growth are thus particularly destabilizing on the distribution of income, concentrating opportunities in the hands of a few. The sustainability of growth is important to mitigate negative inequality effects.

CONCLUSION

This study used a data set on poverty and inequality across 12 Latin American countries over 25 years that is far from perfect. While the authors of the data made remarkable efforts in seeking to achieve consistency across space and time, the data are not as solid as desired, particularly for the rural sector. It should be remembered that the results presented[13] are consequently conditional on the quality of this data set. As better data become available, the estimations we have presented will need to be run again, possibly with different results. Yet, it is remarkable that the data yield strong regularities, confirming many of the theoretical expectations on the relation between growth and poverty and inequality, and qualifying these results by models of Latin American economic development and by contexts in which growth and recession occurred. If the data had simply been white noise, these regularities would not have emerged as systematically and significantly as they did. Removing suspicious data for rural poverty leaves these results unaltered, vouching for the robustness of the findings.

The following table summarizes the income elasticities of poverty and inequality that were obtained in this study.

Income elasticity	Urban poverty	Rural poverty	Inequality
Early growth	–0.32	–0.27	0.32
Recession	–1.11**	–0.60**	–0.44**
Late growth	–1.25**	–0.99**	–0.05

** Significant at the 95 percent level.

---

[13] See Lustig (1994).

There are strong asymmetries in the relations among income and poverty and inequality according to growth episode: recession is systematically devastating on poverty and inequality. A 1-percent decline in GDPpc in a recession episode eliminates the gains in urban poverty reduction achieved by 3.7 percent growth in GDPpc under early growth, the gains in rural poverty reduction achieved by 2 percent growth under early growth, and the gains in inequality reduction achieved by 9 percent growth under late growth. Recession has a particularly strong ratchet effect on inequality since subsequent growth is unable to compensate for the higher level of inequality thus achieved. Reducing aggregate income shocks, in particular by lessening external vulnerability, should thus be an important policy goal, even if the opportunity cost is somewhat lower growth.[14] Economies can indeed be made more resilient to external shocks, and this is all the more important when poverty is high. The dilemma of this trade-off can be lessened by providing the poor with access to risk-coping instruments in order to protect them from the poverty and inequality effects of downturns. This includes building permanent programs of social protection for food security, guaranteeing employment in public works programs, keeping children in school, and maintaining health services whatever the phase of the economic cycle, and minimizing budget cuts in social services during recessions.[15]

The style of growth matters for welfare. Early growth (import substitution industrialization) was not effective for poverty and inequality reduction. Late growth (open economy) is encouragingly very effective for poverty reduction. The precise mechanisms by which this happens need to be analyzed. But late growth is disappointingly ineffective for inequality reduction.

Econometric estimates of income elasticities of poverty and inequality obtained without distinguishing growth episodes are misleading: a negative elasticity may come from recession instead of growth, especially for inequality in general and for poverty under early growth and recession, leading to fallacious policy implications regarding the potential of growth to reduce poverty and inequality under these circumstances.

Aggregate income growth is only effective for poverty and inequality reduction if a set of contextual conditions holds. For urban poverty, aggregate income growth is only effective if the levels of inequality and poverty are not too high, if

---

[14] Altimir (1998).
[15] Nelson (1999).

the levels of secondary education are sufficiently high, and if growth is reinforced by growth in the service sector in a context of sufficiently high equality. For rural poverty, the cost of a recession per percentage point of decline in GDPpc is higher if the income shock is short. And for inequality, short episodes of growth are more destabilizing of the distribution of income.

The overarching conclusion is that inequality needs to be attacked directly by asset redistribution measures in order for growth to be effective for poverty reduction. Latin America remains the region of the world where income is most unequally distributed, and inequality robs growth from creating the expected welfare gains.[16] Education, in particular, has a powerful role to play in reconciling aggregate income growth and poverty reduction.

---

[16] IDB (1998).

References

Aghion, Philippe, and Peter Howitt. 1998. *Endogenous Growth Theory*. Cambridge, MA: MIT Press.

Altimir, Oscar. 1995. *Changes in Inequality and Poverty in Latin America*. Santiago, Chile: CEPAL.

———. 1998. "Inequality, Employment, and Poverty in Latin America: An Overview." In V. Tokman and G. O'Donnell, eds., *Poverty and Inequality in Latin America: Issues and New Challenges*. Chicago, IL: University of Notre Dame Press.

CEPAL. 1994, 1995, 1996. *Social Panorama in Latin America*. Santiago, Chile.

de Janvry, Alain, and Elisabeth Sadoulet. 1998. *Poverty and Inequality in Latin America: A Causal Analysis, 1970–1994*. Working Paper. Department of Agricultural and Resource Economics. University of California at Berkeley, Berkeley, CA.

The Economist. 1996. "The Backlash in Latin America: Gestures against Reform." November 30: 19-21.

Inter-American Development Bank (IDB). 1998. *Facing Up to Inequality in Latin America: Economic and Social Progress in Latin America, 1998–1999 Report*. Baltimore, MD: Johns Hopkins University Press.

Londoño, Juan Luis, and Miguel Székely. 1997. *Persistent Poverty and Excess Inequality: Latin America, 1970–1995*. Working Paper Series no. 357. Inter-American Development Bank, Washington, D.C.

Lustig, Nora. 1994. *Measuring Poverty in Latin America: The Emperor Has No Clothes*. Washington, D.C.: Brookings Institution.

Morley, Samuel. 1995. *Poverty and Inequality in Latin America: The Impact of Adjustment and Recovery in the 1980s*. Baltimore, MD: Johns Hopkins University Press.

Nelson, Joan. 1999. "Shock-Resistant Growth?" ODC Viewpoint. Washington, D.C.: Overseas Development Council.

PREALC/International Labour Office. 1992. *Empleo y transformación productiva en América Latina y el Caribe*. Documento de trabajo no. 369. Santiago, Chile.

Psacharopoulos, George, and others. 1995. "Poverty and Income Inequality in Latin America during the 1980s." *Review of Income and Wealth* 41 (September): 245–64.

Ravallion, Martin. 1997. "Can High-Inequality Developing Countries Escape Absolute Poverty?" *Economic Letters* 56: 51–57.

Ravallion, Martin, and Gaurav Datt. 1996. "How Important to India's Poor Is the Sectoral Composition of Economic Growth?" *World Bank Economic Review* 10 (January): 1–25.

———. 1999. *When Is Growth Pro-Poor? Evidence from the Diverse Experiences of India's States*. Washington, D.C.: World Bank.

World Bank. 1990. *World Development Report 1990: Poverty*. Washington, D.C.: World Bank.

———. 1997. *World Development Indicators*, CD-ROM. Washington, D.C.

CHAPTER THREE

Social Protection for the Unemployed: Programs in Latin America

Gustavo Márquez

Macroeconomic volatility seems to be a recurrent feature of the Latin American economies. There is some evidence that unemployment is more sensitive to downswings than it was in the past. Furthermore, openness exposes workers to more unemployment risks. Traditional legally mandated severance payment mechanisms have failed to provide the income support needed by unemployed and displaced workers primarily because of the narrow scope of its coverage. This has led governments in Latin America, faced with sharp economic instability since 1995, to develop a series of attempts at setting up mechanisms to support the incomes of groups of the population hurt by unemployment and declining incomes. This chapter presents an overview of these programs, pointing out their limitations and potentials.

UNEMPLOYMENT INSURANCE

Table 3–1 presents a summary description of unemployment insurance systems in the region. As can be seen, very few countries in the region have legally or administratively enacted unemployment insurance systems, and even fewer have working unemployment insurance schemes. This is a consequence of the very weak incentives that exist for the development of unemployment insurance and other more socialized forms of income protection, given that severance payments work as privately provided income insurance for workers in full-benefit employment contracts who are laid off.

The author thanks Carola Alvarez (IDB), Gaurav Datt (IFPRI), and three anonymous reviewers for insightful comments and suggestions.

Table 3-1. Unemployment Insurance in the Region

Country	Law	Funding	Replacement rate[a]	Benefit duration	Benefits min/max	Coverage requirements[c]
Argentina	1991 reform 1995	Worker: 1 percent wages Employer: 1.5 percent payroll	60 percent	4-12 months Max: 4 m.w.	Min: 1 m.w.	Employees 1 (12), 2, 3
Barbados	1982	Worker: 1.5 percent wages Employer: 1.5 percent payroll	60 percent 10 weeks 40 percent 16 weeks	26 weeks in a 52-week period		Employees 1 (6) 16–64 years old
Brazil	1986 1990	FAT (65 percent tax on total sales)	1–3 m.w.	4 months	Min: 1 m.w.	Employees 4 (36, 4), 5, 6
Chile	1981	Government	$37 monthly for the first 6 months, $18 last 6 months	Max. 1 year[b]		Employees 2, 4 (12, 2), 5
Ecuador	1958 1988	Worker: 2 percent salary Employer: 1 percent payroll	One-time subsidy, amounts decided each year			Employees 1 (24), 7 (30)
Mexico		Social security pension	95 percent	5 years max		Employees between 60–65 years old
Uruguay	1981	Contributions to social security	Up to 50 percent	6 months	Min: 0.5 m.w. Max: 4 m.w.	Employees 1 (6), 5, 3, 8 in commerce and industry
Venezuela	1989 reform 1998	Worker: .7 percent wages Employer: 1.5 percent payroll	Up to 60 percent	13–26 weeks	Max: $44	Employees 1 (12), 2

m.w. Minimum wage.
a. Percentage of last wage.
b. Beneficiaries receive also family support, medical, and maternity benefits.
c. Requirements: 1 (s) be employed s months before receiving subsidy, 2 availability to work, 3 does not receive other social security benefits, 4 (s, j) not having received more than s months of benefits in the last j years, 5 unemployed for reasons outside the conduct and willingness of worker, 6 subject to economic need, 7 (x) waiting period of x days, 8 at least 12 months between periods of receiving subsidy.
Source: Lora and Pagés (1999); U.S. Dept. of Health and Human Services (1995).

In those countries that do have unemployment insurance systems, coverage is limited to workers that have contributed, while they were employed, to the financing of the system. In other words, only workers in full-benefit employment contracts and working in payroll tax–paying firms enjoy the benefits of the unemployment insurance system. This excludes from the protection a sizable fraction of the workforce that works in the unregulated segment of the labor market, presumably those who because of their human and social capital deficits are the neediest in terms of income protection. The level and duration of benefits provided are low relative to unemployment insurance systems in more developed countries. Replacement rates are normally on the order of 50 to 60 percent of last wage, with caps linked to the minimum wage for higher salaries. Benefits are granted for periods typically not longer than four months.

The unemployment insurance system in Argentina is quite limited in the number of beneficiaries and has remained so in spite of strong increases in the number of unemployed workers. Jacqueline Mazza reports that the number of beneficiaries has remained stable, around 100 thousand to 125 thousand workers, of whom more than 70 percent are prime age males, and more than 50 percent are not household heads.[1] She also reports that an analysis of beneficiaries in their personal and previous job characteristics shows that there is a definite trend toward serving younger and middle-class displaced workers. This suggests that unemployment insurance is not fulfilling a safety net role for the poor in the case of Argentina.

Brazil has the biggest unemployment insurance system in the region, with around 300,000 to 400,000 beneficiaries. Mazza reports that unemployment insurance in Brazil is also serving younger (more than 50 percent of beneficiaries are younger than 30) and more educated (45 percent of beneficiaries have completed eighth grade or higher) workers. As Mazza assesses, the unemployment insurance system reflects wage inequality, in the sense that benefits accrue to the middle deciles in the distribution of income.[2]

In Venezuela, the unemployment insurance system was enacted in 1989, but it was never implemented. The system was reformed in 1998. The new system will protect beneficiaries through a mix of individual and collective insurance operated by competitive insurance providers, but implementation has not yet begun as of this date. Given that only workers with regulated, tax-paying contracts are entitled

---

[1] Mazza (1999).
[2] Mazza (1999).

to benefits, it is likely that the pattern of distribution of beneficiaries will be very similar to that of Argentina and Brazil.

Mexico and Uruguay have unemployment insurance programs operated by the social security system. In both cases coverage is quite limited, and in the former it is just an advance payment of old age pensions for a maximum of five years. In the case of Barbados, the unemployment insurance system is very small in coverage, though quite well adapted to the needs of an island economy with frequent but short episodes of unemployment concentrated in workers in the tourism industry.[3]

In general, unemployment insurance systems lack connection with other labor market intermediation and placement services. Even when the unemployment insurance system is operated through the Labor Ministry (as in Brazil), workers are not required to register in the intermediation service, and payment of the benefit is not contingent on verification of search effort. On the one hand, this lack of connection generates opportunity for fraud. Even if it is illegal to have a job and receive unemployment insurance payments simultaneously, most operators complain of their lack of capacity to control what is perceived to be widespread fraud and collusion between firms and workers.[4] On the other hand, this lack of connection with labor market intermediation services makes the system a pure income transfer that does not ease the transition of the unemployed into a new job.

Most unemployment insurance systems are financed through payroll taxes, which are already quite high in the region. This partly explains why coverage is limited, replacement rates are low, and periods of coverage short. Any expansion of the system to cover hitherto unprotected segments of the population is likely to face substantial opposition by its own present beneficiaries and by firms operating in the regulated sector of the economy. Only in Brazil has some expansion to new groups been made (to traditional fishermen and to workers affected by the drought in the Northeast), but the expansion has been temporary and financed through the use of excess funds. If unemployment insurance is to work as part of the safety net in a crisis, the expansion of coverage would have to be produced just when the flow of benefits to already protected workers was highest, creating financial strains

---

[3] Mazza (1999).

[4] Mazza (1999) reports that some efforts have been made in Argentina to detect if workers receiving unemployment insurance were working, by using a common taxpayer identification number. It was found that a sizable number of workers were not only working but also contributing to the social security plan in a new job while they continued to receive the unemployment insurance payment.

on the system and the need for additional funding. The question is whether to attempt this through the unemployment insurance system or by creating an alternative mechanism for income transfer better suited to the needs of workers with different labor market participation.

It has also been argued that the implementation of unemployment insurance requires considerable institutional resources in terms of accounting and recordkeeping. However, mandatory savings-based schemes in place in Brazil, Colombia, Ecuador, and Peru also require considerable institutional resources of the same type. Furthermore, pension system reforms in several countries in the region have created a network of institutions that hold individual workers' accounts and that can be used for recordkeeping in the unemployment insurance system with few additional costs.[5]

In conclusion, the design and target population of unemployment insurance make it suited to protect workers who have full-benefit employment contracts and who acquire rights to it through their contributions while employed. In terms of labor market distortions, the low level of benefits and their short duration apparently do not create incentives against the search for employment. In fact, the reports on fraud in Argentina and Brazil rather suggest that workers use unemployment insurance as a means to obtain additional income while in a new job. As Hugo Hopenhayn and Juan Pablo Nicolini (in this volume) show, it is possible to design optimal unemployment insurance schedules that do not induce reduction in search efforts. Furthermore, unemployment insurance schemes based on nominative contributions to individual accounts that can be rolled over into retirement funds can minimize negative impacts on search effort.[6]

In terms of ability to expand and contract countercyclically, unemployment insurance expenditure is an ideal mechanism. By definition, outlays increase when unemployment is rising and contract with the recuperation of employment.

The most problematic aspect of unemployment insurance, however, is related to its coverage. Workers must bear at least part of the cost of insurance to prevent moral hazard problems. For high-productivity workers, wages are high enough to make the benefit of paying for unemployment insurance (the expected value of benefits when unemployed) higher than the cost of the current income forgone by pay-

---

[5] Most notably Chile but also Argentina, Uruguay, Peru, and Venezuela.
[6] For a proposal of an unemployment insurance system along these lines, see Cortázar and others (1995) and the Venezuelan social security law of 1997.

ing the contribution. However, for low-productivity workers, the utility gain from an increase in current income will be big enough to generate incentives to negotiate with employers a contract without benefits in exchange for a higher current income.

EMPLOYMENT GENERATION PROGRAMS

Employment generation programs are a natural reaction of governments to increasing unemployment. Politically they show the concern of the government with the workers' plight and, by providing jobs, they directly attack unemployment. For analytical purposes it is convenient to separate labor-intensive public works from wage subsidies to the private sector.

Labor-Intensive Public Works

Labor-intensive public works have been the tools of choice to deal with economywide shocks. The number and variety of programs in place in the region show that governments choose to spend greater additional resources on employment generation than on other mechanisms to provide income support to unemployed workers. One of the main advantages of these programs is that they are self-targeted and, therefore, can be implemented without the delays necessary to implement a targeting mechanism.[7]

Three characteristics of labor-intensive public works are crucial in their success as income support mechanisms. In the first place, these programs are financed by the central government and executed by local organizations—be it local governments or nongovernmental organizations (NGOs)—who normally are in charge of selecting the works to be performed and the selection of beneficiaries. Thus, labor-intensive public works require an extensive and solid network of institutions at the local level, with the technical and operational capacity to choose the works to be done, organize the production process, and channel resources to the needy poor. A large part of the success of these programs hinges on how well structured the relationship is between the central government and the executing agencies. There is not a unique way of designing this relationship. To mention just two examples, Argentina chooses to finance works that are approved by a central government agency and executed mostly by local governments, while Brazil chooses to allocate resources

---

[7] Grosh (1994); Ravallion (1998).

semiautomatically on a regional needs base and have works selected by the subnational governments. In any case, what is important is that the design of the relationship between financing and work execution be adequate to the institutional and political structure of the country. Federalist countries should respect local autonomy in work selection and allocate budgets on objective criteria, while more centralized countries will be more able to select works and distribute resources at the central level while keeping responsibility for execution at the local level.

In the second place, the wage level and the criteria for selection of beneficiaries are set at the central level, while local organizations are in charge of the selection of beneficiaries. Thus, a certain tension prevails between the criteria set at the central level and the local political and social reality within which the selection of beneficiaries takes place. There are multiple ways to solve or at least mitigate the consequences of this tension. Community oversight is useful to ensure that resources are not diverted through political favoritism or other forms of corruption, but there is no guarantee that the needed level of community participation will exist. A useful complement to community oversight is a system of random sampling of projects and beneficiaries by the central government agency in charge of overseeing the program to check whether resources are being diverted. This step implies a nontrivial investment of resources in sampling and supervision, but these resources will pay for themselves in greater transparency and better targeting of beneficiaries.

In the third place, to target resources on needy groups and to avoid inducing distortions in local labor markets, wages in labor-intensive public works are frequently set below the market wage of the relevant labor market. The literature on workfare in the developed world suggests that this targeting mechanism is not without costs in terms of stigmatizing workers who participate in the program, and in terms of political and social discrimination among workers by program administrators.[8] There is no solution to this problem short of raising wages to market levels, which in most cases will be impossible given resource constraints.

In summary, labor-intensive public works do not generate important labor market distortions to the extent that they offer wages below the relevant market and can provide a source of income to workers temporarily unemployed. Their coverage depends on the resources allocated to the program, but there is no intrinsic reason why coverage of low-skill workers could not be as ample as needed to reduce unemployment to the target level. This same property, however, brings us

---

[8] Lightman (1995); Rose (1994).

to the problem of their countercyclical nature. Because the amount of resources dedicated to the program is a political decision, there is no way of guaranteeing that the program will move in sync with the economic cycle, expanding in downturns and shrinking in upturns. In fact, the experience in the region shows that once the programs are in place, it is very difficult to reduce their size. In the well-known cases of programs that were phased out during the 1980s (PEM and POJ in Chile and PAIT in Peru), the closing seems to have been mostly a reaction to widespread problems of design and political manipulation.[9]

Wage Subsidies

Subsidized private sector jobs are much less prevalent than labor-intensive public works programs. Argentina is the only case where wage subsidies were widely used, and their scope has shrunk recently, owing to criticisms from the union movement.

Wage subsidies work through reducing the payroll tax or severance payments in employment contracts for particular groups of workers (youth, women, ex-combatants, and so on). This characteristic makes them suitable for the introduction of more flexible (or precarious) employment contracts in a process of labor market regulation reform. In fact, this was the role these programs fulfilled in Argentina in 1995. But at the same time, this feature makes them the center of a political debate on labor market "flexibility," which in large measure explains why these programs were phased out in the face of union opposition in 1998.

However, because wage subsidies are targeted on particular groups, they change the relative prices of different types of workers in favor of the target group and induce large labor market distortions, not the least of which is the substitution of nonsubsidized for subsidized workers.[10] To mitigate this problem, there is normally an "additionality" requirement, by which subsidies are granted only for net new hires that expand the payroll. In turn, this rule requires the determination of a baseline number of employees and a control on new hires. Theoretically, the Ministries of Labor fulfill this task in the normal course of their business. In practice, the ministries are extremely weak and have a very low enforcement capability. This

---

[9] Graham (1994).

[10] More formally, deadweight effects appear when the subsidized jobs would have been created anyway, without the subsidy, while substitution effects appear when subsidized workers replace nonsubsidized ones. See Calmfors (1994). The additionality requirement addresses the deadweight effect, while substitution effects are only prevented at the margin.

weakness makes it impossible to determine base lines and control hires of subsidized workers, therefore making worker substitution a widespread problem. As a
consequence, it is not clear whether these programs really create more jobs than
would have been created without the subsidy.

In summary, these programs generate large and important labor market
distortions by attempting to change the relative salaries of different types of workers.
Because they have to be explicitly targeted by design, they require a comprehensive and often nonexistent enforcement apparatus, making the problem of targeting the program an intractable one. In terms of their countercyclical nature,
expanding and shrinking the program requires an administrative decision. To
the extent that these programs are often perceived as a mechanism to introduce
more flexible (or more precarious) employment contracts, they can become the
center of an often ardent political debate and make decisions about program implementation politically very costly. This has been the experience of Argentina, where
these programs were phased out jointly with the rejection of more far-reaching
labor regulation reforms during 1998.

Table 3–2 summarizes the employment generation programs in seven countries in the region at the end of 1995. The list was extracted from a joint ILO-IDB
volume on active labor market policies in Argentina, Brazil, Chile, Costa Rica, Jamaica, Mexico, and Peru. These countries represent a wide spectrum of variation in
policy development, operational capabilities, and exposure to volatility in international capital markets. Program descriptions and characteristics are summarized
by Francisco Verdera in that volume, and a more thorough discussion of programs
is presented in the accompanying national reports.[11] An itemized description of the
programs is presented in table 3A–1 in the appendix to this chapter.

Argentina is the country with the most varied set of employment generation
programs, comprising a combination of public works and subsidies to private employment. Public subsidies to private sector employment, in the form of subsidies to
firms that increase the number of employees, were widely used under various mechanisms. Workers displaced from the public sector and unemployed workers receiving
unemployment insurance were given vouchers that employers could use to pay tax
liabilities. Firms could opt for tax rebates if they were hiring particular groups of
workers (youth, women, ex-combatants, and so on) under promotional contractual
forms. Firms in particular activities (like reforestation) were subsidized if they hired

---

[11] Verdera (1998).

Table 3–2. Employment Generation Programs in Seven Countries in the Region

Country	Beneficiaries		Expenditure	
	Thousands	Percent of total labor force	Millions of U.S. dollars	Percent of GDP
Argentina	892.2	9.31	249.2	0.09
Brazil	221.8	0.49	1,188.8	0.21
Chile	4.3	0.10	1.4	0.00
Costa Rica	8.1	0.71	3.3	0.04
Jamaica	6.0	0.61	21.2	0.50
Mexico	1,024.0	4.42	1,802.0	0.51
Peru	27.8	0.93	100.0	0.19

Source: Data from Verdera (1998), modified by author. For a complete listing, see appendix tables in this chapter.

new workers. But the most visible mechanism of subsidization was the use of "promotional employment contracts" established in a series of decrees in 1995. These promoted contracts were more precarious than regular full-benefit contracts, did not originate rights to severance payments, and had lower payroll tax liabilities.

Argentina's federal government also financed labor-intensive public works as an employment generation device. The *Trabajar* and similar programs were financed and supervised by the federal government using the *Fondo Nacional de Empleo* (a fund financed through payroll taxes). The resources were used to build small-scale and labor-intensive public works (in many cases social infrastructure, but also roads and small sanitation works), with the works being executed by a wide variety of agencies, from local and state governments to NGOs.

The *PROGER* program in Brazil is a contrasting mechanism for employment generation. The program operates through the establishment of credit lines offered through the national development banking system to small enterprises, cooperatives, NGOs, and other civil society associations. This mechanism circumvents the subnational governments for execution of works in order to avoid the creation of budgetary entitlements. Partial and incomplete evaluations of *PROGER*, however, are not too optimistic about the results for employment generation.[12]

Chile does not have any employment generation program as such, though it has a number of very small and narrowly targeted programs to address living conditions that may hinder the labor market participation of particular groups.

Costa Rica uses public works, wage subsidies, and credit to small enterprises as mechanisms to promote employment generation. Credit to promote employment generation in small firms is also widely used in Jamaica in a battery of programs, some of which also include a form of short-term training. Jamaica has a training and temporary employment program for unemployed youth, aimed at easing their labor market insertion.

Mexico uses public works (rural roads and other social infrastructure) as employment generation devices. The programs are financed by allocations from general revenues (not from payroll taxes) in the federal government budget, and states and local governments execute the works.

Finally, Peru uses legal incentives, a social investment fund, and a micro- and small-enterprise credit program as tools for employment promotion. The labor law reform of 1991 introduced several more precarious forms of employment contracts, allowing firms to hire workers without generating rights to severance payments under fixed-term contracts. FONCODES, a social investment fund, is also used as an employment generation device that can be quickly adjusted to the situation of local labor markets. However, it is not clear how much capacity or interest FONCODES management has in employment generation as opposed to the physical execution of civil works.[13]

SHORT-TERM TRAINING PROGRAMS

Short-term training programs work as an income support device through the provision of scholarships to trainees during the classroom training and apprenticeship periods, which are normally between four and six months. The scholarships are below the relevant market wage, and the apprenticeships are developed in private firms with which the training providers sign an agreement. The short duration of the classroom training makes these programs more suited to young new entrants

---

[12] Government of Brazil (1998).
[13] Verdera (1998).

in the labor market with job search skills than to workers who need skill updating or upgrading and are being displaced from declining sectors.

The main challenge in the design of these training programs arises from the existence of a national training institution, normally a monopolistic public provider of training financed through a payroll tax, with no incentive whatsoever to adapt the nature of its activities and clientele to the challenges of high unemployment. To circumvent this obstacle the programs are organized through the setting up of a separate pool of resources managed by a specialized agent at the central government level. This agent in turn bids out resources to private providers that execute the training programs in a decentralized fashion. As already mentioned, these decentralized providers must enter into agreements with private sector firms to ensure that trainees will have an apprenticeship stage, making private firms the effective gatekeepers of the quality and relevance of the training programs. Another interesting by-product of this process is the development of stronger connections between firms and training providers, which make the latter effectively providers of job search assistance services.

Training programs tend to be more expensive on a per beneficiary basis than labor-intensive public works, given that a larger part of the resources goes to pay the training provider. However, calculations of benefits should include the long-term change in the structure of the training system and the development of job search assistance services, which are very large positive externalities of these programs.[14]

The organization of the programs makes it easy for the program organizer to administratively target groups of the population, and the programs have been quite successful in attracting unemployed youth. However, the programs can be "too effective" in attracting the target group: in Mexico in 1996 youth participation rates increased so much that even if the employment rate of the group rose, so did its unemployment rate. Although there is no formal proof that this was the result of the expansion of training programs (particularly PROBECAT) in that year, a suggestive association exists among expansion of these programs, decline in school

---

[14] These emergency training programs have created the opportunity to introduce institutional innovation into a training system characterized by the monopolistic power of payroll-tax-financed institutions. Disseminating these innovations to the mainstream vocational training system will make it much more successful in addressing the needs of workers caught in the normal process of job churning, who need to upgrade skills.

Table 3–3. Training Programs in Seven Countries in the Region

| Country | Beneficiaries | | Expenditure | |
	Thousands	Percent of total labor force	Millions of U.S. dollars	Percent of GDP
Argentina	133.0	1.4	95.6	0.04
Brazil	740.5	1.6	310.2	0.06
Chile	36.6	0.8	18.3	0.03
Costa Rica	13.1	1.2	60.6	0.73
Jamaica	43.5	4.4	18.6	0.44
Mexico	410.3	1.8	135	0.04
Peru	1.5	0.1	5.0	0.01

Source: Data from Verdera (1998), modified by author. For a complete listing, see appendix tables in this chapter.

enrollment rates, and increase in labor force participation and employment of the target groups.

In summary, these programs tend to generate positive labor market externalities beyond the training process itself, by easing the entry of young workers and creating experience in the operation of labor market intermediation mechanisms (job search assistance). The nature of the training makes the programs suitable for unemployed youth and, as with any training program, one should not expect them to create new jobs but rather to provide new entrants with some labor market experience. Because youth unemployment is a permanent problem in the labor market, one should not think about these programs as countercyclical devices, but rather as permanent features of a well-functioning labor market intermediation system, which could be expanded and contracted following demand in a countercyclical way.

Table 3–3 presents a summary description of the training programs that were being used as income transfer devices in seven countries in the region by the end of 1995.[15] An itemized description of these programs is presented in table 3A–2 in the appendix to this chapter. Training programs were widely used as a mechanism to

---

[15] Verdera (1998).

transfer income, particularly to unemployed youth, through scholarships during the classroom training period (normally three to six months) and sometimes through job search assistance or apprenticeship in private firms. Most of the time these training programs were financed by the government and delivered by private and NGO training providers, with little or no intervention by the traditional national training institutions.

The basic operational technology of these training programs was based on *Chile Joven*, a pioneering youth training program that combined a scholarship for classroom training with a three-month paid apprenticeship in a private firm. Instead of direct purchasing of training services, resources were used to create a fund that was managed by a central government agency. The managing agency requested proposals for training projects, and funds were granted through open bidding. The proposals had to describe the content of the courses to be taught and include a commitment from private sector firms to accept the trainees as apprentices for a period of time (normally three months). The provision of scholarships served as an income transfer to beneficiaries, took them out of the unemployment queue, and gave them some labor market experience during the apprenticeship. These three beneficial effects of the *Joven* program were quite adequately suited to situations characterized by high youth unemployment rates.[16] However, other countries in the region emulated the contracting methodology of the *Joven* program to cater to the needs of other population groups.

Among the countries in the study reported here, Argentina, Chile, and Peru have programs inspired by the *Chile Joven* design, targeting low-income unemployed youth. Argentina has also used the contracting mechanisms of the *Joven* program to develop training programs for other groups of the population and has granted subsidies to private employers who hire apprentices under promotional employment contracts.

Brazil also uses competitive bidding for training provision, but the program operates in a highly decentralized way. The *PLANFOR* program is financed through the FAT, a payroll-tax-financed fund, and funds are allocated to states and local

---

[16] The contracting mechanism of *Chile Joven* was a way to create incentives for training providers to deliver courses of good quality and with content relevant to the labor market. This created pressures for an institutional and content revamping of the training system, as firms accepting apprentices acted as controllers and gatekeepers of the relevance and adequacy of the training provided. The program was therefore rightly perceived as a tool to modernizing and connecting the training system with productive activities.

governments, who in turn hire different providers (private and public) through competitive bidding. States must present annual training plans to the *PLANFOR* administration, and funds are allocated in proportion to each state's share of the total workforce. This method of allocation is presently being changed to reflect the state level of poverty and education and past experience with the execution of annual training programs. Interestingly, the national training institutions (in Brazil the SENAI-SENAC system) participate in the bidding process as another provider of training services, thus creating a financial and institutional dynamic in the overall training system.

Costa Rica used instead the national training institution (INA) as a channel for delivery of training services to semiskilled and skilled unemployed workers. Thus, INA schedules and provides training programs for low-income workers in marginal urban areas, for displaced public sector workers, and for handicapped workers using its own facilities and instructors. A special line of action was established to enable INA to contract out other training institutions, but no special targeting mechanism has been used.

Jamaica uses several programs to provide training for unskilled and young unemployed workers, but the mechanism for income transfer is temporary jobs rather than scholarships during training.

Mexico has the biggest training with income transfer program in the region, and it has been effectively used as a protective device for unemployed and displaced workers and expanded and contracted according to the economic cycle. The PROBECAT program provides a scholarship for the beneficiaries, and the state offices of the Labor Ministry organize various training programs that are delivered locally. Different program evaluations have found that the program has been somewhat successful as a training program, increasing incomes and likelihood of employment for beneficiaries, even though positive effects tend to increase with higher levels of education of the beneficiaries.[17]

---

[17] Government of Mexico (1995).

Table 3A–1. Description of Employment Generation Programs in Seven Countries in the Region

Country, program	Beneficiaries		Expenditure	
	Thousands	Percent of total labor force	Millions of U.S. dollars	Percent of GDP
Argentina		9.31		0.09
Public works financed with public resources				
Solidarity Assistance Program (PROAS)				
Unemployed household heads in public works; joint program by Ministry of Social Development and state governments	260.0	2.7	54.5	0.020
Occupational Training Program (PRENO)	94.0	1.0	20.0	0.007
Community Service Program (ASISTIR)				
Female household heads in community development activities	25.0	0.3	2.6	0.001
Trabajar Program				
Unemployed household heads in public works; program by local governments and NGOs	233.0	2.4	44.9	0.017
Private sector employment promotion				
Private Employment Program for Small- and Medium-Sized Enterprises				
Subsidy for new jobs for unemployed workers in firms with less than 100 employees	254.0	2.7	42.4	0.016
National Forestation Program (FORESTAR)				
Subsidy for new jobs for unemployed workers in new agricultural/forestry firms	21.0	0.2	4.4	0.002
Labor Reintegration Program				
Subsidy to workers who find a job while receiving unemployment insurance	–		–	
Geographic Mobility Program				
Subsidy to workers who have to move from place of residence to keep job	–		–	
Private Employment Creation Voucher Program (BOCEP)				
Fiscal credit for workers displaced from state's payroll; new employer can use as collateral for credit from public banks	5.2	0.1	73.4	0.027
Brazil[a]	221.8	0.49	1,188.8	0.21
Income and Employment Generation Program (PROGER)				
Special credit lines to MSMEs, cooperatives and informal sector	221.8	0.5	1,188.8	0.21

(continued)

Table 3A–1. (continued)

Country, program	Beneficiaries		Expenditure	
	Thousands	Percent of total labor force	Million of U.S. dollars	Percent of GDP
Chile	4.3	0.10	1.4	0.00
Temporary Work Program				
Child-care and educational services for children of agricultural temporary workers	4.3	0.1	1.2	0.002
Indigenous Microentrepreneur Development Program				
Strengthening of economic networks of indigenous groups through ME creation and support	–		0.2	
Costa Rica	8.1	0.71	3.3	0.04
National Employment Generation Program				
Transfer of a minimum wage to unemployed workers who participate in construction of social services infrastructure and service delivery	2.1	0.2	0.1	0.001
Pro Trabajo Work Training Program				
Incentives for labor reintegration and temporary work–subsidy of 50 percent of minimum wage for on-the-job training for unemployed/vulnerable workers	3.4	0.3	2.1	0.026
Productive ideas–support to ME creation	2.6	0.2	1.1	0.013
Jamaica	6.0	0.61	21.2	0.50
Micro Investment Development Agency (MIDA)				
Credit for ME development	6.0	0.6	7.6	0.181
The Government of Jamaica/Government of the Netherlands Micro Enterprise Project (GoJ/GoN MEP)				
Credit for ME development	–			0.000
The Government of Jamaica/European Union Programme				
Credit for ME development	–		1.4	0.034
Mel Nathan Institute for Development and Social Research (MMI)				
Community development services	–		1.6	0.038
Enterprise Development Trust (EDT)				
Credit for ME development	0.0	0.0	0.2	0.004
The Women's Construction Collective (WCC)				
Training and credit for female construction workers	–		–	

(continued)

Table 3A–1. Employment Generation Programs (continued)

Country, program	Beneficiaries		Expenditure	
	Thousands	Percent of total labor force	Millions of U.S. dollars	Percent of GDP
Jamaica (*continued*)				
ASSIST Ltd.				
Credit for ME development	–		0.1	0.002
Bee Keeping and Honey Bee Project				
Training and employment for youth in				
bee-keeping activities	–		0.3	0.007
SESP				
Training and temporary employment for				
unemployed workers	–		10.0	0.237
Mexico	1,024.0	4.42	1,802.0	0.51
Rural Roads Conservation Program				
Rural public works for unemployed youth,				
federal government-financed works organized				
by state and local governments	712.0	3.1	350.0	0.099
Physical Infrastructure and Productive				
Employment Works Program				
Social infrastructure public works for				
unemployed youth, federal government-				
financed works organized by state and local				
governments	312.0	1.3	1,452.0	0.410
Lions Club and Rotary International Private Social				
Programs	–	–	–	–
Peru[b]	27.8	0.93	0.1	0.19
Microenterprise and Self-employment Program				
(PRODAME)				
Training and credit for ME creation and support	4.2	0.1	0.1	0.000
FONCODES				
Social investment fund builds small public works				
using local workforce	23.6	0.8	100.0	0.002

– Not available

a. PROEMPREGO is excluded from the Brazilian list of employment generation programs as it is an investment program. It obviously has employment consequences, but its primary objective is improvements in sanitation, environmental infrastructure, urban transport, and so on through BNDES lines of credit.

b. Peru has also implemented a number of its employment generation programs as labor-intensive investment subprojects complementary to the normal investment activities of institutions such as the National Development Institute (INADE), National Program of Nutrition Assistance (PRONAA), National Construction Company (ENACE), National Housing Fund (FONAVI), National Institute of Health and Educational Infrastructure (INFES), SEDAPAL, CORDECALLAO, CORDELIMA, INABIF, Municipal Compensation Fund, PROMANACHCS (Agriculture Ministry), and the Transportation Ministry.

Table 3A–2. Description of Training Programs in Seven Countries in the Region

| Country, program | Beneficiaries | | Expenditure | |
	Thousands	Percent of total labor force	Millions of U.S. dollars	Percent of GDP
Argentina	133.0	1.4	95.6	**0.04**
Project Youth				
Scholarships and stage in temporary job for low-income, nonskilled, unemployed youth	53.0	0.6	71.7	0.027
Microentrepreneurship Project				
Entrepreneurship training for experienced, unskilled workers	5.4	0.1	6.5	0.002
Imagen Program (Employment Guidance)				
Job-search assistance	27.0	0.3	1.2	0.000
Occupational Workshops Program (PTO)				
Support to NGOs on setting up training institutions	18.0	0.2	4.2	0.002
Occupational Training Program				
Training of unemployed and SME personnel	24.0	0.3	7.3	0.003
Employment Training Program				
Scholarships and stage in temporary job for low-income, nonskilled, unemployed, and displaced workers	1.7	0.0	2.3	0.001
Learning Program				
Financing of health and accident insurance for young workers hired under *Contratos de Aprendizaje*	1.9	0.0	–	
Starting Program				
Financing of training cost for workers in new firms	2.0	0.0	2.4	0.001
Fiscal Credit Program				
Tax exception for training firms	–		–	
Brazil	740.5	1.6	310.2	0.06
PLANFOR				
FAT-financed training program executed at the federal and state levels by independent training institutions				
State and Federal Programs				
Federal and state programs for vulnerable groups	340.8	0.7	149.8	0.03
Emergency Programs				
Emergencies from drought and declining/restructuring sectors	399.7	0.9	159.4	0.03

(continued)

Table 3A–2. Training Programs (continued)

Country, program	Beneficiaries		Expenditure	
	Thousands	Percent of total labor force	Millions of U.S. dollars	Percent of GDP
Chile	36.6	0.8	18.3	0.03
Chile Joven Youth Employment Program				
Stipend and stage in temporary job for low-income, nonskilled, unemployed youth	17.9	0.4	10.4	0.019
Support Program for Women Heads of Low-Income Households				
Training, daycare, health, and other services to improve labor market insertion of poor women	15.0	0.3	4.9	0.009
Women and Microenterprise Program				
Entrepreneurship training for female household heads with some education	0.1	0.0	0.3	0.001
Labor Reintegration Program				
Job search and relocation assistance to displaced carbon and textile workers	0.2	0.0	0.8	0.002
Regular Scholarships Programs				
Scholarships for training at official institutions for vulnerable groups (temporary workers in agriculture, ports, and fishing)	1.3	0.0	0.3	0.001
Support Project for Labor Reintegration for Handicapped People				
Policy formulation and pilot program for labor market insertion of handicapped workers	0.1	0.0	0.1	0.000
Labor Training and Insertion for Handicapped People	0.6	0.0	0.9	0.002
Rehabilitation, Training, and Labor Insertion Program for Handicapped People	0.2	0.0	0.1	0.000
Labor Training and Formation Program				
Adult training program privately operated	1.2	0.0	0.4	0.001
Costa Rica	13.1	1.2	60.6	0.73
Llave en Mano Training Program				
Contracting out training activities by the public training institution (INA)	–		–	
Training and Restructuring for the Mobilized				
Training for displaced public sector workers	1.5	0.1	–	
Public Workshops				
Training low-income workers in marginal urban areas	6.2	0.6	–	
Professional Training for the Handicapped				
Training handicapped workers	1.0	0.1	–	

(continued)

Table 3A–2. (continued)

Country, program	Beneficiaries		Expenditure	
	Thousands	Percent of total labor force	Millions of U.S. dollars	Percent of GDP
Costa Rica (*continued*)				
Labor and Social Security Ministry's Program for Employment Training Scholarships				
Scholarships for training workers with secondary education	4.4	0.4	0.1	
Jamaica	43.5	4.4	18.6	0.44
Skills 2000				
Training for out-of-school and unskilled unemployed workers	40.0	4.1	11.4	0.3
Special Training Empowerment Programme (STEP)				
Youth training	0.6	0.1	4.6	0.1
Strategies to Rehabilitate Inner Cities through Viable Enterprises (VIABLE)				
Urban youth training	–		–	
National Youth Service (NYS)				
Training for temporary employment for unemployed youth	2.9	0.3	2.6	0.06
Mexico	410.3	1.8	135	0.04
Unemployed Training Scholarship Program (PROBECAT)				
Training and scholarships for unemployed workers	410.3	1.8	135	0.038
Peru	1.5	0.1	5.0	0.01
Youth Labor Training Program (PROJOVEN)				
Scholarships and training for unemployed youth	1.5	0.1	5.0	0.01

– Not available.

References

Calmfors, Lars. 1994. "Active Labour Market Policy and Unemployment—a Framework for the Analysis of Crucial Design Features." *OECD Economic Studies 22.* Paris.

Cortázar, Rene, and others. 1995. "Hacia un nuevo diseño del sistema de protección a cesantes." *Colección Estudios CIEPLAN 40.*

Government of Brazil. 1998. Ministério do Trabalho, Brasília. *Relatório da Força-tarefa sobre Políticas de Emprego – Diagnóstico e Recomendações.* August.

Government of Mexico. 1995. *Capacitación y empleo: evaluación del programa de becas de capacitación para desempleados,* Sec. de Trabajo y Previsión Social, México DF. August.

Government of the United States. 1995. *Social Security Programs throughout the World.* Department of Health and Human Services.

Graham, Carol. 1994. *Safety Nets, Politics, and the Poor: Transitions to Market Economies.* Washington, D.C.: Brookings Institution.

Grosh, Margaret. 1994. *Administering Targeted Social Programs in Latin America.* World Bank Regional and Sectoral Studies. World Bank, Washington, D.C.

Lightman, E.S. 1995. "You Can Lead a Horse to Water, but . . . : The Case against Workfare in Canada." In J. Richards and others, eds., *Helping the Poor: A Qualified Case for Workfare.* Toronto: Howe Institute.

Lora, E., and C. Pagés. 1997. "La legislación laboral y el proceso de reformas estructurales de América Latina y el Caribe." In M. Cárdenas, ed., *Empleo y distribución del ingreso en América Latina, Hemos avanzado?* Bogotá: Fedesarrollo.

Mazza, Jacqueline. 1999. *Unemployment Insurance: Case Studies and Lessons for the Latin American and Caribbean Region.* Technical Study RE2/SO2. Inter-American Development Bank, Washington, D.C.

Ravallion, Martin. 1998. *Appraising Workfare Programs.* Technical Study. SDS/POV, Inter-American Development Bank, Washington, D.C.

Rose, Nancy E. 1994. *Put to Work: Relief Programs in the Great Depression.* Monthly Review Press.

Verdera, Francisco. 1998. "Análisis comparativo de los programas de empleo e ingresos en América Latina y el Caribe." In G. Márquez and D. Martínez, eds., *Programas de empleo e ingreso en América Latina y el Caribe.* Lima, Peru, and Washington, D.C.: Inter-American Development Bank and International Labour Organisation.

CHAPTER FOUR

Heterogeneity and Optimal Unemployment Insurance

Hugo A. Hopenhayn and Juan Pablo Nicolini

The purpose of this chapter is to explore the effects of heterogeneity on the design of optimal unemployment insurance (UI). The problem is by all means important to policymakers. Most existing UI programs offer the same contract to all workers, while optimal contract theory suggests that optimal contracts depend on the risk exposure of agents. The evidence on private insurance markets suggests heterogeneity is important, too: the older one becomes, the more expensive life insurance is; the faster one drives—and therefore the more accidents one has in a given year—the more expensive auto insurance is next year; the closer to California your house is, the more expensive earthquake insurance is. If private firms find it optimal to offer different contracts to customers that have different observable characteristics, why would it be optimal to offer the same unemployment insurance to different workers?

Maybe existing contracts are offering too much insurance to some workers and too little to others. If this is the case, welfare could be increased and distortions on incentives reduced with the same budget, by optimally designing contracts for groups of workers. The purpose of this chapter is to contribute to this discussion.

The provision of insurance has a negative impact on incentives in environments with private information. Thus, UI has effects on average unemployment duration and therefore on equilibrium unemployment rates. In fact, most features of the UI programs have been allegedly designed with the aim of reducing these distortions. For instance, the benefit received is only a fraction of the previous wage and lasts for a limited time. Also, a certain number of previous working periods are required to qualify for benefits.

This paper was prepared for the LACEA/IDB/World Bank Network on Inequality and Poverty. We thank Carmen Pagés for useful suggestions.

In previous work, we used optimal dynamic contract theory under asymmetric information to assess the optimality of the existing restrictions to deal with incentive problems and characterized optimal unemployment insurance contracts when asymmetric information creates a trade-off between insurance and incentives.[1] We showed that along the optimal contract, the benefit the unemployed worker receives is a decreasing function of the length of the unemployment spell. We also showed that a reemployment tax that increases with the length of the unemployment spell could substantially improve the efficiency of the contract.

A major drawback of existing models is that all unemployed workers are assumed to face the same risk in all periods. In this chapter we relax this assumption in two dimensions. First, we use the model to understand how important systematic differences are in workers' reemployment hazard rates for the design of unemployment insurance. Second, we want to understand the effect of cyclical variations in reemployment probabilities.

As we mentioned above, understanding these issues seems critical from a policy perspective. Current unemployment insurance programs give similar profiles to all unemployed workers. However, the unemployment risk is very uneven across the population. For instance, in Argentina the average unemployment rate from May 1992 to May 1995 was 3.6 percent, 9.7 percent, and 14.5 percent for professionals, white-collar, and blue-collar workers, respectively.[2] In addition, there is not much contingency of the program on aggregate conditions, though in some cases the governments make discretionary adjustments.[3] And aggregate conditions vary a lot, particularly in Latin American countries. The experience of Chile in the early 1980s and that of Argentina in 1995, when unemployment rates skyrocketed to 27 percent and 18 percent, respectively, are eloquent examples.

All we know about optimal contract theory suggests that the particular details of the contract are sensitive to variations in the risk exposure of agents, so it is natural to investigate the optimality of unemployment insurance contracts that vary with observable characteristics of unemployed workers. This issue is particularly important when there is policy concern regarding the well-being of the less fortunate in society, since unemployment risk is higher in the low-skill and low-education portion of the working population.

---

[1] See Hopenhayn and Nicolini (1997 and 1999).
[2] See Pessino (1997) for details.
[3] Some U.S. states increase the coverage during recessions discretionally; see Meyer (1990).

The model and approach of this chapter draw heavily on our previous work.[4] We extend the analysis to allow for risk heterogeneity across workers and over time. This chapter proceeds as follows. First, we derive some theoretical results in a simple two-period model, for the purpose of highlighting the main forces at work in the problem of designing optimal unemployment insurance contracts in the presence of risk heterogeneity. A full dynamic treatment of the problem is substantially more complicated and beyond the scope of this chapter. Next we generalize the model to an infinite time horizon and solve it numerically to compute the effects on the optimal contract of variations in the risk exposure of unemployed workers. There is clear evidence that the reemployment probability depends critically on observed characteristics of agents, like education or age. Thus, we first fit a logit equation to unemployment termination rates in Argentina, using data from a household survey (*Encuesta Permanente de Hogares*) to quantify the degree of unemployment risk heterogeneity. We use this evidence to calibrate the model. We particularly draw attention to the dependence of the optimal effort level on the risk characteristics of the agents. After that, we provide a nontechnical summary of the results and discussion of the main policy implications derived from the analysis, together with a discussion of a policy experiment ongoing in Argentina since 1996. Finally, we close the chapter. The reader not interested in the technical discussion should go directly to our closing remarks.

SOME THEORETICAL RESULTS

In this section we characterize the optimal unemployment insurance in a two-period model with two alternative sources of heterogeneity. First, we consider a setup where workers are heterogenous in their unemployment risk exposure. Second, we consider variations of risk exposure over time, depending on aggregate conditions.

As we mentioned in the introduction, the theoretical analysis will be done in a two-period model. This model is straightforward to solve, and the intuition behind the results is very clear. The infinite period version is technically very demanding and beyond the scope of this chapter.[5]

We consider the problem of providing insurance to a worker who is unemployed in the first period. In this same period, the worker chooses the effort de-

---

[4] Hopenhayn and Nicolini (1997, 1998).

[5] For infinite versions of the model without heterogeneity, see Hopenhayn and Nicolini (1997, 1999).

voted to finding a job for the second period. The key feature of the environment is that the probability of finding a new job depends on the effort devoted by the unemployed worker, and the government cannot monitor this effort. A contract specifies an unemployment benefit in the first period, a benefit in the second period if the worker is still unemployed, and a tax in the second period if the worker does find a job. The optimal contract maximizes the utility of the worker subject to a budget constraint for the government. This budget constraint is given by the political will of the government; in particular, it could be zero. This is the case of a self-financed unemployment insurance.[6]

Heterogeneity

We will first study how the optimal contract depends on the risk characteristics of the agents. The preferences of the worker are given by

$$(4\text{-}1) \qquad U(c) - a + \beta[(1 - p - \Delta)\, U(c^u) + (p + \Delta)\, U(c^e)],$$

where $a \in \{0,1\}$ is the search effort chosen by the worker in the first period, p is the probability of finding a job if the search effort is zero, while $p + \Delta$ is the probability if the effort level is 1, c^j is consumption in period 2 in state $j = e$ (employment), u (unemployment), and c is first period consumption. The function U is increasing and concave and β is the discount factor, assumed to be the same one as that used by the government.

In the context of our model, different risk exposures amount to heterogeneity on the probability to get a job when the effort level is high. Thus, let us assume that there are $j = 1, 2, 3, \ldots J$ different classes of workers, such that

$$p^j = p_0^j + \Delta_j.$$

The question we address in this section is how the features of the optimal contract vary when p varies. Heterogeneity may arise from differences in the baseline probability, p_0^j, or in the marginal effect of effort, Δ_j. In this section we will consider variations in both. Note that we allow for the worker to find a job even without

---

[6] Most existing UI programs spend more than what they collect and must be financed with other taxes.

searching. The key is that the probability of finding a job is higher if the worker chooses the high effort level.

We follow the literature and assume that the principal can control the consumption of the agent, so we preclude borrowing and lending contracts. We also assume that jobs are homogeneous and pay a wage w.[7] Even though our emphasis is in heterogeneity, we will suppress individual superscripts j in the notation that follows, since they will not be important in the algebra.

As the effort level is not observable, if the government wants to induce the worker to choose the high effort level, the contract must satisfy the following incentive compatibility constraint:

(4-2) $$\beta\Delta(U(c^e) - U(c^u)) \geq 1.$$

This condition guarantees that the worker will weakly prefer to choose the high effort level. The value for the government, measured in goods, of the contract is given by

(4-3) $$\beta[(p+\Delta)(c^e - w) + (1-p-\Delta)c^u] + c = B.$$

As is well known, there is a family of optimal contracts that are the solution of a Pareto problem. To solve for a point in the Pareto frontier, we can maximize the utility of the worker given a budget B for the government. Alternatively, we can solve the dual, that is, we can minimize the budget given a value for the worker's utility.

Note that the two problems have different interpretations regarding how different workers are treated. If we fix the budget, we are assuming that the government is allocating the same budget to each worker. Thus, along the optimal contract, workers who have lower probabilities of finding a job will have lower utility. However, if the contract fixes the utility of each worker at the same level, then it has to be the case that a higher budget is allocated to workers with lower

---

[7] In the context of this model, this is a harmless assumption if wage offers are observable, since the principal will fully insure the agent against wage risk. If wage offers are not observable, there is an additional moral hazard problem owing to the effect of the insurance on the reservation wage of the worker. However, in Hopenhayn and Nicolini (1998) we show that this moral hazard problem is equivalent to the one we model, and it can be embodied in the analysis without any change in the theory.

reemployment probabilities. Thus, in the first problem there is no redistribution across workers, while in the second one there is. We do not directly address this redistribution issue here, since it may be the object of a broader social security scheme that considers other income risk beyond unemployment risk. We will solve the problem assuming that the government allocates the same budget to each worker. However, it is worth mentioning that all the theoretical results proved in this chapter also hold if we solve the problem assuming that the contract gives all workers the same utility level.

The optimal contract problem is therefore to maximize the utility function 4-1 subject to the incentive compatibility constraint 4-2 and to the budget constraint 4-3, where, as we mentioned before, B is the per worker budget that the government allocates to the UI program. Note that the objective function is concave and the restrictions define a convex set, so the first-order conditions fully characterize the solution.

It is straightforward to verify that the first-order conditions can be combined to yield

(4-4)
$$\frac{1}{U'(c)} = \frac{p+\Delta}{U'(c^e)} + \frac{1-p-\Delta}{U'(c^u)}.$$

This equation and the two constraints can be used to find solutions for c, c^u, and c^e as functions of p and Δ. Note that the incentive compatibility constraint implies that consumption tomorrow if employed must be higher than consumption tomorrow if unemployed. But then, equation 4-4 implies that

$$c^e > c > c^u,$$

which means that the unemployment benefit tomorrow must be lower than today's, while consumption tomorrow if employed must be higher than today's. The intuition for these results is standard in the moral hazard literature. To provide incentives, the contract must punish unlucky workers by lowering the benefit and compensate lucky workers by increasing consumption.[8]

---

[8] These results generalize to infinite periods with repeated unemployment spells; see Hopenhayn and Nicolini (1997, 1999).

State Verifiability

Our focus in discussing optimal unemployment insurance has been the group of workers whose unemployment risk is higher, namely, the less educated and less experienced workers. Often, the members of this group find job opportunities mostly in the informal sector of the economy. Therefore, it may be very hard to monitor the employment status of the worker. Our investigation assumed that while search effort is not observable, employment status is. A strong incentive problem arises when the latter does not hold, since an unemployed worker receiving benefits would not have incentives to disclose having found a job.

One way to cope with this problem is to design programs that require those receiving benefits to appear at the insurance office, perhaps at random times. An extreme version of this is to force the beneficiary to hold a schedule. This can be done through government-sponsored working programs, like the *Plan de Empleo Mínimo* in Chile in the early 1980s or the *Programa Trabajar* currently functioning in Argentina. This last program has been in operation for three years, and its budget is used to fully subsidize labor in social projects managed by nonprofit organizations. These organizations are responsible for other costs of the project, that is, materials and capital. Wages paid are below the minimum wage, which reflects the fact that this program is geared to low-income groups. Furthermore, the regional allocation of the program's budget is affected by regional unemployment rates. The duration of the projects ranges from three to six months. Each worker must dedicate a minimum of six hours a day to working in the project.

Given the discussion above, a program like this one is attractive in that it decentralizes the monitoring of the employment status of the beneficiary in an incentive compatible way. The nonprofit organizations finance the other inputs of the program, so it is in their best interest to enforce the presence of the worker.

In terms of the analysis of this chapter, this program can be understood as an unemployment insurance contract plus a technology to monitor the working status of the worker. To the extent that the problem of monitoring employment status is more problematic for low-income groups, it is reasonable that these programs should be focused on these groups.

An alternative way in which this monitoring takes place is by requiring unemployed workers who collect benefits to attend educational and retraining programs. Note that the main objective may not be the instruction per se (although the more it increases the marginal productivity of the worker, the better), but the monitoring services it supplies. It is not clear, though, how the monitoring in these programs is performed, since it is not obvious that it is in the best interest of the school to monitor participants' attendance.

It should be emphasized that these monitoring schemes may come at a cost. In the analysis performed in this chapter, the key variable that increases the probability of reemployment is the effort of the worker. Although it is not obvious that effort is just measured as total daily time allocated to search activities, this is indeed a natural interpretation. Under this interpretation, then, by forcing the worker to allocate a significant fraction of the time endowment to the monitoring technology, the time left to allocate to search activities is very low. Thus, while the programs do ensure that the worker is not taking advantage of the insurance while working, they also reduce the available time for search activities and eventually reduce the reemployment probability. This is only a problem if the recommended action is the high effort level. On the contrary, if the optimal effort level is zero, which, as we suggested in this chapter, may be the case, these mechanisms can be a reasonable way to solve the monitoring problem.

In the case that the time interpretation of effort is appropriate, a possible way out of the trade-off between monitoring the employment state and letting the unemployed worker allocate a sizable amount of time to search activities is a part-time job. The idea is to force the worker to allocate the minimum possible amount of time to the monitoring technology and minimize the probability that the worker is in fact employed. Examples of strategies that could be used with that purpose are part-time jobs whose time requirements each week are stochastic. Thus, the worker has half a day to allocate to search activities but does not know, ex ante, when. Under the assumption that working requires a stronger commitment to a time schedule than searching, this may improve upon the efficiency of the program.

It should also be mentioned, however, that the time interpretation of effort that we considered in the previous paragraph is not the only way to interpret the moral hazard problem. And this is important to assess the potential cost in terms of a reduction of the reemployment probability of the program. An alternative interpretation, which is formally equivalent, is that job offers exogenously come to the unemployed worker with a certain probability.[15] The wage of each offer is drawn from a given probability distribution, so with certain probability the worker receives low wage offers, and with other probability high wage offers. As is standard in job search models, the worker will accept the high wage offers and reject the low

---

[15] See Hopenhayn and Nicolini (1999) for details.

wage ones. In fact, the optimal behavior of the worker is characterized by a reservation wage, such that all offers above that wage will be accepted and all offers below that wage will be rejected.

In such an environment, an unemployed worker receiving benefits will be more demanding than a worker without coverage, so the probability of accepting a job will be lower. This incentive problem can be cast along the lines of the model analyzed in this chapter and exactly the same theoretical results follow. In fact, if we observe time series of the working status of the agents and of which of the unemployed workers is receiving benefits, it is impossible to tell from the data if the moral hazard problem is due to a reduction in the time devoted to search or an increase in the reservation wage.

From a theoretical standpoint, this equivalence does not present any complications, since, as we have mentioned already, the results do not depend on the source of the moral hazard problem. However, it is key to assess the effect that forcing the unemployed workers to allocate time to monitoring activities has on their reemployment probability. In the case that the moral hazard problem is due to reduced time devoted to search, taking the worker's time reduces the chances of reemployment, while if it is due to increases in the reservation wage, it does not.[16]

A final word regarding the monitoring problem. Note that the insurance scheme discussed above contemplates levying a tax on the workers once they get a job. Thus, if it is too costly to monitor the worker's employment status, incentives for self-reporting must be given. As in any problem with private information, the fact that one of the parties can reveal information can be used in the optimal design problem. Contributed funds have been suggested as a way of curtailing this problem. The idea of the contributed funds is that each worker has a personal account, very similar to a pension plan, to which the worker contributes in the working state and withdraws from in the unemployment state. Thus, the incentives to contribute arise from the effect present contributions have on future benefits. This program shows how the future benefits can be used to provide incentives to the workers to reveal their state. However, if these funds simply replicate outside saving opportunities, workers would have very little incentives to report. Hence, additional benefits should be provided to induce self-selection. This could be done by

---

[16] Note that in the shorter search scenario, it is perfectly reasonable for unemployed workers to refuse to enter into this program, particularly those who have a marginal effect of effort that is high. This creates an adverse selection problem because the ones that more willingly participate in this program are the ones who get a small increase in their employment probability by choosing the high effort level.

subsidizing the return or providing an option value by conditioning future unemployment benefits to specific employment durations.

In most cases these funds, as is the case in pension plans, are fully funded by each individual. That is, total contributions and total withdrawals satisfy a present value condition for each individual account. As such, there is no insurance provided. Full insurance only imposes ex ante present value conditions, using fair prices to value alternative states of nature. Thus, while the contributions can definitely have informational content that is valuable in the design of the optimal mechanism, imposing ex post present value conditions amounts to providing no insurance. When informational constraints are relevant, full insurance is not optimal, but in the trade-off between incentives and insurance, there is no presumption that the solution is the corner with no insurance.

References

Hopenhayn, Hugo, A., and Juan Pablo Nicolini. 1997. "Optimal Unemployment Insurance." *Journal of Political Economy* 105 (April): 412–38.

———. 1998. *Optimal Unemployment Insurance: The Adverse Selection Case.* Working Paper. Universidad Torcuato Di Tella, Buenos Aires, Argentina.

———. 1999. *Optimal Unemployment Insurance and Employment History.* Working Paper. Universidad Torcuato Di Tella, Buenos Aires, Argentina.

Meyer, B. 1990. "Unemployment Insurance and Unemployment Spells." *Econometrica* 58 (July): 757–82.

Pessino, Carola. 1997. "Argentina: The Labor Market during the Economic Transition." In Sebastian Edwards and Nora Lustig, eds., *Labor Markets in Latin America: Combining Social Protection with Market Flexibility.* Washington, D.C.: Brookings Institution.

CHAPTER FIVE

Helping the Poor Manage Risk Better: The Role of Social Funds

Steen Lau Jørgensen and Julie Van Domelen

In a world of increasing opportunities and risks because of globalization and technological and political change, there is a need to reassess what role social funds should play. Social funds have established themselves as important instruments for social protection in many parts of the developing world. This chapter will show the important role that social funds can fulfill in an approach to social protection, which moves us away from simply looking at social protection as a response to adverse shocks toward a more holistic, institution-oriented definition that puts social protection squarely at the center of the fight against poverty and social exclusion.

Initial steps have been made, with fairly comprehensive qualitative information available on most social funds through beneficiary assessments. Improvements in quantitative information, particularly about benefits to poor households and sustainability of social fund investments, are under way in several countries with support from the World Bank–financed Social Funds 2000 Impact Evaluation Study.

WHAT IS A SOCIAL FUND?

There is no universally agreed definition of a social fund. We propose to define social funds as follows: agencies that finance projects in several sectors targeted to benefit a country's poor and vulnerable groups based on a participatory manner of demand generated by local groups and screened against a set of eligibility criteria. There are agencies that would meet these criteria but are not called social funds, and there are agencies called social funds that do not meet these criteria.

In general, social funds present the following characteristics. Social funds establish menus, procedures, and targeting criteria to support investments benefiting the poor. They appraise, finance, and supervise the implementation of small social projects but do not (in general) identify, implement, and maintain or operate the projects. Almost all social funds insist on cofinancing from the beneficiaries to ensure that projects are not just responding to need but to demand. However, while they respond to demand from local groups (community groups, nongovernmental organizations [NGOs], local governments, or local representatives of regional or national governments), most have a set menu of eligible projects or a negative list of ineligible projects. Even though most are part of the public sector, the funds often have operational autonomy and enjoy exceptions from public sector rules such as civil service rules or procurement and disbursement rules. Most tend to be like private firms in their operational practices, with a small staff employed on the basis of performance contracts, higher salaries, and higher performance standards. Management is usually private sector style, that is, driven more by results than by rules. Because of their operational autonomy, most funds operate under strict accountability and transparency criteria through independent audits and intense public scrutiny. Although most social funds are heavily dependent on external financing, they are run by nationals of the country and do not rely on long-term expatriate technical assistance.

Since the first internationally known social fund, the *Fondo Social de Emergencia* in Bolivia, was established in 1987, the world has seen an explosion in the number of these institutions and a proliferation of objectives and modes of operation. Today almost all countries in Latin America and the Caribbean have social funds or development projects (such as the one in North-East Brazil) that share the same operational characteristics as social funds. In Sub-Saharan Africa, at last count social funds or their sister Public Works and Employment Projects (AGETIPs, by their French acronym) existed in 24 countries, with at least half a dozen more countries at various stages of preparing or piloting social funds.[1] In the Middle East and North Africa there are four social funds operating, one of which, the Egypt Social Fund, is the world's largest, with at least two more under preparation. In Eastern Europe and Central Asia, about five are currently in operation, with another half dozen at various stages of preparation. The region that has the fewest social funds is Asia, with only three agencies in operation that are called social funds and with five more under preparation. However, several agencies do exist in countries such as India and Indonesia that share many operational characteristics with social funds.

---

[1] Frigenti and Harth (1998).

Table 5–1. Portfolio Distribution of Social Fund Investments in the Middle East and North Africa

Percent

Program	Micro-enterprise	Roads	Other infras-tructure	Education	Health	Water and sanitation	Other
West Bank and Gaza–Community Development Project		40	24	20	6	10	
West Bank and Gaza–NGO Project				54	28		17
Yemen SFD	8		4	56	11	20	1
Egypt–SFD Phase I	58	4	20	6	5	2	5
Algeria Safety Net Program		40	31			21	7

Source: Van Domelen (1998).

In terms of the level and focus of activity of social funds, they are most widely known for their investments in social infrastructure, particularly health, education, water supply, and sanitation, although this allocation varies greatly by country. For the regions where summary statistics are available, Latin America and the Middle East and North Africa, tables 5–1 and 5–2 summarize the distribution of investments. Investment in health, education, and water supply (infrastructure and noninfrastructure) is the leading area in all funds except those in Egypt, Chile, the West Bank, the Gaza Community Development Project, Algeria, and the original Emergency Social Fund of Bolivia.

Growth in the number and volume of activity of social funds makes them one of the most successful examples of institutional replicability and adaptability in the short history of development efforts.[2] While international agencies were largely responsible for the extension of the basic model between regions, the homegrown demand from countries for this type of program has fueled their adoption and adaptation to local circumstances. The fact that social funds allow governments to build on local groups' ability and resources, and thereby leverage scarce fiscal or aid money, has meant that these funds are now occupying important niches in many countries.

---

[2] The Inter-American Development Bank and the World Bank alone have invested more than $3.5 billion in social funds.

Table 5–2. Portfolio Distribution of Selected Social Fund Investments in Latin America and the Caribbean

Percent

Program	Economic infrastructure	Social infrastructure	Productive projects	Other
Bolivia				
ESF (1986–91)	44	43	3	9
SIF (1991–95)		85		15
Chile				
FOSIS (1991–95)			46	54
Ecuador				
FISE (1993–95)	11	85	4	
El Salvador				
FIS (1990–96)		84	13	3
Guatemala				
FIS (1993–95)	3	62	2	33
Haiti				
FAES (1995–96)	26	67		7
Honduras				
FHIS (1990–95)	10	65	7	18
Nicaragua				
FISE (1991–94)	19	63	1	17
Peru				
FONCODES (1991–96)	22	53	13	12

Source: Goodman and others (1997).

However, as part of a country's social protection strategy, it is worth pointing out that social funds remain a very small part of the social protection activities in the vast majority of countries. In a recent review of social funds financed by the Inter-American Development Bank, only one fund in Latin America spent more than 1 percent of GDP (Nicaragua).[3] On average in the Latin American region, less than U.S.$10 is spent per year per poor person through social funds. In the Middle East and North Africa, in spite of the presence of one of the world's largest social funds in Egypt, which has committed roughly U.S.$1 billion since its inception in 1991, social fund spending is a relatively small share of total effort on safety net pro-

---

[3] Morley in Bigio (1998, p. 46); Goodman and others (1997).

grams. In general, social funds remain highly dependent on external resources. Exceptions to the rule are Chile, with under 10 percent from foreign sources, Colombia with 20 percent external financing, FONEPAZ in Guatemala at 12 percent, and Peru's FONCODES, with 58 percent donor support. Only Egypt has moved to shift more of the share of financing to local sources, from only 6 percent at the outset to 22 percent at present. Data for Africa, Eastern Europe, and Asia are not available.

Originally, social funds were set up to provide temporary employment and provide "a bridge over the crisis," through labor-based income transfers and the subsidization of social services and infrastructure.[4] As the institutions have evolved, most are now seen as more permanent components of a country's social development strategy. The social funds still respond to emergencies, such as Hurricane Mitch in Central America, the fall-out from the wars in Cambodia and Angola, an earthquake in Armenia, or a drought in Zambia.

Although many social funds were initiated with fairly simple objectives, today most social funds must balance multiple objectives, all of which fall broadly under the umbrella of efforts to improve the living conditions of the poor. Most social funds incorporate to a lesser or greater extent objectives in the five categories listed below. Please note that these objectives are not mutually exclusive, and several social funds have changed emphasis over time:

1. The improvement in a country's *infrastructure*, such as the current Bolivian Social Investment Fund and the funds in Central America, Peru, Ethiopia, Malawi, Armenia, Angola, and Cambodia. These funds have tended to focus on addressing unmet needs of poor communities through basic social and economic infrastructure.

2. The *employment* funds, typical of the initial stage of funds created in response to emergencies, such as in Bolivia and Egypt. In the absence of an emergency, job creation also appears as a prime objective in other funds, such as the AGETIPS in Africa or the planned Bulgaria fund, whose main objective is the provision of short-term employment primarily through the repair of infrastructure.

3. Broader-based *community development*, exemplified in Argentina, Romania, Malawi, and Zambia, where a major objective of the social funds is to build community capacity to demand and manage development resources. This is most frequently done through a "learning-by-doing" process where the social funds finance mainly infrastructure projects that the communities manage and implement.

---

[4] Avila and others (1992).

4. Improvement in the delivery of *social services*, as typified by the funds in Chile, Argentina, and Romania, where a major emphasis is put on financing private-public partnerships in social service provision, including a large emphasis on training.

5. *Support for decentralization*, promoted by the funds in Chile, Honduras, Bolivia, and Ethiopia, where a major objective of the fund is to work closely with local governments to support the decentralization effort of the country. Some funds pass on their expertise to governments (Zambia, Honduras), while others (like Chile) transfer successful pilot interventions to local governments.

There is hardly a uniform trend in where social funds are going, and any knowledgeable social funds person will be able to come up with a dozen funds that are not following any of the trends given here. In any case, in a general sense some of the trends that can be observed are as follows:

• Social funds are generally becoming more permanent, more integrated into a country's overall social and economic development efforts—this implies more and better coordination with line agencies, local governments, and civil society.

• There is a relative increase (but from a very small base) in the share of resources from social funds that go to social services.

• Increasingly social funds pay more attention to popular participation, both to enhance sustainability and to build social capital.

• Social funds are increasingly seen as, and are moving to operate more as, supporters of decentralization.

• Social funds are faced with increasing demand for income-generating subprojects, but the experience so far has been mixed. The funds with better performance in the microfinance area have usually done a combination of two things. First, they have selected appropriate intermediaries, and second, they have adopted policies that take into consideration best practice in the microfinance area. The Chile social fund presents an interesting case in terms of its successful support for income generation.

From ten-plus years of experience with social funds, several stylized facts can be developed about what works and what does not.[5] On the positive side, social

---

[5] While these stylized facts are the authors' own, many are supported by the findings of assessments such as Bigio (1998); Frigenti and Harth (1998); Goodman and others (1997); Pradhan, Rawlings, and Ridder (1998); and Subbarao and others (1997).

funds have proved very good at adjusting to changed circumstances, as decentralization moves forward or as a natural disaster happens.[6] Funds tend to be more participatory than other development projects, but they have the potential to do even better, and there is wide variety across social funds. Social funds are well targeted to the poor and have reached the poor in many cases. They have low overheads and administrative costs and generally manage to provide infrastructure at much lower costs than traditional public sector agencies. In terms of both financial and public accountability the funds tend to outperform other development interventions, and where they work well, they help generate trust in the public sector among communities and build social capital. Funds can work in very different situations: for example, in Armenia, Argentina, Cambodia, Rwanda, and Haiti.

Social funds have a mixed record on sustainability. Social funds that started as emergency operations rarely focused on sustainability as a prime issue. As funds have evolved and become more focused on medium-term impacts, sustainability has become a systemic concern, particularly given the poor track record of the line ministries and local governments often responsible for operating and maintaining the investments after the social fund intervention. On health and education investments they tend to do better than traditional ministries owing to the emphasis on community participation; on economic infrastructure they do as well or as poorly as other agencies depending on the institutional framework in the country.[7]

Originally, autonomy from line ministries was seen as fundamental for a social fund to operate. However, there are several successful counterexamples, including social funds in Chile and Zambia under the Ministries of Planning and the Argentina social fund, which is a program of the Ministry of Social Development. In terms of operating procedures, some funds work more directly with community groups (Peru, Argentina, Zambia, Malawi, Romania, and Armenia), while others work more closely with intermediaries like local government (Honduras, Nicaragua, and Bolivia). In terms of the types of investments included in social fund menus, some funds focus more narrowly on social infrastructure, while others have more

---

[6] Some examples include Honduras, where in response to Hurricane Mitch the FHIS shifted to emergency assistance and reconstruction by changing procedures and quadrupling its capacity; Chile, where after a strategic planning exercise FOSIS revised its menu of eligible interventions and shifted to a geographic rather than programmatic focus; and Bolivia, where the FIS now works solely with local governments in response to the new decentralization policies.

[7] Bigio (1998).

expanded menus to include significant investments in productive activities, training, and social services. In general, it appears that optimal institutional design is better determined by country need and circumstance than standard prescription.

Social funds generally have not done well in microcredit activities, and they are not well integrated with the rest of the public sector. Because of their operational autonomy, in some cases funds have ended up running as almost parallel governments, confusing beneficiaries and not contributing to capacity building. While most social funds were designed as temporary instruments, there has been little success in training and transferring the positive aspects of social fund experience to line ministries. Some critics claim that the operational success of the social funds has distracted attention from the longer-term institutional reforms necessary in the permanent public agencies.

While social funds have been very successful at reaching underserved areas and marginal populations, there has also been leakage of benefits to the nonpoor and gaps in coverage of the poorest of the poor (while social funds do in fact reach the lowest income deciles, not all people in those deciles benefit from social fund interventions). These observations are largely due to the demand-driven model, which relies upon community initiative and capacity; the focus on providing access to broad public services (health, education), where exclusion of less-poor community members is not feasible; and inclusion of certain types of programs that may be less well targeted by their nature (for example, small and microenterprise support, urban sewerage).

Social funds have also been less adept at providing massive assistance, especially in terms of employment generated. Moreover, targeting of employment benefits has tended to exclude women and be less pro-poor than programs that use wages lower than market-based wages.

Two of the main difficulties in coming to hard and fast conclusions about social funds are the diversity of experience and the dearth of effective evaluations of social fund performance and impact. The last point may seem contradictory when one looks at the lengthy bibliographies and research pieces devoted to social funds. However, most evaluations have been limited by the lack of data on what is happening to program participants at the household level and a lack of information that would allow comparison of social funds to other delivery mechanisms. To address the second point, the World Bank launched the Social Funds 2000 Impact Evaluation Study in 1998 to evaluate social fund performance in terms of poverty targeting, impacts of benefits at the household level, sustainability of these benefits, and cost effectiveness of interventions compared with other delivery mechanisms in each of six case study countries (Bolivia, Honduras, Zambia, Armenia, Nicaragua, and Peru). Results are expected for the first quarter of 2000.

For social funds to remain effective contributors to social protection, the institutional issues raised above will need to be addressed in a sustained fashion. Where social funds have a narrower sectoral focus, sharing tools and information and joint evaluations with line ministries and local governments may lead to either better rationalization of efforts, mutual strengthening of institutional capacity, and/or eventual phasing out of social fund support in certain areas.[8] In other instances, closer social fund integration with local governments, combined with greater decentralization, may lead to an absorption of social fund financing within fiscal transfer schemes. In other circumstances, social funds may take on a more pre-eminent role in assisting poor communities to organize and express their demands. By addressing these institutional coherency and effectiveness issues, social funds may evolve into more permanent actors in a country's social protection and poverty reduction framework.

SOCIAL FUNDS IN A SOCIAL RISK MANAGEMENT FRAMEWORK

One of the reasons for the relative success of social funds has been their ability to work with a wide variety of agencies, private contractors, line ministries, local authorities, decentralized agencies, international and local NGOs, community-based organizations, and the communities themselves. Social risk management is focused on helping individuals manage risk better, but individuals' risk management strategies employ a variety of institutions or economic agents. The most basic unit is the family—where a lot of the information asymmetries are minimized. NGOs and community-based organizations also help through information intermediation between the families in a community and the outside world. Similarly, market-based institutions are employed through the labor or financial markets. Finally, social funds work with various public sector agencies. It is not surprising that the beneficiaries (and sometimes the public at large) often regard social funds as fully responsive to community and household priorities and, therefore, as an important agent of public support for their own risk management.[9]

---

[8] An example of transfer of models back to line ministries is Chile's FOSIS support for forestry initiatives.

[9] Van Domelen and Owen (1998). As funds evolve toward becoming more permanent instruments, they run the risk of losing some of the characteristics that have made them so popular in the first place, namely, agility and flexibility.

FIGURE 5–1.

Social Funds in the Social Risk Management Framework

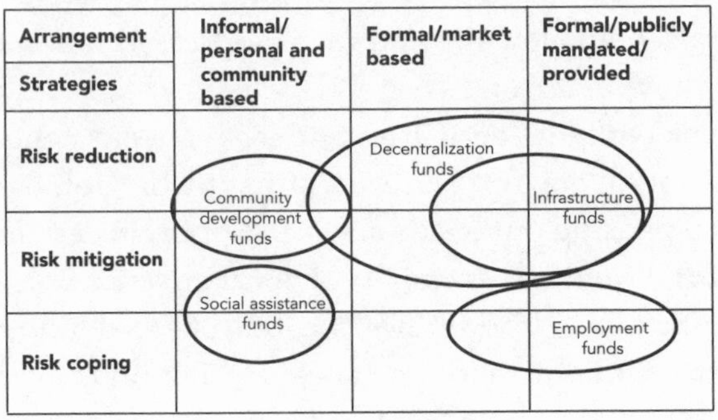

Arrangement Strategies	Informal/ personal and community based	Formal/market based	Formal/publicly mandated/ provided
Risk reduction		Decentralization funds	
Risk mitigation	Community development funds		Infrastructure funds
Risk coping	Social assistance funds		Employment funds

Figure 5–1 shows a mapping of the different types of social funds into a matrix of social risk management. The employment funds are set up to help people cope with the effect of crises. What differentiates social funds from traditional public works programs is that active participation from the private sector and civil society is encouraged through the use of private sector contractors and civic organizations as sponsors, and thus the social funds are able to move out of the bottom right corner of the matrix toward the middle of the last row. Some recent social funds with a public works component, such as the Malawi Social Action Fund, have managed to include some elements of community participation, spreading the coverage of these funds into the first column as well.

The community development funds fit within the cells of support to informal mitigation and reduction mechanisms. They help in mitigation by building social capital (one more asset for the portfolio of the vulnerable) and in reducing certain risks such as local conflict through the support for locally generated joint efforts.

The social assistance funds have so far mainly focused on supporting households' informal coping mechanisms (such as support for AIDS victims, helping the poor get access to existing transfers) or within mitigation (through support for building human capital through nutrition, training, and other human development services). The support for decentralization funds is working across the market-based and public sector aspects of risk mitigation and coping. By building the capacity of local governments to interact better with the private sector and with communities, the funds are helping lower the information gap, which has in the past caused government failure in the provision of some social risk management services at this level.

The trends in social funds' characteristics toward more permanent impacts beyond temporary employment, more social services, more participation, more decentralization, and more income generation would seem to indicate that social funds are shifting upward in the matrix toward risk reduction as opposed to risk coping.

Several social fund–type mechanisms have been created with temporary employment as a prime objective, for instance, in Bolivia after the closure of the tin mines, in Egypt to deal with the effects of the Gulf War, in the West Bank and Gaza in response to closures of the border with Israel, and in Ecuador as a response to the economic contraction during adjustment. To think of a social fund within a social risk management framework means to assess, first, whether temporary employment is needed (for example, is open unemployment the issue for the vulnerable?), and then, whether a social fund instrument is better at delivering such services than other perhaps more centralized and top-down interventions.

Even though social funds have done well on many scores, employment creation has not been their strong suit.[10] For instance, social funds have not been very effective in targeting a specific type of worker to benefit from these temporary jobs, be they ex-miners or redundant public sector workers. Although considered "vulnerable," such groups often have coping mechanisms (severance pay, higher skill and education levels, and so on) which make direct employment generation through public works less attractive. In general, even the larger social funds with explicit employment creation objectives have generated temporary jobs equivalent to well below 1 percent of the labor force. While funds may serve as an important political tool during difficult periods of transition and shocks, as a social risk minimization strategy its effects reach a relatively small number of households at risk.

The same holds true for social fund operations as a poverty alleviation or compensation measure. Although the number of people benefiting from improved access to and quality of social infrastructure and services is far greater than the potential employment impacts, the amounts disbursed are minor. One study discussed above found that the value of goods and services being transferred by a social fund to the poor typically averages well below 5 percent of the per capita income of the poor.[11] The finding is similar to a recent review of social funds in the Middle East and North Africa region, which finds that in all cases the annual amount transferred was less than 4 percent of the poverty line income.[12] Therefore, the so-

---

[10] For the results on Bolivia, see Newman, Jørgensen, and Pradhan (1991).

[11] Goodman and others (1997).

[12] Van Domelen (1999).

cial protection effects of social funds, either in terms of employment creation or in the provision of basic services to the poor, have been important for the beneficiaries but limited in their coverage.[13]

WHITHER SOCIAL FUNDS?

Social funds can be an effective tool to support risk mitigation at the community level since there are more assets available for a community to manage in a portfolio sense after the social fund has financed new or improved infrastructure. To move the social funds squarely into the risk-reducing area, their investments need to help prevent shocks. This would mean making sure that the water supply system indeed does provide clean water over a period of time to prevent water-borne diseases, and making sure that learning is taking place in the school, so the risk of future low earnings is reduced. In other words, social funds need to pay more attention to the flow of benefits from the infrastructure they have created, including more attention to operation and maintenance.

Education investments account for a significant share of current social fund portfolios. In most cases, grants are given for school rehabilitation or construction of new classrooms at the primary level. The potential impacts of these investments vary between projects. These benefits range from extending the useful life of a building to creating space for increased enrollment, increasing the number of years offered at the school, and improving teacher and community morale and hence the quality of education. Under a social risk management strategy, the benefits of building repair are far outstripped by the benefits of increasing enrollment and number of years completed, as these will have the largest effects on the capacity of poor households to reduce risks over time.

Taking social risk management as a primary consideration, social funds would become more discerning in their education investments, placing relatively more resources in projects that had greater potential to affect either enrollment (directly, through creating more spaces, or indirectly, through reduced drop-out rates) or years of schooling completed. By focusing their attention on impacts in educational attainment, social funds will be better able to steer themselves away from becoming simply a substitute for national school construction and maintenance programs.

---

[13] Bigio (1998).

To date, social funds have been more focused on outputs than outcomes, understandable in the context of social crises and the need to prove their operational capacity. Moving to a greater focus on outcomes will require that social funds become better "learning organizations" capable not only of action but in-depth monitoring and evaluation. Mainstreaming impact evaluation methodologies and ensuring that learning takes place across social funds, local governments, and sectors is a significant challenge for the future.

Given the limited resources available to social funds compared with the poverty problems of the countries, difficult decisions about whom to reach are unavoidable. In general, the targeting strategies of social funds use a broad focus on poor communities, not distinguishing by vulnerability. To improve their effectiveness at risk management, social funds should seek to identify communities, households, and individuals within the broad pool of the poor, which are by their nature more vulnerable and marginalized. If one of the goals of social risk management is to improve equity, assisting the most vulnerable will increase the impact of social fund investments. This will be difficult given the demand-driven nature of the funds and fierce competition for resources coming from eligible communities. Nonetheless, social funds should consider several strategies, many of which are already used by selected social funds. Such strategies might include a sliding scale of community contributions, with less counterpart required of the most marginalized participants; expansion of the menu to include projects explicitly oriented to such vulnerable groups as the elderly or indigenous groups; and a greater emphasis on resources to enable communities to tap into other government programs.[14]

Using a social risk management approach calls for a reconsideration of the menu of eligible social fund micro projects. Priority investments would include those interventions that have the most profound effect on reducing the risks faced by the most vulnerable populations. This means an expansion from the traditional area of social infrastructure investment. Financing projects that address such issues as legal assistance to help vulnerable groups obtain property rights, financing transportation to facilitate remote communities' access to health and education ser-

---

[14] Romania's Social Development Fund is financing programs that allow marginalized groups to get access to existing government benefits such as child or elderly allowances. The Argentina Participatory Social Fund finances empowerment and leadership workshops for women's groups that have, among other elements, training for how to access municipal services. Another Argentine example is a subproject that provides legal services to an indigenous group to enable its members to have national identity cards and hence access to entitlement programs.

vices, and supporting empowerment training for women are examples that might be envisioned under a social risk management strategy.

To date, there has been relatively less emphasis placed on community economic development (which would help reduce and mitigate risk) than on short-term employment creation and delivery of basic social infrastructure. There are some notable exceptions, such as the cases of Egypt, Chile, and Albania, where significant resources have gone to microfinance and technical support to entrepreneurs. These programs help to accumulate assets at the household level, a key element in a social risk management strategy. If social funds accept their place in a broad social risk management strategy for a country, this will mean more emphasis on support for community economic development, an area where social funds have done less well in general.[15]

PARTICIPATION AND CAPACITY BUILDING

Social funds contribute to social risk management through the creation of local capacity. Besides the impacts of the investments themselves, social funds further this local capacity building in two important ways. First, social funds have been an important source of resources and learning by doing for decentralized, locally based entities, including local governments, NGOs, local offices of line ministries, and community groups. This is consistent with the notion that vulnerable communities are better served by public interventions that are executed in a decentralized fashion. The impact of local agencies more able to address local problems is difficult to quantify but has been observed in many impact assessments of social funds.

To maximize this impact, the design of social funds should go beyond a more narrow focus on local agencies and groups as executing agencies, or channels for investments, and seek to obtain further institutional impacts. Many social funds have made important strides. For example, in Zambia, district officers are fully integrated in the project cycle and receive an important complement of training. In Argentina, participatory provincial and local councils have been established to further coordination, information sharing, and resource optimization around social investments, including those made by the social fund. In Honduras, the FHIS has

---

[15] Where microfinance or other income-generating activities have been successful, the majority of beneficiaries are women, especially women heads of household, so a move in this direction would also help develop more gender-balanced social risk management. That men do not apply is not only because of targeting but also because market failure is less prevalent for men than for women.

sponsored one of the first forays into town hall type meetings, or *cabildos abiertos*, to identify community needs and priorities in a participatory fashion.

The second area of process impact is on the "social capital" of poor communities. Due to their demand-driven, participatory approach, social fund interventions may increase both household and community social capital by increasing community cohesion, furthering community propensity to act jointly for the benefit of members of the community, and building trust and empowerment. In most cases, this effect is attributable to processes that increase social capital through the skills, networks, and confidence gained by the community at large in the identification of its needs and by project committee members who manage the implementation of the micro projects. This increased community capacity to address problems is often observed in increased participation rates in community-initiated activities and improved perception of the community by its residents, as borne out in beneficiary assessments carried out on social funds.[16] For instance, in Malawi, a beneficiary assessment of community participants found that their trust in government in general had increased because of their experience in working with the Malawi social fund, MASAF.

Social funds that have been more successful at building social capital appear to be those that have processes that give maximum responsibility to communities for the design and implementation of micro projects. For instance, many funds use a formal community assembly mechanism to identify and prioritize needs. Several funds channel financing directly to community project committees, who are then responsible for project implementation, including selection of contractors or service providers, administration, and supervision. These mechanisms have helped raise awareness of the broad range of community perceptions of needs, forge links of shared concerns between community members, mobilize general participation, and give valuable organizational experience to selected community members.

In some instances, there may be an apparent trade-off between building capacity of local agencies and increasing social capital of poor communities. For instance, social funds that channel money directly to community groups are often criticized as short-circuiting local government's prerogatives. However, social funds, which rely to a large degree on intermediaries (be they governmental or nongovernmental agencies), usually have less intense community participation and responsibility built into their project cycles. In fact, optimal social fund design should

---

[16] Van Domelen and Owen (1998).

seek to combine the two elements. Strengthening both local institutional capacity and social capital of communities would best further the goal of social risk management.

CONCLUSION

Social funds have played a role in social risk management in the past, but mainly in the area of risk coping, with some impact on risk mitigation. Their relative operational efficiency and ability to work with a variety of actors involved in social risk management makes them potentially important vehicles for risk reduction and mitigation as well.

References

Avila, Seifert, and others. 1992. *Un puente sobre la crisis*. La Paz, Bolivia: Fondo Social de Emergencia.

Bigio, A., ed. 1998. *Social Funds and Reaching the Poor–Experiences and Future Directions*. Washington, D.C.: World Bank.

Frigenti, L., and A. Harth. 1998. *Local Solutions to Regional Problems: The Growth of Social Funds and Public Works and Employment Projects in Sub-Saharan Africa*. Washington, D.C.: World Bank.

Goodman, M., and others. 1997. *Social Investment Funds in Latin America: Past Performance and Future Role*. Washington, D.C.: Inter-American Development Bank.

Newman, J., S. Jørgensen, and M. Pradhan. 1991. "How Did Workers Benefit from Bolivia's Emergency Social Fund?" *World Bank Economic Review* 5 (May).

Pradhan, M., L. Rawlings, and G. Ridder. 1998. "The Bolivian Social Investment Fund: An Analysis of Baseline Data for Impact Evaluation." *World Bank Economic Review* 12 (September): 457–82.

Subbarao, K., and others. 1997. *Safety Net Programs and Poverty Reduction: Lessons from Cross-Country Experience*. Washington, D.C.: World Bank.

Van Domelen, J. 1998. *Review of Social Investment Funds in the MENA Region*. Working Paper. World Bank, Washington, D.C.

———. 1999. "Social Funds in the Middle East and North Africa." Draft internal report. Washington: World Bank (January).

Van Domelen, J., and D. Owen. 1998. *Getting an Earful: A Review of Beneficiary Assessments of Social Funds*. Social Protection Discussion Paper Series 9816. Social Protection Unit, World Bank, Washington, D.C.

CHAPTER SIX

Insuring the Economic Costs of Illness

Paul Gertler

One of the most sizable and least predictable shocks to the economic opportunities of families is major illness. There are two important economic costs associated with illness: the cost of the medical care used to diagnose and treat the illness and the loss in income associated with reduced labor supply and productivity. The size and unpredictability of both of these costs suggest that families may not be able to smooth their consumption over periods of major illness, especially in developing countries where few individuals are covered by formal health and disability insurance.[1] The possibility that there is less than full consumption smoothing through these mechanisms suggests a potentially large loss in welfare from this shock to the household's resources. Many developing countries, recognizing this potential loss in welfare and the failure of private health insurance markets, have or are considering social insurance to help smooth the economic costs of illness.

This chapter investigates the potential welfare gain from social insurance. In particular, it pays attention to the possibility that social insurance may crowd out or replace private informal insurance. While families with sick members in developing countries are not able to gain access to formal insurance markets, they do rely on private informal coping mechanisms such as drawing on savings, selling assets, transfers from their family and social support networks, and borrowing from local credit markets.[2] Estimates of the welfare gain from social insurance must net out the crowd-out effect.

I am grateful to John Giles for useful comments and advice. The views expressed are mine alone.
[1] World Bank (1993, 1995a).
[2] Morduch (1999) provides a useful summary of this literature.

The extent to which families are able to smooth consumption over periods of illness is also important for the design of social insurance programs. In particular, as is discussed later, the extent to which families are able to smooth small health shocks has implications for user fees and the ability of social insurance to finance the rarer expensive health shocks.

To determine the extent to which households are able to employ private informal insurance mechanisms to smooth health shocks, the ability of families in Indonesia and China to smooth consumption over periods of major illness is investigated. To do so, the chapter uses unique panel data that contain excellent measures of health status combined with data on consumption.

While there is a growing literature on consumption smoothing in developing countries, little explicit attention has been paid to smoothing of health shocks.[3] Robert Townsend includes in his regression analysis the "percentage of the year sick" and finds no effect on consumption changes. Anjini Kochar models wage income and informal borrowing as a function illness, as measured by a member of the family experiencing a loss of work due to illness.[4] She finds that illness to the male lowers wage income and increases informal borrowing during peak periods in the agricultural cycle, but that there are no effects during slack periods and no effects of female illnesses. These studies appear to indicate that families living in low-income countries are able to smooth illness shocks fairly well.[5]

A key limitation of past work, however, is that the measures of health employed may reflect only small, and even potentially anticipated, changes in health status, not the kind of unexpected major illnesses that may be difficult to smooth. Paul Gertler and Jonathan Gruber overcome these problems by using measures of individuals' physical abilities to perform activities of daily living (ADLs).[6] ADLs have been proved reliable and valid measures of physical functioning ability in both developed and developing countries and distinguish the type of serious exogenous health problems that are likely to be correlated with changes in labor market and consumption opportunities. Gertler and Gruber find that while households are able to smooth 70 percent of the costs of moderate health shocks, they can only smooth about 40 percent of the costs of serious illness.

---

[3] See Morduch (1995) and Townsend (1995) for reviews of the consumption smoothing literature.
[4] Townsend (1994); Kochar (1995).
[5] In contrast, Cochrane (1991) finds that consumption in the United States is sensitive to major illness, defined as being ill for more than 100 days.
[6] Gertler and Gruber (1997).

POLICY FRAMEWORK

The classic reason for most governments to intervene in health care markets is the inherent uncertainty in health status. No one knows what tomorrow will bring. Seemingly healthy individuals can be struck by cancer, injured in accidents, or experience severe diarrhea. The uncertainty is compounded the longer one looks into the future and the less one knows about one's current health. While the costs associated with most illnesses are small, the costs associated with rare serious illness can be quite large. When a serious illness hits unpredictably, the economic consequences for the family can be significant. Given aversion to risk, families prefer to insure these risks and thereby have predictable, smooth nonmedical consumption. Despite the demand, families have difficulty purchasing insurance from private sources because of two problems created by information asymmetries: adverse selection and cream skimming.[7] Private insurance market failure suggests the potential for welfare gains from government intervention. The main problem in insurance market failure is that participation is voluntary, so that good risks can choose not to buy insurance and bad risks can be denied coverage. Many countries solve this problem through mandatory social insurance (SI). In developing countries, SI takes two main forms.

The first is universal publicly financed and delivered health care modeled after the British National Health System. In these systems, governments provide medical care through public facilities that are accessed by paying at most a nominal user fee. These systems are financed through some combination of general tax revenues and payroll taxes. There is a heated policy debate about raising user fees at public health care facilities. Governments have or are actively considering raising user charges at public facilities as a means of financing improvements in the

---

[7] Rothschild and Stiglitz (1976). Adverse selection arises because insurers are not able to observe differences in health status among different people, so they are forced to offer insurance based on the population's average medical care expenditures. The terms of the contract are good for bad-risk individuals, but bad for good risks. The incentive is for the good risks to drop out of the market, leaving the bad to insure among themselves. This substantially drives up the price of insurance, making it potentially unaffordable to large segments of the population. Cream skimming occurs when insurers can observe poor health. Insurers try to select good risk and avoid individuals with pre-existing conditions such as cancer or AIDS, who are bad risks with predictably high medical care expenditures. In addition, since insurance contracts are usually written for discrete periods of time, individuals who develop serious illness are prohibited from renewing their insurance.

health sector.[8] Vocal opponents are concerned that increased fees will adversely affect the poor's access to medical care and, consequently, their health outcomes.[9] This debate, however, has ignored the possible role of public subsidies as insurance. Subsidies reduce risk by spreading the medical costs of uncertain illness across healthy and sick times; taxes are incurred when individuals are healthy and are used to finance medical care purchased when individuals are sick. As a result, raising user fees in a world of imperfect consumption insurance has an important welfare cost: higher user fees "tax families while they are down," imposing higher costs at exactly the point where the marginal utility of consumption is highest.

The second approach is to finance medical care through mandatory payroll taxes and allow beneficiaries to purchase medical care from both private and public providers. The movement toward this model has been motivated by the desire to reduce financial pressure on government budgets.[10] SI is seen as a way to shift a portion of the public burden of delivering and financing health care to the private sector. SI reduces the out-of-pocket prices at the time of purchase of higher quality private care relative to lower quality public care. As a result, SI provides an incentive to choose the private sector over the public sector, thereby lowering the demand for publicly delivered services. Since SI is financed through additional off-budget earmarked taxes, it also relieves pressure from the general budget.

Low-income countries, however, have limited abilities to tax. Therefore, the resources available for SI are severely constrained, which greatly diminishes their ability to provide insurance. In such poor environments, there is a strict budget constraint on SI benefits. SI plans thus face the trade-off between providing a large number of individuals with a small benefit or a small number of people with a large benefit. This means that a very large deductible (and possibly a large copayment) would be required to provide uncapped benefits for the rare large financial risks (for example, those associated with rare catastrophic illnesses such as cancer). The high deductible would ensure that benefits were available for expensive catastrophic illnesses and were not used up on less expensive higher-probability events (for example, influenza). Because of the budget constraint, lowering the deductible would require capping benefits. In the limit, a zero deductible implies the lowest possible benefit cap and least effective insurance against catastrophic illness.

---

[8] For example, World Bank (1987); Jiménez (1996).
[9] For example, Cornia, Jolly, and Stewart (1987); Ready (1996).
[10] Gertler (1998).

All the same, this is exactly what many countries have done. Paul Gertler and Orville Solon show that many low-income countries have adopted first-dollar coverage and therefore have placed the lowest cap possible on benefits.[11] In essence, they have chosen to provide the minimum benefits for all illnesses rather than full insurance for rare high-cost illnesses.

A number of powerful political interest groups see a first-dollar capped benefit design as in their self-interest. The most obvious interest group is the collection of international donors and other political groups who are worried about the poor and who want to use the health care system as a means of redistribution.[12] First-dollar coverage ensures universal access to medical care regardless of income. It alleviates the widespread concern that even small out-of-pocket costs may deter utilization, especially among the very poor.[13] Politicians also support first-dollar coverage. Since the median voter is poor in most of these countries, first-dollar coverage puts money into more voters' pockets. Employers also have strong financial incentives to support capped-benefit first-dollar coverage. Typically, social insurance premiums are cofinanced by employers. In many countries, large employers historically have provided workers with limited health benefits as a means of reducing absenteeism.[14] However, quick treatment of minor illnesses reduces absenteeism more than the treatment of catastrophic illnesses. Employers capped benefits since it was cheaper to fire severely ill individuals who had little chance of returning to work. For similar reasons, employers benefit more from the capped first-dollar coverage that is more likely to reduce absenteeism than from catastrophic coverage with high deductibles that is less likely to affect workforce productivity.

The solution to both the user fee debate and the debate over first-dollar coverage depends in part on the extent to which families are able to smooth the costs of small health shocks. If yes, then there is little welfare loss to charging small user fees or using co-pays and deductibles.

---

[11] Gertler and Solon (1998).

[12] Besley and Gouveia (1994).

[13] Cornia, Jolly, and Stewart (1987). Indeed, a good portion of public intervention in health care markets is justified by the tenet of universal access to basic minimum medical care, regardless of income, as embodied in the populist slogan "health for all by the year 2000." Most countries recognize that poor individuals may not be able to afford health care and therefore subsidize the participation of poor individuals in universal insurance schemes. This explains, in part, why most countries set up large universal public health care delivery systems that charge at most nominal user fees (Jiménez 1987; World Bank 1987).

[14] Gertler and Sturm (1997).

WELFARE MEASUREMENT

One measure of the welfare cost of not being able to fully insure the costs of illness is the amount that households are willing to pay to eliminate consumption variability owing to illness. This measures households' ex ante valuation of insurance that would fill the gap in existing insurance markets for the income loss due to illness, arising either through reduced earnings or increased medical expenditures.

The willingness to pay is calculated in a certainty equivalence framework. Let C^* be consumption when healthy and $L(H_i)$ be the economic cost of illness with severity H_i, which occurs with probability π_i. Then the welfare loss from uncertain illness is the amount W, such that the welfare from getting $C^* - W$ with certainty is equal to the expected welfare when the loss is uncertain:

(6-1)
$$u\left(\frac{C^*-W}{C^*}\right) = E\left[u\left(\frac{C^*-L(H_i)}{C^*}\right)\right].$$

However, the willingness to pay formula overstates the welfare gain from social insurance because it ignores the fact that households will smooth some of the shocks through private informal mechanisms. So, if we let γ represent the share of the loss that cannot be smoothed, then (6-1) can be written as

(6-2)
$$u\left(\frac{C^*-W}{C^*}\right) = E\left[u\left(\frac{C^*-\gamma L(H_i)}{C^*}\right)\right].$$

Assuming a constant relative risk aversion form for the utility function, where ρ is the coefficient of relative risk aversion, (6-1) can be rewritten as

(6-3)
$$\frac{\left(\frac{C^*-W}{C^*}\right)^{1-\rho}}{1-\rho} = \Sigma_j \pi_j^* \frac{\left(\frac{C^*-\gamma L_j}{C^*}\right)^{1-\rho}}{1-\rho},$$

where there are j discrete health states. Rearranging terms, the certainty equivalent can be expressed as a percentage of consumption when healthy:

(6-4)
$$\frac{W}{C^*} = 1 - \left(\Sigma_j \, \pi_j{}^* \left(\frac{C^* - \gamma L_j}{C^*} \right)^{1-\rho} \right)^{\frac{1}{1-\rho}} .$$

W/C^* measures the value of insurance that fully smoothes consumption across illness states as a percentage of baseline consumption. This measure is a lower bound of the willingness to pay for insurance, however, since it is calculated based on the variation in consumption due to illness after families have already used informal mechanisms to smooth some of the costs of illness. These smoothing activities themselves have costs that are not reflected in the calculation. For example, there is some cost to family and friends from private transfers of resources to the ill household head; similarly, if consumption smoothing is occurring through increased labor supply by family members, the value of the reduced leisure to those family members is not reflected here.

The key to estimating (6-4) is γ, the share of the costs of illness that cannot be insured. Here it is estimated in the context of the theory of full insurance, as discussed by John Cochrane, Angus Deaton, and Robert Townsend.[15] This theory posits that households will fully share the risk of idiosyncratic shocks so that the growth in household consumption will not depend on changes in household resources once the change in aggregate community resources has been taken into account. This is formalized in the next section.

INDONESIA

Indonesia is the fourth most populous country in the world, with tremendous cultural and economic diversity. Until recently, economic growth has been impressive with an average real annual per capita growth rate of 3.9 percent over the past 15 years. Despite this growth, per capita incomes were still low, even before the onset of the crisis, at U.S.$880 per year in 1996.[16] Indonesia had also seen remarkable improvements in health status.[17] Between 1960 and 1990 life expectancy at birth increased by 24 percent to 59 years, and child mortality decreased 68 percent to 111 per thousand.

---

[15] Cochrane (1991); Deaton (1992a); Townsend (1994).
[16] Asian Development Bank (1997).
[17] World Bank (1993).

Indonesia has invested heavily to develop a comprehensive government-operated health care delivery system that individuals are able to access by paying a modest user fee. In 1991, there was at least one primary health center and several subcenters in each of Indonesia's 3,400 subdistricts. A large network of government-operated hospitals at the district, provincial, and central levels backs up this large primary care system. Despite this system, Indonesia's health care expenditures remain low relative to those of its neighbors.[18] In 1990 annual expenditures on health care from both public and private sources were only about $12 per person, which amounts to roughly 2 percent of GDP.

Few individuals in Indonesia are covered by health insurance other than the implicit insurance provided through the almost free public health care system; on average, user fees at public facilities amount to 5 percent of average costs.[19] While the public health care system provides extensive primary care services, its hospital care is more limited. Moreover, many individuals opt to pay out of pocket for higher quality private sector services, as over half of all utilization is provided by the private sector.[20] About 10 percent of the population is covered by health insurance provided to civil servants. However, this insurance only covers utilization at public facilities and, therefore, the benefit to the individual is only to cover the small user fees. An additional 4 percent of the population is covered by health insurance offered through employers, but this insurance typically has capped benefits, minimizing absenteeism for minor illnesses but not paying the costs of major illness.[21] Similarly, there is limited disability insurance as there is no government program, more than two-thirds of workers are self-employed, and few firms provide extensive sick leave.

Data and Sample

The data used in this analysis, collected as part of the Indonesian Resource Mobilization Study (IRMS), come from a panel survey of households designed to evaluate an experimental increase in user fees charged at public medical care facilities in two of Indonesia's 27 provinces. The two study provinces are West Nusa Tengarah (NTB), which is composed of the two islands just east of Bali, and East Kalimantan

---

[18] World Bank (1993).
[19] World Bank (1995b).
[20] Gertler and Molyneaux (1996).
[21] Dow and Gertler (1997).

(KalTim), which is located on the east coast of the island of Borneo. Together they account for about 6 million residents. KalTim has the third highest per capita income among all 27 provinces, while NTB ranks twenty-second. The data were collected in 1991 and 1993, allowing us to examine health, income, and consumption changes over a two-year period. The data were collected for each household at the same point in the year in both waves, so that seasonality effects are conditioned out of the differences models.

The sample consists of all households that were in the survey in both rounds, whose heads were at least 18 years old in the second round, and who have nonmissing data on the health measures described below. Paul Gertler and Jack Molyneaux, and William Dow and others discuss attrition from this sample and conclude that it does not cause significant sample selection problems.[22]

The Risk of Illness

The key to the analysis is that there are unusually good measures of the change in the health status of household members. The analysis explores the effects of two types of health measures: self-reported illness symptoms (symptoms) and limitations in the physical ability to perform activities of daily living (ADLs). Self-reported illness symptoms are similar to the measures used by the previous literature. Illness symptoms are measured by a dummy for whether the individual reports any symptom (ill), and a dummy for whether they report a symptom that has lasted more than one month (chronically ill). This measure aggregates the 10 categories of self-reported specific symptoms (for example, fever, respiratory congestion, and so on) for adults.

As an alternative the analysis therefore relies on a second measure that assesses an individual's physical ability to perform activities of daily living. These physical functioning measures are based on individuals' self-ratings of ability to engage in specific activities, not based on general assessments of illness symptoms that are more likely to be endogenous to labor supply decisions. Initially developed for studying levels of disability among the elderly, these measures are used increasingly to study the health status of all adults. Physical functioning measures have been tested extensively for reliability (consistency between tests and interviewers) and validity (consistency between individual assessments of differ-

---

[22] Gertler and Molyneaux (1996); Dow and others (1996).

ent skills). In addition, in contrast to self-reported symptoms, these measures tend to be negatively correlated with income and education in both the United States and low-income samples.[23]

Activities of daily living are divided into two categories. Intermediate ADLs consist of the ability to carry a heavy load for 20 meters; sweep the floor or yard; walk for five kilometers; take water from a well; and bend, kneel, or stoop. Basic ADLs consist of the ability to bathe yourself; feed yourself; clothe yourself; stand from sitting in a chair; go to the toilet; and rise from sitting on the floor. A limitation in any of these activities, particularly basic ADLs, clearly represents a major change in health status.

The responses to these questions on the survey are coded as "can do it easily" (a value of 1), "can do it with difficulty" (2), and "unable to do it" (3). The responses to these questions were then combined in accordance with the following algorithm developed for the RAND Medical Outcome Study:[24]

$$Health = \left(\frac{Score - \text{Min } Score}{\text{Max } Score - \text{Min } Score} \right),$$

so that the ADL index takes on a value of 1 if the individual can perform all ADLs without difficulty, and zero if the individual cannot perform any ADLs. This chapter's central model uses an overall index of ADL limitations. Results for a dis-aggregation of this ADL index into both its intermediate and basic components are presented below.

The means and standard deviations of the health outcome measures are presented in table 6–1, part A. The table shows the means for period 1 levels, and for changes from period 1 to period 2. In period 1, a large proportion of adults, 29 percent, reported some ADL limitation. In addition, substantial change in health status occurs over time. Between 1991 and 1993, more than 33 percent of the sample reported changes (either upward or downward) in ADL limitations.

---

[23] See Strauss and others (1993); Kington and Smith (1996); Gertler and Zeitlin (1996). In the United States and South East Asia, ADLs have been found to be reliable and valid self-assessments with a high degree of internal consistency. See Andrews and others (1986); Guralnik and others (1989); Ju and Jones (1989); Strauss and others (1993); Ware, Davies-Avery, and Brook (1980). They are routinely used in studies of labor supply in the United States (for example, Bound 1991; Bound, Schoenbaum, and Waidman 1995; Stern 1989), and are the key measures of health status in the new Health and Retirement Survey. See Wallace and Herzog (1995).

[24] Stewert and others (1990).

Table 6–1. Means and Standard Deviations of Health Outcome Measures, Earnings, and Medical Care Expenditures in Indonesia

Variable	Mean
Part A. Means of health measures	
Period 1 levels	
ADL index	0.966
	(0.082)
Some ADL limitations	0.29
Illness symptoms	0.60
Chronic illness symptoms	0.14
Changes	
Change in ADL index	0.005
	(0.088)
Any ADL change	0.337
Change in illness	–0.015
Change in chronic illness symptoms	0.161
Part B. Means of other variables in period 1	
Nonmedical consumption per capita	36,350
	(31,868)
Head's hours of work	36.6
	(24.6)
Head's earnings per capita	17,573
	(19,256)
Head not working	0.19
Family medical spending per capita	335
	(1,020)
Male	0.86
Married	0.79
Spouse's age	35.8
	(11.6)
Family size	4.80
	(2.13)
Education	
None	0.33
1–5 years	0.32
6 years	0.19
7 years or more	0.16

Note: Tabulated by the author from IRMS data. Standard deviations are in parentheses. N = 3,933.
Source: Author's calculations.

If one looks at the self-reported symptom measures, one finds that more than one-half of the sample reported an illness symptom last month in the first survey round. This raises questions about the usefulness of this indicator for investigating consumption smoothing as its huge frequency indicates that it is picking up many minor health problems that do not need expensive medical care or affect labor supply. However, a much smaller share reports chronic symptoms lasting more than one month. While there is some reduction in symptoms across these two years, there is a very large increase in chronic symptoms, which may be expected to some extent as this cohort ages.

The Cost of Illness

A prerequisite for there to be an effect of illness on consumption through imperfect consumption insurance is that there must be a sizable cost of illness. In this section, the cost of illness is quantified in terms of reduced labor supply, lost earnings, and increased medical spending.

Earnings and medical care spending equations can be estimated using the following fixed effects specification:

(6-5) $$\Delta L_{ij} = \beta \Delta h_{ij} + v_j + \varepsilon_{ij},$$

where ΔL_{ij} is the change in labor supply (or earnings, or medical care spending) for individual i living in community j, Δh_{ij} is the change in health for that individual, and v_j is a community-level error component.

Equation 6-5 regresses first differenced labor outcomes and medical care spending against the change in health and aggregate determinants of labor supply (or medical spending). A full set of community dummies is included to control for these aggregate determinants.[25] Also included are demographic controls to capture other secular trends in the labor supply of household heads: the head's sex, age, education, and marital status; the wife's age and education; and the change in log family size. To measure a change in the indicator variables for symptoms, a variable is defined which is 0 if there is no change, 1 if the person moves from ill to healthy, and −1 if the person moves from healthy to ill. The change for ADLs is simply the change in the ADL index value.

---

[25] Communities for our purposes are defined as IRMS "enumeration areas," which are village sampling clusters.

The model is a fixed effects specification, and as such controls for unobserved heterogeneity. In particular, the first differencing sweeps out correlation from omitted unobserved individual characteristics (such as preferences and health endowments) that confound identification of the effect of illness on labor market outcomes. However, there may be unobserved correlates of income changes and changes in health outcomes that confound identification. One major source of spurious correlation, shocks to the local community economy, such as weather, which affect both permanent income and health, is controlled by including a set of community fixed effects.[26]

Labor supply is meaningful in two ways: as the changes in hours worked and as a dummy for participation in the labor force. Earnings and wages are only reported in the IRMS data for the one-third of heads who work in the market. We impute wages to all workers based on these market rates by first taking an average of hourly market wages by province (NTB or KalTim), age (<25, 25–49, 50+), education (the four categories denoted at the bottom of table 6–1, part B), and gender. This cell-specific average wage is then matched to all persons in the cell, regardless of whether they worked in the market.[27] This imputed hourly wage is then multiplied by hours per week to get weekly earnings, and by 4.3 to get monthly earnings, in order to match our monthly consumption figures.

The means and standard deviations of the earnings and medical care expenditures variables are reported in table 6–1, part B. Earnings are measured in real per capita terms in order to match the consumption specification below.[28] Among heads, average hours of work are almost 37; more than 80 percent of heads work in period 1.

Spending on medical care is measured as the product of reported medical utilization and prices from the sites at which medical care was delivered, following Gertler and Molyneaux.[29] Descriptive statistics for both are reported in table 6–1, part B. Spending on medical care is quite low, averaging less than 1 percent of

---

[26] A related source of concern is idiosyncratic changes in household income that feed back into health; for example, job loss that results in a deterioration of health (perhaps through mental depression). But our pattern of results suggests that this alternative explanation does not account for our findings. In particular, we find that larger health shocks are associated with bigger income losses and larger consumption losses. Therefore, if our results reflect effects of labor supply on health, this feedback mechanism would have to operate more strongly the larger the negative income shock. This means, for example, that the effect on health from a job loss would be bigger for high-wage individuals than low-wage individuals. This type of feedback seems to us to be unlikely.

[27] The valuation of nonmarket work at the market wage is only appropriate if labor markets clear; this assumption is supported for Indonesia by Pitt and Rosenzweig (1986) and Benjamin (1992).

[28] All figures are reported in 1991 urban NTB rupiah.

[29] Gertler and Molyneaux (1996).

Table 6–2. Coefficients for Illness and Change in Hours Worked, Indonesia

	Model		
Variable	1	2	3
Change in symptoms	−0.52		
	(0.80)		
Change in chronic symptoms		−1.04	
		(1.02)	
Change in ADLs			30.85
			(5.08)
Male head	3.14	3.23	3.21
	(2.28)	(2.32)	(2.30)
Age of head	−0.26	−0.26	−0.31
	(0.21)	(0.21)	(0.21)
Age squared/100	0.22	0.22	0.26
	(0.20)	(0.20)	(0.19)
Education			
None	2.78	2.66	2.82
	(1.62)	(1.62)	(1.62)
1–5 years	2.69	2.64	2.76
	(1.47)	(1.46)	(1.46)
6 years	4.71	4.59	4.67
	(1.59)	(1.59)	(1.59)
Single	0.39	0.47	0.05
	(3.27)	(3.27)	(3.26)
Wife's age	−0.08	−0.08	−0.08
	(0.07)	(0.07)	(0.06)
Change in log family size	−1.49	−1.39	−1.51
	(2.28)	(2.28)	(2.27)

Note: Standard errors are in parentheses. Estimates are from models such as (6-2) in the text. N = 3,933.
Source: Author's calculations.

nonmedical consumption. This reflects both low levels of utilization and the extensive subsidization of medical care costs by the public sector. Even conditional on having some positive spending, mean spending on medical care is only about 2 percent of nonmedical consumption, although roughly 5 percent of sample households spend more than 10 percent on nonmedical consumption.

Table 6–2 reports the full regression specification for our first measure of labor supply, change in hours worked. For symptoms, there is a negative effect of becoming ill on hours of work, but neither coefficient is significant. The result suggests that having chronic symptoms is associated with a reduction in labor supply of 1 hour per week.

Table 6–3. Coefficients for Illness, Labor Supply, and Medical
Spending, Indonesia

Variable	Symptoms	Chronic symptoms	ADLs
Change in hours	−0.52	−1.04	30.85
	(0.80)	(1.02)	(5.08)
Change in labor force participation	0.031	0.029	−0.738
	(0.012)	(0.014)	(0.080)
Change in earnings (in Rp. 10,000)	−0.128	−0.060	2.02
	(0.060)	(0.076)	(0.35)
Change in medical spending (in Rp. 10,000)	0.022	0.015	−0.118
	(0.004)	(0.006)	(0.026)

Note: Standard errors are in parentheses. Coefficients are for change in health in the regression that includes all covariates shown in table 6–2. N = 3,933.
Source: Author's calculations.

The third column shows the results for the ADL measures; here, illness is represented by a reduction in the index, so that a positive coefficient indicates that illness reduces labor supply. There is a sizable and significant effect of ADL changes. The coefficient implies that moving from completely healthy (index = 1) to completely sick (index = 0) would lower hours of work by almost 31 hours per week, which is a fall of 84.3 percent of baseline hours worked. In other words, if the head moved from being able to perform all of the ADLs to being unable to perform even one ADL, his hours of work per week would fall by 2.8 hours (7.6 percent of baseline hours).[30] The control variables are generally insignificant, except that the most educated heads are found to work more hours.

Table 6–3 presents the coefficients of interest for other measures of labor supply. The first row replicates the findings from table 6–2. The next row shows the results for change in labor force participation. The finding parallels that of table 6–2: positive effects of symptoms (becoming ill raises nonparticipation), and negative effects of ADL changes (improved physical functioning lowers nonparticipation). In this case, the effects are significant for all of our health status measures, although much stronger for ADLs. Indeed, moving from being able to perform all of the ADLs to being able to perform none implies a 74 percent likelihood of becoming a

---

[30] Note that this evaluation can be done for all of the ADL coefficients by simply multiplying the coefficient by 0.0909, which is the change in the ADL index arising from a movement from being able to do all ADLs to being completely unable to do one ADL.

nonparticipant, while experiencing an illness symptom or chronic illness increases the likelihood of not participating by about 3 percent.

The third row of table 6–3 shows the effect on imputed earnings, expressed in 10,000 rupiah units. Surprisingly, the effect of chronic symptoms on earnings is actually lower than for nonchronic symptoms, despite a larger effect on hours worked. This implies that the population for which chronic symptoms are associated with reduced work is a relatively low (predicted) wage population. Although the imputation of wages by demographic characteristics limits the generality of this result, it is consistent with the notion that individuals who are marginally attached to the labor force are justifying their exit from the labor force by reporting a chronic symptom.

For ADL change, the coefficient is once again much stronger. It implies that moving from being completely able to perform ADLs to being completely unable to perform ADLs would lower earnings by Rp. 20,170. This is roughly as large as baseline mean earnings, suggesting that such a shift would (unsurprisingly) leave the head with small earnings. Moving from being completely able to perform all ADLs to being unable to perform one ADL lowers earnings by Rp. 1,834, or about 10 percent of baseline earnings.

Finally, the last row of table 6–3 shows the effects of illness on medical spending. There are significant effects in the expected direction for all three measures (having symptoms = more spending; lower ADLs = more spending). But these effects are trivially small relative to the effects on earnings. This is not surprising since publicly provided care is heavily subsidized (that is, user fees are well below the cost of care).

Do Households Fully Insure Consumption?

The previous sections demonstrated that major illnesses as measured by changes in basic ADLs are associated with large financial costs to households. This section tests whether households are insuring consumption against these unexpected costs of illness.

The empirical specification is derived from the theory of full insurance, which casts consumption insurance in terms of interhousehold risk sharing.[31] In practice, however, the empirical specification used here follows the previous developing

---

[31] See, for example, Cochrane (1991); Deaton (1994); and Townsend (1994).

country literature in examining consumption *smoothing*, either through insurance from others or through self-insurance (that is, savings). Indeed, the empirical tests do not distinguish between these two channels of consumption smoothing. The reason for briefly laying out the full insurance model is to highlight a key assumption of the empirical testing: state independence in consumption.

The key empirical insight of the theory of full insurance is that mechanisms for pooling risks will equalize the growth in the marginal utility of consumption across households within communities. The easiest way to derive this condition is from the first-order conditions to the central planner's problem of allocating resources under uncertainty given a set of household social weights. The first-order conditions in logarithmic form are $\ln(MU(C_{ijt})) = \ln(\lambda_{jt}) - \ln(\omega_{ij})$, where $MU(C_{ijt})$ is marginal utility of consumption of household i living in community j, λ_{jt} is the Lagrange multiplier associated with the aggregate resource constraint for community j in period t, and ω_{ij} is the social weight associated with the household. The social weight does not vary over time and therefore is just a household fixed effect. Taking differences of both sides of the first-order conditions to eliminate the fixed effect finds that with full insurance $\Delta \ln(MU(C_{ijt})) = \Delta \ln(\lambda_{jt})$. In words, the growth rate of each household's marginal utility within a community is equalized.

The empirical analogue depends on the shape of the marginal utility function and other factors that affect intertemporal and interhousehold differences in tastes. Here a form of the constant relative risk aversion utility function suggested by Deaton, where the utility of per capita consumption is multiplied by the size of the family, is used.[32] Letting n_{ijt} be the number of household members, the utility function is

$$U_{ijt}(C_{ijt}) = \theta_{ijt} n_{ijt} \left(C_{ijt} / n_{ijt} \right)^{1-\rho} / (1-\rho),$$

where θ_{ijt} is an unobservable taste parameter that accounts for other variations in preferences.

In this case, the differenced logarithmic first-order condition becomes

$$\Delta \ln\left(\frac{C_{ij}}{n_{ij}} \right) = \frac{1}{\rho} [\Delta \ln(\lambda_j) - \Delta \ln(\theta_{ij})],$$

---

[32] Deaton (1994).

which can be expressed as

$$\Delta \ln\left(\frac{C_{ij}}{n_{ij}}\right) = \frac{1}{\rho}\Delta \ln(\lambda_j) + \varepsilon_{ij}.$$

This implies that while the growth in the marginal utilities of consumption is constant within a community, the growth in household consumption will differ due to intertemporal and interhousehold differences in preferences (due, for example, to aging or change in family size). Therefore, the theory of full insurance implies that the growth in each household's consumption will not depend on changes in household resources that are uncorrelated with shifts in preferences once the growth in community resources has been taken into account.

With the use of the above results one can test whether families are able to insure consumption against illness by estimating the following equation:

(6-6)
$$\Delta \ln\left(\frac{C_{ij}}{n_{ij}}\right) = \alpha\Delta \ln(C_j) + \beta\Delta h_{ij} + \varepsilon_{ij},$$

which is a regression of the growth in per capita (nonmedical care) consumption against the change in health (h_{ij}), controlling for the growth in community resources by including the change in community-level consumption. In addition, preference shifts associated with changes in family size or structure are controlled for by including the change in log family size and a series of measures of the change in the shares of the family that are male or female family members ages 0–5, 6–17, 18–49, and 50 plus. And, as above, other potential taste shifters that might be correlated with illness are controlled for: the head's sex, age, education, and marital status; and the wife's age and education. Conditional on these taste shifters, then, if there is full smoothing of illness, there will be no effect of the change in health on the change in consumption.

The dependent variable for the analysis is the change in the log of monthly nonmedical consumption per capita. The means for consumption expenditures are shown in table 6–1, part B. Like earnings, consumption is reported in real terms by deflating for price differences across locales and over time.

The estimates of equation 6-6 are presented in table 6–4. For illness symptoms, the hypothesis of full insurance cannot be rejected. The coefficients on both measures are insignificant; indeed, they are wrong-signed, indicating that illness is associated with higher levels of consumption, not lower.

Table 6–4. Regression of the Growth in Nonmedical Care Consumption, Indonesia

Variable	Model 1	Model 2	Model 3
Change in symptoms	0.004		
	(0.012)		
Change in chronic symptoms		0.013	
		(0.014)	
Change in basic ADLs			0.194
			(0.080)
Male head	0.020	0.019	0.021
	(0.037)	(0.037)	(0.037)
Age of head	0.002	0.002	0.002
	(0.003)	(0.003)	(0.003)
Age squared/100	−0.003	−0.003	−0.002
	(0.003)	(0.003)	(0.003)
Education			
None	−0.028	−0.028	−0.028
	(0.023)	(0.023)	(0.023)
1–5 years	−0.019	−0.019	−0.018
	(0.022)	(0.022)	(0.022)
6 years	0.033	0.033	0.033
	(0.024)	(0.024)	(0.024)
Single	0.080	0.079	0.079
	(0.052)	(0.052)	(0.052)
Wife's age	0.0003	0.0003	0.0003
	(0.001)	(0.001)	(0.001)
Change in log family size	−0.464	−0.465	−0.464
	(0.036)	(0.036)	(0.036)
Change in community consumption	0.366	0.365	0.370
	(0.033)	(0.033)	(0.033)

Note: Standard errors are in parentheses. Coefficients on change in share of family in age/sex groups are not reported. N = 3,933.
Source: Author's calculations.

In contrast, when the ADL index is used, the full insurance hypothesis is strongly rejected. Changes in the ADL index have a significant and sizable effect in the expected direction; negative increments to health are associated with reductions in consumption. Moving from being able to perform all ADLs to being able to perform none of them would lower consumption by almost 20 percent. A move from being completely able to being unable to perform one ADL would lower consumption by 1.8 percent.

The control variables show the expected pattern of effects. Consumption growth rates are higher for male heads, for older heads (although the effect increases with age at a diminishing rate), and for more educated heads. Per capita log consumption changes fall with the change in log family size, indicating some economies of scale in consumption; there is no clear pattern to the (unreported) coefficients on the changes in demographic shares, which are mostly insignificant. And there is a strong positive association with community consumption, but the estimated coefficient is much less than one. This is consistent with the rejection of full consumption smoothing at the community level in Townsend and Deaton.[33]

Moreover, the more severe illnesses measured by ADL changes are very strongly associated with consumption changes. This provides a striking refutation of the full insurance hypothesis at the household level. These latter types of illness changes appear to represent shocks to a family's opportunity set that cannot be smoothed.

How Incomplete Is Insurance?

The results in tables 6–1 through 6–4 provide a convincing demonstration that there is incomplete consumption smoothing of illness in Indonesia. The natural question to ask is "how incomplete is this insurance?" This magnitude is critical for assessing the importance of these findings for welfare and for considering their policy implications. Therefore, the magnitude of lack of consumption smoothing against illness as the share of the costs of illness that are financed out of consumption is measured. To do so, the previous consumption smoothing literature is followed by estimating a model of the effect of changes in (net of medical spending) income on the growth of nonmedical care consumption:

$$(6\text{-}7) \qquad \Delta \ln\left(\frac{C_{ij}}{n_{ij}}\right) = \alpha\Delta \ln(C_j) + \mu\Delta \ln(n_{ij}) + \gamma\Delta y_{ij} + \varepsilon_{ij},$$

where y_{ij} is earnings minus medical care expenditures. Then the share of the costs of illness that are financed out of reduced consumption is simply γ/C_{ij}.[34]

---

[33] Townsend (1994); Deaton (1992a).

[34] The level of income is used instead of the log, since roughly one-quarter of cases where there is a change in the ADL index have zero earnings in one period and these cases should not be excluded.

Table 6–5. Estimating Magnitude of Consumption Insurance, Indonesia

Type of estimation	Coefficient	Implied effect of income changes on consumption changes, γ/C_{t-1}
OLS	0.008	0.03
	(0.004)	
IV: ADL	0.096	0.35
	(0.042)	
IV: Symptoms	−0.025	
	(0.070)	
IV: Chronic symptoms	−0.099	
	(0.113)	

Note: Standard errors are in parentheses. Regressions include all controls shown in table 6–4 and the note to that table. Coefficients are for change in earnings of head minus change in medical spending from regressions of the form of equation 6-7. The first row estimates this model by OLS, while remaining rows estimate 2SLS models, with the instrument mentioned.
Source: Author's calculations.

Estimating equation 6-7 by OLS forms the basis for Townsend's and Deaton's test of full insurance.[35] The results from this estimation are shown in the first row of table 6–5. They show only the coefficient of interest—that on change in income— from regressions that include all of the regressors shown in table 6–4; income is expressed in units of Rp. 10,000. In fact, a significant, but very small, relationship is found between income changes and consumption changes and is consistent with Townsend's results. A Rp. 10,000 increase in income is estimated to increase consumption by only 0.8 percent, or Rp. 300. That is, as shown in the second column, this implies that for each rupiah that income falls, consumption falls by only Rp. 0.03. This is a trivial change, which would indicate very close to full consumption smoothing.

However, there are two potential problems with estimating equation 6-7 by OLS, both of which would bias toward a finding of consumption smoothing. The first, as noted by Jonathan Morduch, is that the growth in income is correlated with the error term through the production process; risk adverse families may choose the variation in income so that consumption can be smoothed using available mechanisms.[36] The second is measurement error in the growth of income, particularly since earnings have been imputed in the data.

[35] Townsend (1994); Deaton (1992a).
[36] Morduch (1990).

To solve these problems, an instrumental variables approach is used, which uses the change in the illness variables to instrument for the change in income. This instrument is valid given that the utility function is not state dependent, that there is no feedback from changes in consumption to changes in health, and that measurement error in health changes is uncorrelated with measurement error in income changes. The first two of these conditions are demonstrated by the tests above for the change in the ADL index, while the last seems reasonable. In this case, this regression allows an assessment of whether the major changes in income due to illness are smoothed differently than average income changes.

Once income is instrumented by the change in ADLs in the second row of table 6–5, the coefficient rises dramatically and becomes significant. The estimate indicates that for every Rp. 10,000 of income lost due to illness, there is a fall in consumption of 9.6 percent, or Rp. 3,490. That is, for each rupiah that income falls, consumption falls by Rp. 0.35 (as shown in the second column). This suggests that families are able to smooth only 65 percent of the loss in income from ADL changes on average.

The other illness measures are used in the remaining rows of table 6–5. As one could infer, the estimates here are actually wrong-signed and are insignificant. As noted earlier, there are two alternative explanations for this finding of no impact of illness-induced income changes on consumption. Either these types of high frequency/low severity illness events are easily smoothed, or these are not exogenous shifts in the family's opportunity set (and thus they are not valid instruments for this exercise). In order to consider the first alternative in more detail, the chapter next considers the impact of variations in our ADL measure.

The results thus far have aggregated all of the available ADL information into one index. While this provides a convenient summary measure, it masks underlying heterogeneity in the response of consumption to different types of health changes. In particular, households may be better able to smooth the modest income loss associated with minor health changes than they are the larger income loss associated with major health changes. This would arise if individuals had available limited self-insurance (for example, savings) that can only cover small income losses, or if consumption insurance (for example, transfers and loans from extended family) were available in small but not large amounts.

This issue is explored in table 6–6 by disaggregating the ADL index into changes in intermediate and changes in basic ADLs. As noted earlier, the latter set of limitations are much more serious; while 24 percent of the sample has some intermediate ADL limitation, only 2 percent has some basic ADL limitation. There-

Table 6–6. Heterogeneity, Indonesia

Index	γ	γ/C_{t-1}
Overall ADL index	0.096	0.35
	(0.042)	
Intermediate ADL index	0.079	0.29
	(0.039)	
Basic ADL index	0.165	0.60
	(0.095)	

Note: Standard errors are in parentheses. Each regression includes the controls shown in table 6–4 and the note to that table. The coefficient in the first column is that on change in earnings of head minus change in medical spending from regressions of the form of equation 6-7, for the instruments mentioned. Figures in the second column are implied effects of income changes on consumption changes.
Source: Author's calculations.

fore, the instrument set used to estimate equation 6-3 is varied by IV. The coefficients in the table are estimates of the effect of income variation on consumption, where the instruments are not just the overall ADL index, but also the separate indexes for basic and intermediate ADLs. The IV coefficients in each case therefore represent the impact of income variation induced by less and more severe changes in illness. In other words, they provide an assessment of whether there is better ability to smooth less severe health changes (the intermediate ADL changes in row 2) than more severe health changes (the basic ADL changes in row 3).

The results suggest that the impacts of basic ADL limitations on consumption are much more sizable. They find that each Rp. 10,000 of income loss due to intermediate ADL changes causes consumption to drop by 7.9 percent, but that each Rp. 10,000 of income loss due to basic ADL changes causes consumption to drop by 16.5 percent. That is, the findings estimate that families can smooth 71 percent of the income loss associated with intermediate ADL changes, but only 40 percent of the loss associated with basic ADL changes. This is a striking difference, and it suggests that there is definite heterogeneity in the ability of families to smooth illness shocks.

Insurance Market Policies

The results thus far demonstrate that families are not able to smooth the economic costs arising from serious illness to the household head, and as the extent of ability to smooth falls, the larger the shock. This incompleteness in private insurance markets suggests the potential for welfare gains from government provision of insurance against income loss and medical illness. In this section, the magnitudes of these welfare gains from social insurance are considered. It abstracts from the fundamental issue of the justification for public intervention, except to note that there is a substantial and well-known literature on insurance market failures in this context.[37] In addition, the section focuses solely on the welfare gains from more complete insurance and abstracts from other important potential welfare gains such as improvements in health status and gains in social welfare from redistribution.

This section implements the welfare measurement approach discussed earlier. It considers two alternative social insurance policies, disability and medical insurance. In each case, both the application of the policy to the overall change in ADLs and the application to just basic changes in ADLs are considered to reflect the fact that a policy more tightly targeted to the most severe changes will have the largest welfare gain relative to payouts. The benefits of providing disability insurance to everyone, and just to workers (as is done in most developed countries) are also considered.

Disability Insurance

This section contrasts the benefits and costs of formal disability insurance that fully smoothes consumption over the loss in earnings arising from illness. The gain to the household from such insurance is the expected value of the transfer from the insuring agency plus the welfare gain from consumption smoothing. The cost to the government is the expected value of the transfer plus a markup for administrative costs, the cost of moral hazard through increased reported illness in response to the existence of this program, and any deadweight loss from financing these benefit payments. That is, the expected benefit payout is just a transfer from the government to households; the ultimate efficiency of disability insurance policy rests on a comparison of the welfare gains from consumption smoothing and the inefficiencies inherent in operating a disability insurance program. Measuring these inefficiencies is beyond the scope of this chapter. But, by comparing the welfare gain from consumption smoothing to the expected benefits payout (the transfer), the chapter can offer a sense of how large these costs would have to be in percentage terms to offset the consumption smoothing benefits of disability insurance.

---

[37] See, for example, Rothschild and Stiglitz (1976).

Table 6–7. Welfare Gains from Disability and Medical Insurance, Indonesia

Type of insurance	Expected insurance payouts (percent of consumption)	Welfare gain (percent of consumption)	Gain/cost
Disability insurance for all			
Overall ADLs	0.89	0.36	0.40
Basic ADLs only	0.25	0.18	0.72
Disability insurance for workers only			
Overall ADLs	0.99	0.51	0.52
Basic ADLs only	0.32	0.40	1.25
Medical insurance for all			
Overall ADLs	0.30	0.14	0.47
Basic ADLs only	0.13	0.11	0.85

Note: The first two columns show, as a percentage of consumption, the expected insurance payout and welfare gain (respectively) of providing full insurance against either disability or medical expenditures. The last column shows the ratio of welfare gains to expected insurance payouts.
Source: Author's calculations.

The section begins by estimating the expected payout from a disability insurance policy that fully replaces the earnings loss to those who become ill by the ADL metric. The loss in earnings from an illness, L_j, is measured by using the estimates of equation 6-2 reported in the third row of table 6–3 to predict the loss in earnings from downward movements in the ADL indexes.[38] The probability of experiencing the loss, π_j, is measured using the observed frequency distribution of downward movements in the ADL indexes. The expected loss in earnings, then, is the sum of the π_j times L_j. The estimate for the expected insurance payout for earnings losses is 0.89 percent of baseline consumption.

The estimated insurance payouts, which are equivalent to overall expected earnings losses from illness, are reported in the first column of table 6–7. The expected payout for overall changes in ADLs is about 0.9 percent of consumption. The expected payout for more serious illnesses, as measured by movements in ba-

---

[38] It is inappropriate to incorporate the consumption increases from upward movements in health, which simply reflect recovery from earlier downward shifts. The results for the consumption smoothing effects of changes in the ADL index are very similar if we just use downward shifts to identify our estimates.

sic ADLs, is 0.25 percent of consumption. These results are quite small as a share of consumption. Despite the fact that the expected earnings loss conditional on occurrence of an ADL change is very high, the frequency of occurrence of serious illness is very low, so that overall expected insurance payouts are low as well. Similarly, the expected payouts for more serious illnesses are much lower than for less serious illnesses; this reflects the fact that more serious illnesses occur with much less frequency.

Next, equation 6-4 is used to estimate the private willingness to pay to eliminate the variation in consumption due to the income loss from serious illness. This chapter has already discussed how π_j and L_j are measured. The coefficients reported in the second column of table 6–5 are used as estimates of γ. There is no direct estimate of the coefficient of relative risk aversion, ρ. Instead, we evaluate equation 6-4 for a range of values from 2 to 4, which is the range estimated by most previous studies using individual microdata.[39] The results are fairly insensitive to values in this range.

The results of this exercise for $\rho = 3$ are presented in the second column of table 6–7. We first show the welfare loss from illness, which is (as noted above) a lower bound on the willingness to pay for insurance as a percentage of ex ante consumption. For overall changes in ADLs, this is 0.36 percent of consumption. This is once again quite small, despite the large economic cost of these rare illnesses, due to the infrequency of illness. This also reflects the fact that individuals can smooth 65 percent of the cost of illness through other mechanisms, so that to some extent disability insurance will crowd out those other sources of support. We calculate that if no smoothing from other sources were available, the welfare gain from complete disability insurance would be 1.2 percent of consumption.

But, while small as a share of baseline consumption, this welfare gain is fairly large relative to expected insurance payouts, as shown in the third column of table 6–7. The welfare gain amounts to roughly 40 percent of insurance payouts. Restricting the analysis to only the most serious basic ADL changes, there is once again a very small welfare loss from illness, 0.18 percent of consumption. However, the welfare gain from insuring these more severe illnesses is 72 percent of the insurance payout under disability insurance.

The second panel of table 6–7 restricts the analysis to workers only. In this case, not only do we find that there is a larger payout under disability insurance, but the welfare gains are larger as well. Indeed, for overall ADL changes, the wel-

---

[39] Zeldes (1989); Engen (1993).

fare gains from insurance amount to over one-half of insurance payouts. For basic ADL changes, the welfare gains are actually larger than the insurance payouts.

These findings of large welfare gains from insurance, relative to expected payouts, suggest the potential for welfare improvements from government insurance provision. Only if the deadweight loss of government provision, through administrative costs, moral hazard, and the marginal cost of public funds, amounts to half or more of expected payouts will there be no welfare improvement from formal disability insurance. And, if the government is able to target the disability program to workers and to the most severely disabled, there will be welfare improvements so long as these incremental costs (including, of course, the costs of targeting) do not exceed 125 percent of the transfer.

The Insurance Value of Public Medical Care Subsidies

There is a heated policy debate in developing countries about raising user fees for services obtained at public health care facilities. Governments have or are actively considering raising these charges as a means of financing improvements in the health sector and improving the efficiency with which medical care is delivered.[40] Vocal opponents are concerned that increased fees will adversely affect the access of the poor to medical care and, consequently, their health outcomes.[41] Policymakers are also promoting lowering subsidies for hospitalization and shifting them to primary and preventive care.[42] This proposal is justified based on the argument that primary and preventive care are more cost-effective methods of improving a population's overall health.

This debate, however, has ignored the possible role of public subsidies as consumption insurance. Subsidies reduce risk by spreading the medical costs of uncertain illness across healthy and sick times; taxes are incurred when healthy people finance medical care purchased when sick. As a result, raising user fees in a world of imperfect consumption insurance has an important welfare cost: higher user fees "tax families while they are down," imposing higher costs at exactly the point where the marginal utility of consumption is highest. Thus, given the imperfect consumption smoothing that we document, there may be an additional consumption smoothing motivation for low user fees.

---

[40] See, for example, World Bank (1987); Jiménez (1996).

[41] See, for example, Cornia, Jolly, and Stewart (1987); Ready (1996).

[42] World Bank (1993).

These consumption smoothing models indicate that families are able to fully smooth the costs of medical care associated with small health shocks that do not affect physical functioning. However, since families are not able to smooth rare large shocks, shifting subsidies away from the treatment of these illnesses will come at a cost of reduced welfare from lower insurance.

This section estimates the insurance value of these public medical care subsidies. First, it estimates what medical care expenditures would be in a world with no subsidies. User fees at public facilities are estimated to be about 10 percent of the cost of providing care.[43] Using these same data, Gertler and Molyneaux estimate the price elasticity of demand for medical care to be −0.4.[44] Therefore, if prices were increased to the full costs of care—a tenfold increase—this would raise medical spending by 600 percent. The unsubsidized medical care expenditures for each change in ADLs is measured by the subsidized expenditure predicted from table 6–3, increased by a factor of 6.

Using the estimates of $\pi_{j'}$ the expected unsubsidized medical care expenditures arising from ADL changes are calculated. The results are reported in the first column of the third panel of table 6–7. Even unsubsidized, expected medical care expenditures are only about one-third of the expected loss in earnings from illness.

The willingness to pay to eliminate the variation in consumption due to medical care expenditures in a world with no formal disability insurance is reported in the second column of the third panel of table 6–7. The willingness to pay computation follows that above, but uses the unsubsidized value for medical care expenditures in addition to the earnings loss, raising the welfare cost of imperfect consumption smoothing. Then the difference between the willingness to pay to insure total income loss, including unsubsidized medical spending, and the willingness to pay to insure the earnings loss only is taken.

Not surprisingly, the welfare gain from full medical insurance as a percent of consumption is small; for overall ADLs, it is only 0.14 percent of consumption. However, the welfare gain as a percentage of expected medical care expenditures is quite large. Overall, this gain is almost 50 percent as large as expected expenditures. For basic ADL changes, the gain is 85 percent as large. The welfare gains are large relative to payouts because the unsubsidized medical care losses are incurred on top of income losses. This is the point where the marginal utility of consumption is highest and, therefore, the welfare loss per dollar is highest.

---

[43] World Bank (1995a).
[44] Gertler and Molyneaux (1996).

These results suggest that user fees for frequent small illnesses are affordable in the sense that families are able to smooth consumption over these shocks. This also suggests that user fees for primary and preventive care are affordable. However, since families are not able to afford rare large shocks, shifting subsidies by raising user fees for hospitalization will come at a cost of reduced welfare from lower insurance. Our results suggest that there is likely to be some welfare gain from subsidizing inpatient care for rare expensive illnesses, which families are least able to smooth and for which there is the lowest moral hazard cost.

CHINA

During the 1980s and 1990s, China astonished the world with annual GDP growth rates averaging over 8 percent in most years. These numbers mask the tremendous differences in economic growth across China's regions, as rural areas of the hinterland witnessed much slower growth over this period. Much of the same story can be told with respect to both access and quality of health care during the reform period. Variation in access can be quite striking—in 1993, for example, the number of hospital beds per thousand was 5.50 for Shanghai and 6.24 for Beijing, but only 1.1 in China's rural areas.[45]

Improved access to health care services actually predated the reform era. China's rural residents benefited from a 1965 State Council directive that called for health reform and more emphasis on rural services and led to the training of barefoot doctors and extension of basic health services down to the village.[46] Dramatic improvements in health outcomes followed. The under-five mortality rate, for example, fell from 144 per thousand live births in 1965 to 60 in 1980, and further to 44 by 1990.[47] Since 1980, the basic institutions of the rural health care system developed in the 1960s have remained preserved within the postreform township and village institutions.

The upper tier of the rural health care system run by the County Public Health Bureau is composed of one or more general hospitals, an epidemic prevention station, and a maternal and child health station. Township health centers (*weishengyuan*) form the middle tier of the rural health care system and generally include a small

---

[45] State Statistical Bureau (1994); Ministry of Public Health (1994).

[46] West (1997).

[47] World Bank (1996). The under-five mortality rate is defined as the number of children who die between birth and their fifth birthday.

hospital, an outpatient clinic, and an office for maternal and child health care. Finally, the lowest tier of the rural health system is the village health office *(weishengsuo)*. Part-time rural health aides typically treat only common medical problems and refer serious illnesses to the township health center. Besides family planning services, rural health aides are responsible for immunization treatment and provide general health education.[48]

On the eve of reform in the late 1970s, costs of health care for rural residents were quite low, and collective insurance coverage was quite broad. Dating to the 1950s, one of three forms of insurance was available to rural residents. Government health insurance *(gongfei yiliao)*, available to state cadres, teachers, and township government workers, was funded through cost reimbursement. Labor health insurance *(laodong baoxian)* was provided to any rural residents employed in state-owned enterprises. Finally, cooperative health insurance *(hezuo yiliao)* was set up by villages and managed in coordination with township health centers.[49] By the early 1980s, the majority of China's rural population had access to some form of risk-pooling arrangement that guaranteed access to care. Various estimates place the uninsured population at between 10 and 29 percent in 1981.[50] With introduction of the household responsibility system in agriculture and the dismantling of the communal welfare fund that supported cooperative health insurance, however, the uninsured population exploded to almost 80 percent of rural households by 1993.[51] The villages used in the analysis of this chapter reflect this trend. As of 1997, residents in only one-quarter of them participated in any type of health insurance plan.

At present, the Ministry of Public Health is experimenting with different types of community-financing programs for rural residents. Most small-scale experiments provide a form of coinsurance requiring residents to pay part of the cost of health services at the point of service.[52] Whether health insurance should be compulsory or not has been a matter of debate within policy circles. While a 1994 policy announcement emphasized that participation in community-organized coinsurance programs should be voluntary at the individual level, there have been reports of experiments with compulsory participation as well.[53]

---

[48] West (1997).
[49] Wei (1995); World Bank (1996).
[50] West (1997); World Bank (1984).
[51] Wei (1995).
[52] World Bank (1996).
[53] *Peoples Daily*, July 2, 1994.

Data

The analyses of health shocks in this chapter use household survey data provided by the Survey Department of the Research Center on the Rural Economy (RCRE) at the Ministry of Agriculture in Beijing. Annual household surveys from 104 villages of Shanxi, Jiangsu, Anhui, Shandong, Henan, and Shaanxi provinces and the Shanghai suburbs spanning the period from 1986 to 1997 are used to both analyze the impact of health shocks on household consumption and evaluate potential demand for health insurance in rural China.

RCRE has collected data from a panel of households since 1986, but the survey was not conducted in 1992 or 1994 because of funding difficulties. Households are asked a range of questions regarding income from on-farm activities and off-farm employment, household consumption, land use, asset ownership, savings, formal and informal access to and provision of credit, and transfers from both village members and friends and family outside the village. Values of nonmarketed grain that show up in income, consumption, and grain balance sections of the survey are adjusted to reflect market prices following a procedure outlined by Shaohua Chen and Martin Ravallion.[54] County agricultural research offices that collect expenditure, income, and labor allocation information from households on a monthly basis monitor the household survey. A staff person from the office works with households to clear up inconsistencies in the survey.

In the analysis below, changes in expenditures on health care are used to identify the occurrence and severity of a health shock. While small expenditures generally reflect routine preventative care administered at village or township health offices, large expenditures reflect catastrophic shocks that require visits to more expensive fee-for-service hospitals at the township or county level.

Health Care Costs

Until the mid-1980s the rural health care system was financed largely through transfers from the central government. Since the mid-1980s, however, there has been increasing pressure on local governments to contribute matching funds for the construction of health centers and offices. With respect to the provision of services, a switch from salaried compensation from local government budgets to fee-for-ser-

---

[54] Chen and Ravallion (1996).

vice financing exacerbated the effect of deteriorating mechanisms for risk pooling at the village level and contributed to the growth in household out-of-pocket expenses. Nationally, patient fees represented roughly 14 percent of total expenditures on health care in rural areas in 1980, but by 1992 patient fees accounted for 34 percent of total expenditures on health care.[55] Data from the RCRE household survey also reflect this trend. From table 6–8 we see that in constant 1986 yuan, the share of households spending more than 100 yuan on health expenditures doubled between 1987 and 1997. For the households in this sample, an expenditure of 100 yuan is roughly 8 percent of total household expenditures for the year, making this a sizable health shock.

As in other countries around the world, the data from this survey indicate that most expenditures on health care are devoted to treating the catastrophic illnesses faced by a small proportion of the population. The Lorenz curve plots the cumulative share of the population versus the cumulative share of health expenditures (figure 6–1). It is evident from figure 6–1 that roughly 20 percent of the population in this sample accounts for 75 percent of the expenditures on health care. Lorraine West has noted that in 1993 the household portion of payment for major surgery was roughly 150 yuan, implying that expenditures of over 100 yuan signify major shock.[56]

While households might be able to cover small health shocks relatively easily, catastrophic shocks have become a more serious problem with the introduction of fee-for-service payment schemes in China's rural hospitals. To cover fees for serious illnesses, households must deplete savings, if they exist, or rely on informal loans from family members. Financing medical care to cover the serious illness of a family member can have significant long-term consequences for households in rural China. As the health policy community in Beijing strives to develop a new rural insurance system, the clear task it faces is to find a way to insure against the economic impact of catastrophic shocks.

Consumption Smoothing and the Welfare Loss from Lack of Insurance

In the case of Indonesia the illness shocks were observed directly. In China only medical care expenditures are observed. Moreover, since income is not observed, the impact of illness on income cannot be estimated and equation 6-5 cannot be

---

[55] West (1997).
[56] West (1997).

Table 6–8. Increase in Household Expenditures on Health Care, 1987–97, China

Values in 1986 RMB yuan

Expenditure	1987	1989	1991	1993	1995	1997
Average household consumption of nondurable goods	1,360	1,280	1,221	1,221	1,433	1,342
Average household health care expenditure	31	32	37	45	54	60
Share of household health expenditures over 100 RMB yuan	0.09	0.11	0.11	0.14	0.17	0.18

Note: Nondurable goods include food, clothing, fuel, and services.
Source: RCRE Rural Household Survey.

directly estimated. Instead, (6–5) must be estimated by replacing the change in income with the change in medical care expenditures. The coefficient times baseline consumption, then, is interpreted as how much consumption falls for each yuan of medical care spending. However, the falls in consumption might be due either to medical care spending or to associated reductions in income from lost work due to illness. In the case of China the two cannot be separated.

The change in medical care expenditures is used in place of the change in income in (6–5) to avoid the measurement error problem. However, there could be feedback from the change in consumption to the change in medical care spending. Families with higher income spend more on medical care. The first-order effect is solved by using a difference model that controls for heterogeneity in permanent income. Then by including village-time fixed effects, community-level changes in permanent income are controlled for, as are changes in human capital at the household level. Therefore, the remaining sources of concern include changes in household-level idiosyncratic shocks to permanent income. While feedback from changes in consumption to medical care expenditures cannot be completely ruled out, the degree to which it is likely to affect the results is limited. Moreover, feedback from consumption to medical care expenditures should be positive, while the effect of medical expenditures on consumption should be negative. Therefore, to the extent there is feedback, it biases the coefficient toward zero. This suggests that results are biased toward finding insurance. Hence, the estimates of the welfare loss from not being able to insure the economic costs of illness are lower bound estimates.

Table 6–9 reports the results for two specifications of equation 6-5. The first specifies the changes in medical care expenditures linearly, and the second specifies

FIGURE 6–1

Lorenz Curve of Health Care Expenditures

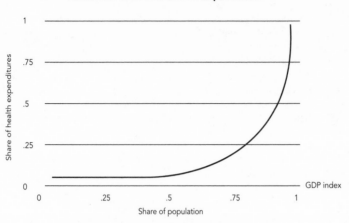

Source: RCRE Household Surveys, 1987-97. Ministry of Agriculture, Beijing

them as piecewise linear splines with knots at 50 and 250. The splines allow nonlinear responses to the health shock. This specification tests the hypothesis that households are able to smooth small shocks, but less able to smooth big shocks.[57] The results overwhelmingly indicate that households are not able to fully insure medical care expenditures. In the linear specification, the coefficient on medical care expenditures indicates that 94 percent of medical care expenditures come out of household consumption, or that households can smooth only about 6 percent of medical care costs. The spline specification, however, indicates that households are fully able to smooth small health shocks under 50 yuan, but not able to smooth larger shocks above 50 yuan. In fact, consumption falls by 1.06 yuan for each yuan of medical spending for spending levels between 50 and 249 yuan, and consumption falls by 1.11 yuan for each yuan of medical spending for levels above 250 yuan. The latter results could be interpreted as households not being able to insure all medical care costs above 50 yuan or that there are other costs associated with large expenditures such as lost income, transportation, and food costs associated with inpatient stays in hospitals.

---

[57] Note that about 27.9 percent of the households have no medical care expenditures in a given year, 53.3 percent have expenditures of less than 50 yuan, 16.3 percent have expenditures between 50 and 250 yuan, and 2.5 percent have shocks greater than 250 yuan.

Table 6–9. Smoothing the Consumption Effects of Shocks to Nondurable Consumption in Rural China

Item	Model 1	Model 2	Mean [standard deviation]
Lag household prime laborers	−0.031	−0.031	2.522
	(0.001)	(0.001)	[1.138]
Lag household dependents	−0.005	−0.005	1.852
	(0.001)	(0.001)	[1.158]
Lag male share of prime laborers	0.026	0.026	0.516
	(0.008)	(0.008)	[0.216]
Lag land per capita	0.002	0.002	1.434
	(0.003)	(0.003)	[1.012]
Lag share of laborers with elementary education	0.006	0.007	0.352
	(0.006)	(0.006)	[0.329]
Lag share of laborers with lower middle school education	0.015	0.015	0.323
	(0.007)	(0.007)	[0.325]
Lag share of laborers with upper middle school education	0.010	0.010	0.071
	(0.010)	(0.009)	[0.188]
Lag share of laborers with special skill	0.007	0.007	0.102
	(0.008)	(0.008)	[0.205]
Change in health expenditures	−0.00071		36.530
	(0.00002)		[80.110]
Small changes in health expenditures (less than 50 yuan RMB)		0.00009	
		(0.00008)	
Medium changes in health expenditures (50 to 249 yuan RMB)		−0.00080	
		0.00005	
Large changes in health expenditures (greater than 250 yuan RMB)		−0.00092	
		(0.00003)	
Number of observations	45,263	45,263	45,263
R^2	0.051	0.053	
Village*year fixed effects, $F_{(780, 44,473)}$	9.567	9.626	

Note: The dependent variable is Δln(nondurable consumption). Average nondurable consumption was 1,321 RMB yuan per household (in 1986 yuan), with a standard deviation of 705 RMB yuan. Standard errors are in parentheses.
Source: Author's calculations.

The willingness to pay is calculated to eliminate the variation in consumption due to medical care expenditure shocks using the methods presented earlier. The results of the spline model are used to estimate γ, and the frequency distribution of medical care expenditures to estimate π_j and L_j. Using the same estimates of risk aversion as in the Indonesian case, it is estimated that households are on average willing to pay 1.87 percent of household consumption. This is approximately six times average medical care spending.

CONCLUSIONS

Using data from Indonesia and China, this chapter finds that while households are able to insure the economic costs of small health shocks, they are not able to insure the costs of major illness. The results indicate that there are large welfare gains from reducing the variation in consumption from the economic costs of major illness. However, households are unable to purchase insurance from the private sector due to market failures. This suggests a role for government to improve welfare through social insurance for income loss due to disability and medical care expenditures. The fact that households are able to insure against the costs of small illnesses suggests that employing user fees to finance the expansion of publicly delivered health care services will have little impact on welfare. Moreover, this result implies that first-dollar capped social insurance benefit structures provide little welfare gain. Indeed, such benefit structures just crowd private informal insurance. Rather, the big welfare gains are from insuring the rare large illnesses.

References

Andrews, G., and others. 1986. *Aging in the Western Pacific*. Manila, Philippines: World Health Organization.

Asian Development Bank. 1997. *Asian Development Outlook 1996 and 1997*. Manila, Philippines: Asian Development Bank.

Attanasio, Orazio, and Steven Davis. 1996. "Relative Wage Movements and the Distribution of Consumption." *Journal of Political Economy* 104 (December): 1227–62.

Benjamin, Dwayne. 1992. "Household Composition, Labor Markets, and Labor Demand: Testing for Separation on Agricultural Household Models." *Econometrica* 60 (March): 287–322.

Besley, Timothy, and Miguel Gouveia. 1994. "Alternative Systems of Health Care Provision." *Economic Policy* (October): 201–58.

Bound, J. 1991. "Self-Reported versus Objective Measures of Health in Retirement Models." *Journal of Human Resources* 26: 106–38.

Bound, J., M. Schoenbaum, and T. Waidman. 1995. "Race and Education Differences in Disability Status and Labor Force Participation." *Journal of Human Resources* 30: S227–S267.

Chen, Shaohua, and Martin Ravallion. 1996. "Data in Transition: Assessing Rural Living Standards in Southern China." *China Economic Review* 7 (Spring).

Cochrane, John. 1991. "A Simple Test of Consumption Insurance." *Journal of Political Economy* 99 (October): 957–76.

Cornia, G., R. Jolly, and F. Stewart. 1987. *Adjustment with a Human Face*. Oxford: Clarendon Press.

Deaton, Angus. 1992a. "Saving and Income Smoothing in Côte d'Ivoire." *Journal of African Economics* 1: 1–24.

———. 1992b. *Understanding Consumption*. Oxford: Clarendon Press.

———. 1994. *The Analysis of Household Surveys: Microeconometric Analysis for Development Policy*. Monograph. World Bank, Washington, D.C.

Dow, William, and Paul Gertler. 1997. "Private Health Insurance and Public Expenditures in Indonesia." RAND, Santa Monica, CA. Unpublished.

Dow, William, and others. 1996. "Health Care Prices, Health and Labor Outcomes: Experimental Evidence." RAND, Santa Monica, CA. Unpublished.

Dynarski, Susan, and Jonathan Gruber. 1997. "Can Families Smooth Variable Earnings?" *Brookings Papers on Economic Activity* 1:1997, 229–304.

Engen, Eric. 1993. "A Stochastic Life-Cycle Model with Mortality Risk: Estimation with Panel Data." UCLA, Los Angeles, CA. Unpublished.

Gertler, Paul. 1998. "On the Road to Social Health Insurance." *World Development* 26 (4): 717–32.

Gertler, Paul, and Jonathan Gruber. 1997. *Insuring Consumption against Illness*. Working Paper. National Bureau of Economic Research, Cambridge, MA.

Gertler, Paul, and Jack Molyneaux. 1996. "The Effect of Medical Care Prices on Utilization and Health Outcomes: Experimental Results." RAND, Santa Monica, CA. Unpublished.

Gertler, Paul, and Orville Solon. 1998. "Who Benefits from Social Insurance in Developing Countries?" Haas School of Business, UC-Berkeley, Berkeley, CA. Unpublished.

Gertler, Paul, and Sturm. 1997. "Private Health Insurance and Public Expenditures." *Journal of Economics* 77 (2): 237–57.

Gertler, P., and J. Zeitlin. 1996. "The Returns to Childhood Investments in Terms of Health Later in Life." RAND, Santa Monica, CA. Unpublished.

Gruber, Jonathan. 1996. *Cash Welfare as a Consumption Smoothing Mechanism for Single Mothers.* Working Paper no. 5738. National Bureau of Economic Research, Cambridge, MA.

———. 1997. "The Consumption Smoothing Benefits of Unemployment Insurance." *American Economic Review* 82 (March): 182–205.

Guralnik, J., and others. 1989. "Physical Performance Measures in Aging Research." *Journal of Gerontology* 44 (September): 141–46.

Hayashi, Fumio, Joseph Altonji, and Laurence Kotlikoff. 1996. "Risk Sharing between and within Families." *Econometrica* 64 (March): 261–94.

Jiménez, E. 1987. *Pricing Policy in the Social Sectors: Cost Recovery for Education and Health in Developing Countries.* Baltimore, MD: Johns Hopkins University Press.

———. 1996. "Human and Physical Infrastructure." In J. Behrman and T. N. Srinavasan, eds., *Handbook of Development Economics.* Amsterdam, Netherlands: North Holland.

Ju, A., and G. Jones. 1989. *Aging in ASEAN and Its Socio-economic Consequences.* Singapore: Institute of Southeast Asian Studies.

Kington, R., and J. Smith. 1996. "Socio-Economic Correlates of Adult Health." *Demography* 33 (1): 25–36.

Kochar, Anjini. 1995. "Explaining Household Vulnerability to Idiosyncratic Income Shocks." *American Economic Review* 85 (May): 159–64.

Mace, Barbara. 1991. "Full Insurance in the Presence of Aggregate Uncertainty." *Journal of Political Economy* 99 (October): 928–56.

Ministry of Public Health (MPH). 1994. *Chinese Health Statistical Digest,* 1993.

Morduch, Jonathan. 1990. "Risk, Production, and Saving: Theory and Evidence from Indian Households." Harvard University, Cambridge, MA. Unpublished.

———. 1995. "Income Smoothing and Consumption Smoothing." *Journal of Economic Perspectives* 9 (Summer): 103–14.

———. 1999. "Between Market and State: Can Informal Insurance Patch the Safety Net?" *World Bank Research Observer* 16 (2): 122–34.

Nelson, Julie. 1994. "On Testing for Full Insurance Using Consumer Expenditure Survey Data." *Journal of Political Economy* 102 (April): 384–94.

Paxson, Christina. 1992. "Using Weather Variability to Estimate the Response of Savings to Transitory Income in Thailand." *American Economic Review* 82 (March): 15–33.

Pitt, M., and M. Rosenzweig. 1986. "Agricultural Prices, Food Consumption, and the Health and Productivity of Farmers." In I. Sing, L. Squire, and J. Strauss, eds., *Agricultural Household Models: Extensions and Applications.* Baltimore, MD: Johns Hopkins University Press.

Ready, Sanjy. 1996. "A Critical Review of User Charges for Basic Services." *Policy Review* 136.

Rothschild, Michael, and Joseph E. Stiglitz. 1976. "Equilibrium in Competitive Insurance Markets: An Essay on the Economics of Imperfect Information." *Quarterly Journal of Economics* 90 (November): 629–50.

Schultz, T. P., and A. Tansel. 1997. "Wage and Labor Supply Effects of Illness in Côte d'Ivoire and Ghana: Instrumental Variable Estimates for Days Disabled." *Journal of Development Economics* 53 (August): 251–86.

Sindelar, J., and D. Thomas. 1991. *Measurement of Child Health: Maternal Response Bias.* Discussion Paper no. 663. Economic Growth Center, Yale University, New Haven, CT.

State Statistical Bureau (SSB). 1994. Zhongguo Tongji Nianjian *1994* (A statistical survey of China). Beijing, China: Zhongguo Tongji Chubanshe.

Stern, S. 1989. "Measuring the Effect of Disability on Labor Force Participation." *Journal of Human Resources* 24 (Summer): 361–95.

Stewert, A., and others. 1990. *Measurement of Adult Health Status: Physical Health in Terms of Functional Status.* Cambridge, MA: Harvard University Press.

Strauss, John, and Duncan Thomas. 1996. "Human Resources: Empirical Modeling of Household and Family Decisions." In J. Behrman and T. N. Srinavasan, eds., *Handbook of Development Economics.* Amsterdam, Netherlands: North Holland.

Strauss, J., and others. 1993. "Gender and Life-Cycle Differentials in the Patterns and Determinants of Adult Health." *Journal of Human Resources* 28 (Fall): 791–837.

Townsend, Robert. 1994. "Risk and Insurance in Village India." *Econometrica* 62 (May): 539–91.

———. 1995. "Consumption Insurance: An Evaluation of Risk-Bearing Systems in Low-Income Economies." *Journal of Economic Perspectives* 9 (Summer): 83–102.

Wallace, R., and A. Herzog. 1995. "An Overview of Health Status Measures in the Health and Retirement Survey." *Journal of Human Resources* 30 (Winter): S84–S107.

Ware, J., A. Davies-Avery, and R. Brook. 1980. *Conceptualization and Measurement of Health Status for Adults in the Health Insurance Study: Vol. IV, Analysis of Relationships among Health Status Measures.* R-1987/6-HEW. RAND, Santa Monica, CA.

Wei, Ying. 1995. "An Introduction to Health Financing Patterns in China." National Health Economics Institute (Beijing). Paper presented at a health care conference in Beijing, (May).

West, Lorraine. 1997. "Provision of Public Services in the PRC." In Christine P. W. Wong, ed., *Financing Local Government in the People's Republic of China.* Asian Development Bank and Oxford University Press.

World Bank. 1984. *China: The Health Sector.* A World Bank Country Study. World Bank, Washington, D.C.

———. 1987. *Financing Health Services in Developing Countries.* World Bank Policy Study. World Bank, Washington, D.C.

———. 1993. *World Development Report: Investing in Health.* Oxford: Oxford University Press.

———. 1995a. *Averting the Old Age Crisis.* Oxford: Oxford University Press.

———. 1995b. *Indonesia: Public Expenditure, Prices and the Poor.* Washington, D.C.: World Bank.

———. 1996. *China: Issues and Options in Health Financing.* Washington, D.C.: World Bank.

Zeldes, Stephen P. 1989. "Consumption and Liquidity Constraints: An Empirical Investigation." *Journal of Political Economy* 97 (April): 305–46.

CHAPTER SEVEN

Coverage under Old Age Security Programs and Protection for the Uninsured: What Are the Issues?

Estelle James

The majority of workers and old people in developing countries are uninsured by formal social security programs. Coverage ranges from less than 10 percent in Sub-Saharan Africa and South Asia and less than 30 percent in most of East Asia to 50–60 percent in the middle-income countries of South America, 70–80 percent in the Eastern European transition economies, and 90–100 percent in the small group of countries in the Organization for Economic Cooperation and Development (OECD).[1]

Economic development is the major determinant of coverage rates, but policies chosen by governments also matter. The structure of industry, the limited taxing capacity of governments, and the high discount rate and liquidity constraints faced by low earners limit the feasible scope of contributory schemes in developing countries. We argue that they also limit the desirability of contributory schemes for low-income workers in these countries. If the contribution rate is borne by workers, it may reduce their take-home pay at a point in the life cycle when they need more income rather than less; and if borne by employers, it may reduce the number of jobs in the economy. A low contribution rate and a high rate of return can reduce these disincentives and distortions that inhibit optimal coverage.

The uninsured fall into two main groups: workers who have labor market jobs that are not covered by contributory programs (for example, the self-employed, the informal sector), either because they cannot find covered jobs or because they (or their employers) prefer to operate in the informal sector where

---

[1] World Bank (1994).

taxes and regulations are smaller; and women who have worked in the household rather than the labor market for most of their lives, expecting to be supported by the family system, which may fail them in old age. The second group can be protected by requiring the purchase of survivors' insurance and joint annuities by workers in the contributory scheme—thereby institutionalizing the informal family system into the formal social security system. In a multipillar scheme, this cost would be borne by the married workers directly involved, rather than being passed on to others. For the first group of uninsured, social assistance programs targeted toward the lowest earners outside of the formal system seem to be essential—creating the need to design such programs efficiently and take their costs into account in planning the reform. The challenge is how to maximize the proportion of money that reaches the targeted groups while minimizing leakage and moral hazard problems.

This chapter discusses how contributory social security systems imply a class of uninsured; argues that a high coverage level under mandatory contributory schemes is neither necessary nor desirable for low-income countries; examines voluntary programs and universal benefits as alternatives to mandatory contributory schemes; suggests institutionalizing the implicit family contract into formal pension systems to protect women who have worked in the home rather than the formal labor market—requiring spouses to purchase survivors' insurance and joint annuities; and analyzes the use of social assistance for the lowest-income groups who are left out of the formal system. Salient issues include the trade-off between social assistance and human capital creation, how to provide social assistance without diminishing the incentive to be in the contributory scheme (the moral hazard problem), how to target benefits while keeping transactions costs and other leakages low, and how much priority to give to social assistance to the old versus young families with children.

HOW SOCIAL SECURITY CREATES A CLASS OF UNINSURED

Most countries, including almost all developing countries, finance old age security through earmarked taxes, called "contributions," rather than through general revenues. This emphasis on contributory systems with benefits contingent on contributions is used to increase the public's willingness to pay and to decrease distortionary, evasionary techniques. But it has the side effect of creating a class of uninsured or partially insured individuals who have contributed little or nothing in their working years and may be left in poverty in old age.

Why Are Most Social Security Schemes Financed by Earmarked Payroll Taxes, or "Contributions"?

Most mandatory pension schemes, including almost all those in developing countries, are financed by payments that people make specifically for this purpose, rather than through general revenues. The payments are mandatory and in this sense they are taxes, but they are earmarked for a specific service and for this reason are usually called "contributions." The programs are for those who make contributions rather than universal, and the benefits they pay depend on the level of contributions.

The basic idea is that when people perceive that they are getting a specific service in return for their payments, they are more willing to pay and less anxious to evade. Both political opposition and economic distortions are likely to be smaller for earmarked taxes than for general taxes. In this sense, the government's spending frontier is extended when earmarked taxes linked to size of benefits are used. For this reason, such arrangements are common for the financing of quasi-public services such as education, medical care, and old age insurance, where exclusion and differentiation in type of service is feasible. People who do not contribute do not get access to these services.

The earmarked tax or contribution for social security is usually based on wages, subject to a ceiling and occasionally a floor. The returns to capital are not taxed to finance these programs, nor is property taxed. Benefits also depend on wages—sometimes lifetime wages and sometimes final year wages. The theory, again, is that this indirectly links benefits to contributions, thereby increasing peoples' willingness to pay the price.

But why use a payroll tax base? Why not base contributions on total income or on some flat amount? One rationale for using a payroll base is that pensions in old age are designed to replace the wages that people receive when they are able to work, hence the benefits should be tied to wages. A close benefit-contribution linkage then requires that contributions also be based on wages. If benefits depended on wages but were financed by general revenues, capital as well as labor would be taxed, thereby making the programs more redistributive. Holders of capital would oppose this financing method, giving us a second, political economy, reason for its infrequent use. A third, more pragmatic, reason for payroll tax finance is that such deductions are the easiest way administratively to reach large segments of the population, who do not file income tax returns in many countries. A sales or value-added tax would also be administratively feasible, but would make it more difficult to keep track of the taxes paid by each individual, and hence to connect benefits and contributions. Payroll taxes, in contrast, can be collected from employers while records are maintained on each worker—administratively an easier job.

To some extent this theory is violated by reality. On the one hand, some groups have been able to extract benefits that far exceed their contributions, due to easy eligibility, lax disability requirements, and early retirement. These behaviors ultimately made the system unsustainable in Latin America and led to a wave of multipillar reforms that tied benefits more closely to earmarked contributions.

On the other hand, the political economy of some countries (for example, Australia, Denmark, Switzerland) has allowed them to use general revenue finance or to forego a ceiling on taxable wages, thereby delinking benefits from contributions and making the system more redistributive from rich to poor. But in recent years, fiscal pressures have caused these arrangements to be downsized and supplemented by contributory pillars. Most mandatory systems now include components that require wage-based taxes and return benefits that depend in some way on wages or contributions.

The Consequence: Groups without Formal Labor Market Experience Are Not Covered

While possibly ameliorating the political and economic limits to taxation and government spending, contributory programs based on earmarked payroll taxes create a new problem—a distinction between covered and noncovered groups that depends on labor market experience. The uncovered group consists of two subsets:

- Those who engage in home work, instead of market work (primarily women).
- Those who engage in market work but whose jobs are not covered by contributory schemes (for example, the self-employed and agricultural workers), either because they cannot find covered jobs or because they (or their employers) choose to operate in the informal sector in order to avoid taxes and regulations.

Women presumably expect their monetary needs to be met through the family system, so they work in the household, without earning wages or pension rights. Their problem is that this expectation in their youth may not be realized when they grow old. Workers who engage in market work that is not covered earn wages to satisfy their monetary needs when young but fail to accumulate pension rights that

FIGURE 7–1

Relationship between Public Pension Coverage and Income per Capita

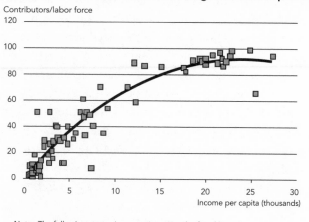

Note: The following regression equation gives the fitted line:
$y = -0.17X^2 + 7.79x - 0.34$
$R^2 = 0.89$
Source: Calculations by R. Palacios and M. Pallares, Washington, D.C., World Bank.

will provide an income when they grow old. Sometimes they contribute just enough to qualify for benefits, albeit modest, and evade thereafter, thereby making the system fiscally unsustainable even though their pension remains modest.

In all these cases, the family system has been the traditional means of old age support, but if this system breaks down, these groups are in trouble, and if they are living at the edge of poverty, their problem becomes a social problem. Indeed, a mandatory old age system developed in part to gather the resources to avoid this social problem. What can be done about these groups who are outside the formal old age systems?

IS INCREASED COVERAGE BY CONTRIBUTORY SCHEMES THE SOLUTION?

Should governments seek to increase coverage in the contributory scheme? While this is possible within limits, I argue that vastly increased coverage is neither feasible nor desirable in low-income countries.

Figure 7–1 demonstrates the close relationship between per capita income and coverage of workers under formal social security programs. Per capita income alone explains 89 percent of the variance in coverage. We observe that in low-income countries such as India and Sri Lanka, coverage of the adult population is as low as 10 percent, while in high-income countries it is close to 100 percent. We also observe some (small) variance in coverage for any given level of income. This suggests that, while coverage can be influenced to a minor degree by country policies, structural factors tied to stage of development play the major role in determining coverage by contributory programs. These structural factors come from two sources—the low tax-collecting capacities of governments at early stages of development combined with the prevalence of small enterprises and self-employment, which make it infeasible to extend coverage; and the fact that it may not be in the best interest of low-income workers to participate in contributory old age schemes, which makes coverage undesirable as well. It is very difficult to implement a mandatory program unless most workers perceive it as in their best interest.

The Difficulties in Collecting from Small Enterprises and the Self-Employed

The rationale for mandatory old age programs is that people may be myopic, may not make provisions themselves on a voluntary basis, and may hope to fall back on society's largesse should the need arise. The government mandate is designed to overcome these problems of myopia and moral hazard. But it leaves the government with a large enforcement problem, as workers try to evade the mandatory payments that they would not have made on a voluntary basis. Governments in developing countries often lack the necessary enforcement capabilities. The structure of the economy makes it difficult for them to compel compliance. Thus they face a trade-off between maximizing nominal coverage and minimizing evasion. After some point the increase in evasion may exceed the increase in nominal coverage, so effective coverage may decline if the government tries to expand the system beyond its capacities—evasion is a contagious social disease.

It is relatively easy to collect from large companies but more difficult to collect from small enterprises or the self-employed or subsistence agriculture or transient workers. Small enterprises have short life spans; they may come and go before they are registered and taxed. The self-employed, who must pay both the worker's and employer's share, have a double incentive to evade and find it easy to underreport their earnings. Keeping track of transient workers who work irregularly for different employers is a daunting task. Self-employment, small enterprises, subsistence production, and transient workers dominate in agriculture, the mainstay of most developing economies.

These problems exist in industrial countries as well, but they are multiplied in developing countries, where the "difficult" groups are disproportionately large and the government's capacity is weak. Many developing countries do not even try to cover these groups, and those that try often fail. For example, the self-employed, who constitute about a third of the labor force, are not covered in Chile.[2] They are covered in Argentina, which is considering excluding them because of high evasion. In many Asian countries employers with fewer than 10 or 20 workers are not covered. In most African countries only employees of the government and large state or multinational companies are covered. It may be wise for developing countries to concentrate their limited enforcement capacities in sectors where they are most likely to succeed—but this leaves the majority of workers uninsured.

Rational Reasons for Nonparticipation among the Poor

Even if increased effective coverage were feasible, it might not be desirable. The costs of coverage must be paid either by workers or employers, depending on the elasticity of labor supply and demand. Many workers may be better off outside the formal retirement old age security system, with higher take-home pay, which would be reduced by social security contributions. And the economy may be better off with more jobs, coming from lower labor costs, if employers operate outside the social security system. Policymakers thus face a trade-off between higher coverage and higher take-home pay for workers, hence greater current consumption; and between higher coverage and lower labor costs for employers, hence greater employment. While this trade-off may be decreased if a low target replacement rate and required contribution rate are chosen, some trade-off always remains.

Low-income workers may have perfectly rational utility-maximizing reasons for preferring to stay out of the old age system and for evading contributions if they are nominally covered. Often they are living close to the poverty level. They have relatively short expected lifetimes, so it may make more sense for them to use their meager incomes to survive at present rather than saving for the distant future, when they may not be alive. This effect is accentuated if, at the annuity stage, they are merged with high-income workers who have greater expected longevity, thereby depressing benefits and returns for the poor. This practice is common in mandatory social security systems, making it rational for low-income workers to evade such systems.

---

[2] World Bank (1994); Queisser (1998).

Moreover, even when they save, the best rate of return for them may come from investing in land, homes, tools, or the education of their children, who will return the loan by supporting them in the future. In most low- and middle-income countries, older people live in multigenerational households and their consumption level therefore depends on the earnings of their children more than on their own pensions. Investing in the human capital of their children may be the best old age security program for them. Investing in a family business may be the next best alternative. Lacking access to well-functioning credit markets and facing a high risk premium, farmers, the self-employed, and low-income groups generally are forced to pay exceedingly high borrowing rates or to use personal savings to finance these investments. They may, understandably, be reluctant to lock up their modest savings in a long-term retirement program that will not be available to meet shorter-term investment, educational, health, or other emergency needs.

Consistent with this hypothesis, a study of contribution patterns in Peru shows that the self-employed, farmers, and low-income workers are less likely to contribute regularly.[3] Empirical evidence from saving programs targeted to the poor in Mexico and Indonesia shows that these groups will indeed save, but they place a high value on liquidity and therefore choose short- rather than long-term financial instruments. Moreover, such savings are invariably small, much less than needed for old age security.[4] Experiments with informal systems show that workers are willing to save small amounts to meet short-term contingencies, in contrast to old age security arrangements that require large long-term illiquid payments.[5] Extending coverage by requiring low-income informal sector workers to contribute to old age security programs would not be in the best interests of these workers in such circumstances, even if the government had the capacity to enforce the mandate.

Usually employers are responsible for part of the contribution, giving them an incentive to operate out of the system if they see this as a way to reduce labor cost. While the market may eventually require a compensating wage increase for employers who are outside the formal old age system, employers may not perceive this in the short run, or even in the long run if they can attract workers who do not place a high value on social security benefits. If employers can keep their labor costs low by staying out of the system, this increases their international competitiveness and consequently the level of employment—especially important in coun-

---

[3] Queisser (1998).
[4] Aportela (1999).
[5] Van Ginneken (1999).

tries with high levels of unemployment or underemployment. Governments must weigh carefully the questions of who will bear the payroll tax if effective coverage is extended and how high the tax can be to avoid negative consequences on employment.

Will a Closer Link between Benefits and Contributions Encourage Participation?

Multipillar social security reforms in recent years have featured a strengthening of the benefit-contribution link. A second, funded defined-contribution pillar has been added, in which benefits ultimately depend exclusively on contributions plus investment income. In addition, these schemes usually include a public pillar that is redistributive and applies only to those who have contributed to the second pillar; it provides a safety net to the low earners among the contributors. In a sense, this can be regarded as an example of the risk category differentiation mentioned above. The hope is that this will increase the incentive of low-earning workers and their employers to participate in the formal sector and thereby reduce the number of uninsured.

These reforms should enable revenues to cover obligations and hence make the system more sustainable for those who do participate. Since fiscal sustainability is a precondition for responsible coverage expansion, these reforms may set the stage for actions by the government to extend coverage. Moreover, they may encourage compliance among long-term workers and their employers and enhance the welfare effects of participation, owing to the smaller tax element and the hope of a higher rate of return.

However, compliance may be discouraged among those who no longer receive windfall gains—some of whom were rich and some poor. And benefits are reduced substantially for those who contribute for only part of their working lives, and hence may not be eligible for the redistributive first pillar. Thus, pension coverage among the old poor may actually decrease.

For example, Chile provides a minimum pension guarantee of 25 percent of the average wage to workers who have contributed for at least 20 years to their individual accounts in the second pillar, and many other countries have followed this example. Accumulations in the second pillar are supplemented by the government to bring the annual benefit to this level. This guarantee will protect low-income covered workers, especially those who have contributed for only 20 years. For this reason, many low-income workers may stay in the system for 20 years. But workers who do not anticipate 20 years of participation will have a continued incentive to stay out of the system. A guarantee that increased with years of contributions might have been more equitable and effective at constraining evasion.

The Brazilian social security system has long included an "age" pension which, at a specified age (65 and 60 for urban men and women, 60 and 55 for rural men and women, respectively), pays 70 percent of the wage base to workers who have contributed for at least five years. The typical pension was one times the minimum salary, which is about 30 percent of the average wage. The Brazilian system also included a much more generous pension based on length of service, which required 30 years of covered employment and paid five to six times the minimum salary (150 percent of the average wage) to the average beneficiary. The "length of service" pension went mainly to urban men who worked in the formal labor force for most of their lives and earned relatively high salaries. The age pension went mainly to women, especially low-income rural women. For example, in 1997 out of 5.2 million recipients of the age pension, 75 percent were rural dwellers and 62 percent were women, while 83 percent of the 2.9 million recipients of the length of service pensions were urban men.[6]

Because of its low employment requirement, the age pension was a near-universal benefit, targeted toward rural areas and women. However (as a consequence of this and other features), Brazil faces severe fiscal and evasion problems as workers were increasingly tempted to escape to the informal sector, contribute for only five years, and collect the age pension. As part of the reform process that began in the mid-1990s and is ongoing today, the contribution requirement for the age pension will gradually increase to 15 years.[7] This change will likely improve urban compliance and sustainability, but rural women and others who do not have a chance to participate in the formal labor market for 15 years may become uninsured.

As another example, Uruguay previously had an age pension that required 10 years of covered employment, but the required contributory period was raised to 15 years in Uruguay's recent pension reform.[8] Undoubtedly, this will have the same beneficial effects on fiscal sustainability, but the fate of the uninsured is unclear.

---

[6] Instituto Nacional do Seguro Social (1998).
[7] World Bank (1998).
[8] Queisser (1998); Law 16.713, chapter II, article 68.

Policy Changes That Might Increase Coverage at the Margin

Figure 7–1 shows that per capita income strongly influences but does not completely determine coverage by formal programs. What kinds of policies might increase coverage, in an enforceable and welfare-enhancing way, at the margin?

Low contribution and target replacement rates. Many developing countries choose a relatively high replacement rate target of 60–70 percent, which requires a high contribution rate for sustainability. A lower target replacement rate and contribution rate would decrease the trade-off with take-home pay and unemployment, thereby encouraging workers and employers to participate. Thailand recently instituted a scheme for private sector workers with a target replacement rate of 20 percent.

Paying a high rate of return on funded plans. One would expect that workers would be more likely to use retirement savings accounts if the rate of return were high and administrative costs low. However, since these funds are committed for the long term, workers would have to trust that high returns would continue for many years; it is not clear that such assurances could be given.

Increasing the credibility of the contributory scheme. The incentive to participate in the system will increase if workers believe it is financially sustainable and will survive to pay the promised benefits in the future when they retire. That is one object of multipillar systems—but it may take many years for their credibility to be established.

Permitting borrowing against retirement funds or lump sum withdrawals upon retirement. This would make retirement funds more liquid and therefore diminish resistance to participation—but these depleted accounts might never be replenished and lump sums might be quickly spent, defeating the original purpose of the old age program.

Offering better terms to low earners in view of their lower life expectancy and higher opportunity cost. This may take the form of lower contributions or higher promised benefits. Such incentives are widely viewed as redistribution. They may alternatively be an implicit recognition of the fact that low earners belong in a different risk category from high earners, because they are likely to live shorter lives; hence if both groups face the same contribution-benefit ratio, perverse redistribution from poor to rich goes on, and it is quite rational for the poor to try to stay out of the system.

Differentiated risk categories have, in effect, been introduced in the multipillar systems of many countries: the Netherlands has a flat benefit formula in the first pillar; Mexico makes a flat contribution to each worker's individual account; Switzerland places a ceiling on first-pillar benefits while having no ceiling on taxable wages; and in Uruguay, low- and middle-income contributors to the new funded pillar receive an extra benefit.[9] In Colombia a "solidarity tax" of 1 percent is imposed on salaries above a specified level and used to finance subsidies to low-income contributors.[10]

These better annual payoffs or lower charges may marginally encourage participation by low earners—although the high discount rate and liquidity demand of this group limit this effect. At the same time, if such measures are viewed as redistribution rather than risk categorization, they may encourage evasion by high earners and may simply not be viable for political economy reasons. Moreover, if the differentiation is not justified on actuarial grounds, it may make the system financially unsustainable. Thus, there are real limits to the ways in which policies can be shaped to make inclusion in a contributory program desirable for large groups of workers in low-income countries.

In sum, until the government's capacity to enforce tax collections increases, the structure of the economy changes to facilitate this, and the earning capacity of the bottom half of the labor force grows—all of which occurs with the process of economic development—it is difficult and not necessarily desirable to extend contributory old age security coverage to the entire population.

VOLUNTARY AND UNIVERSAL SOLUTIONS OUTSIDE THE CONTRIBUTORY SCHEME

Some analysts have urged that voluntary contributions should be permitted to extend pension insurance to those who do not have covered jobs. In Japan, men are encouraged to make flat contributions for their wives in exchange for the promise of a flat benefit. In China, workers in township and village enterprises are subject to social pressure to contribute to their individual accounts on a "voluntary" basis. Making coverage voluntary avoids the evasion and unemployment problems discussed above. In several countries community organizations such as nongovernmental organizations (NGOs) have tried to set up small-scale self-help schemes for informal sector workers.[11]

---

[9] Queisser (1998).

[10] Valdes-Prieto (1998).

[11] Van Ginneken (1999).

Are Voluntary Contributions the Answer to the Coverage Problem?

While the availability of voluntary retirement savings instruments is probably util-ity improving, I believe we should not expect them to accomplish very much. After all, a basic reason for the existence of mandatory programs is that many people, especially low-income people, will not save voluntarily for their retirement, and the basic reason for limited coverage is that, even when the program is mandatory, many workers and employers will try to avoid contributing because they believe that participation does not make them better off. In addition, the transactions costs of collecting many small voluntary contributions might be relatively high. Voluntarism and self-help schemes are more likely to succeed in programs when the costs are small and the benefits immediate (as for microfinance or primary health care). It is likely to be only a small part of the solution to a large long-term old age security problem.

In addition, I would offer at least three caveats to this approach. First, if annu-ities are promised in the voluntary program, they should be actuarially fair, except for deliberate redistribution that is planned and funded from the start; otherwise, the voluntary program could explode into a large, unfunded, unexpected obliga-tion. Second, in an individual account saving plan, workers should be given accu-rate information about the real rate of return they will receive and the replacement rate it will provide. In China, where some new enterprises have begun to cover workers on a "voluntary" basis (augmented by social pressure to pay), workers have been led to expect a high nominal rate of return based on the assumption of a high rate of inflation. Workers may not realize that this nominal rate will fall if inflation falls, so its real value is minuscule. Third, voluntary contributions are likely to be small, at best. In China, the negative real rate of return combined with the small size of the voluntary contributions will not provide much security in old age.

Will Universal Benefits Solve the Problem of the Uninsured?

Some countries do not have a problem of "uninsured old" because they have uni-versal flat (uniform) or very broad means-tested old age security benefits. These include many OECD countries, such as the Netherlands, Denmark, Norway, Canada, New Zealand, and Australia. In these countries, employment and contributions are not required for inclusion. Instead, the old age benefit is typically financed out of general revenues, and all residents are eligible to receive it once they reach the specified age. When these countries adopt a multipillar system, this universal benefit in effect becomes their first pillar. This approach solves the problem of coverage since there are no uninsured, and it eliminates poverty in old age so long as the benefit is above the poverty line.

However, it poses several other problems, chief among them being fiscal problems. Universal flat old age benefits are costly and will become more costly as populations age. A contributory program with earmarked taxes and with more narrowly targeted redistributions would cost less. To finance these large expenditures with aging populations requires either a large increase in tax rates, which may be distortionary, or a cut in other important social programs. This approach also poses political economy problems, stemming from the need to reach a collective agreement on the level of the uniform benefit and from the redistribution inherent in such programs.

Are universal uniform general-revenue-financed old age benefits a good option for developing countries? Recently Bolivia established such a first pillar in the form of the "bonosol," a universal benefit financed from the proceeds of a "collective capitalization fund" that contains the government's shares of state enterprises in the process of being privatized. The benefit initially was slated to be 11 percent of the average wage, 50–85 percent of the income of poor workers.[12] However, it was quickly cut, and it is even less clear what will happen when the capitalization fund is exhausted. Probably for most developing countries, a universal flat old age benefit is a luxury they cannot afford, nor is it the best use for their limited public resources.

The great income inequality in developing countries also makes a universal uniform benefit implausible, because it would be hard to reach a collective decision on its size and method of financing. When income is unequal, a uniform benefit that is reasonable from the point of a poor worker would be negligible for a rich worker, who would therefore be uninterested in supporting it. But a benefit that is high enough for the rich worker would exceed the wage level of a poor worker and would be very expensive for the economy as a whole. Relatedly, when incomes are very unequal, typically only a minority of people pay general taxes, and these people would oppose financing a universal benefit—making it infeasible from a political economy point of view. Bolivia, where incomes are very unequal, tried to avoid these problems by using proceeds associated with a privatization program, but it is not clear that the bonosol will last. Note that the OECD countries with universal benefits all have a high degree of income equality.

---

[12] Queisser (1998); von Gersdorff (1997).

HOW TO PREVENT POVERTY AMONG OLDER WOMEN: FORMALIZING THE INFORMAL FAMILY SYSTEM

What, then, will work? This chapter proposes two solutions—one aimed at women who are married to covered men and the other aimed at members of both genders who did not have covered jobs when young and are close to the poverty line when old.

The majority of old people are women, and this is even truer of the very old. Among the old that are poor and uninsured, women are disproportionately represented. They often lack the labor force participation that would entitle them to contributory benefits, and even if covered, they are usually only "partially insured" because their levels of education, wages, and years of service are low. They are less likely than men to have inherited property, and in some cultures, assets acquired by women are taken over and owned by men. Their greater longevity means that they are dominant among the very old, who are most likely to be poor, having used up whatever savings they previously accumulated.

The absence of labor force participation and asset ownership among women was part of a traditional family system in which husbands participated in the formal markets and wives worked in the home. Women provided nonmonetized services, especially when young, while their monetary needs were supposed to be covered by their spouses, and eventually their children. But in many cases this system fails, especially in old age, when women are at the receiving end of the lifetime contract. Marriages break up, and the husband is the one with the formal income. Husbands die earlier than wives, with their retirement benefits used up, and often do not leave adequate resources to support the surviving spouse.[13] Children move away or have income problems of their own. In these cases, the monetary support that the family was supposed to provide is not forthcoming, and the low personal income of women becomes a social problem.

Social security systems could be designed to enable women to enforce the implicit family contract that was agreed to earlier in life. Eventually women are likely to participate more broadly in the labor market and to be covered on their own, but in the meantime public policies can ensure that the family support system they counted on when young continues into old age.

---

[13] For evidence that families do not choose adequate survivors' insurance, even in countries where this is available, see Auerbach and Kotlikoff (1991).

Some traditional defined-benefit social security systems provide dependents' and survivors' benefits to wives of covered workers; the wives are covered by virtue of their husbands' coverage. But this means that society at large, rather than the individual husband, takes responsibility for dependent wives. The benefits to housewives are financed partially by taxes paid and benefits foregone by unmarried men and by wives who participate in the labor market—a high implicit tax that discourages female labor force participation and accentuates the problem. Men who marry much younger women late in life are heavily subsidized, and women who are not married to covered men do not receive any benefit. This system may work well when almost all men and women are married, at socially determined ages, and few females work in the formal labor market. But it raises serious efficiency and equity problems when marital and labor force participation patterns change and become more discretionary.

In the context of these changing individualized patterns and multipillar systems, which attempt to link the individual's benefits with his or her contributions, the following measures might be considered to incorporate the informal family contract into the formal old age security system:

• The required purchase of adequate survivors' benefits by those inside the contributory system and the availability of low cost survivors' benefits to those outside

• The requirement that insured workers contribute toward the personal accounts of their nonworking spouses or that mandatory retirement savings be considered the joint property of both spouses

• Mandatory joint annuitization, with price indexation, so that the money accumulated in workers' accounts is not quickly used up and the lifetimes of both spouses are covered

• The use of unisex mortality tables, so that women do not receive lower annual benefits than men because of their greater longevity (this implies a redistribution from men to women that will be controversial and may be difficult to implement in a competitive annuities market)

• Splitting the accrued benefits and retirement accumulations between the spouses, a provision that becomes especially important in case of divorce

• Increased emphasis on female education and labor market equality to augment the earning power and pensions of women

• Changing inheritance, property, and divorce laws to give women equal rights.

Measures such as these would take care of the needs of the largest group that is not covered—spouses who have not participated in the labor market for much of their lives—and as such would go far toward eliminating poverty among the uninsured old.

SOCIAL ASSISTANCE AND MEANS-TESTING

For individuals who remain outside the formal old age system and are poor, we are driven to the need for means-tested social assistance that is universal and noncontributory. Indeed, most countries have some such social assistance program, aimed at the poorest groups. And these programs have been increasing in some countries to supplement new multipillar systems with a close benefit-contribution link.

In recent years several OECD countries have replaced their single-pillar universal systems with multipillar systems because of the growing fiscal strain. That is, the universal flat benefit, in reduced form, has become the first pillar, while a second mandatory pillar that is contributory, funded, and privately managed has been added. (In these countries, the second pillar generally builds on preexisting plans established by collective bargaining and now extended by government.) The existence of the second, contributory, pillar permits cutbacks in the size of benefits from the first, universal, pillar, but it also creates a new problem of the "partially uninsured." Commonly, this has been addressed by offering larger means-tested benefits for those who are not in or who receive only small benefits from the contributory second pillar.

For example, Denmark recently decided to raise contributions to funded occupational defined-contribution plans (its second pillar) to 9–12 percent of wages, which should eventually provide a replacement rate of 40–45 percent, and to decrease the size of the universal flat benefit (its first pillar) to 25 percent of the average wage. Of course, this means that those with limited employment experience (women, self-employed, farmers) will receive smaller benefits than others in their cohort and less than they would have previously. In this sense, they are only partially insured. To offset this result, the government will offer a means-tested benefit to those without second-pillar pensions. So, it is supplementing the first (public universal) pillar with a second (private contributory) pillar on the one hand, and a means-tested "zero" pillar for the partially insured on the other hand.[14] The United

---

[14] Ploug (1993) and discussions with author, 1998.

Kingdom has decreased the value of its flat basic pension relative to the average wage and increased the roles of both private defined-contribution pensions and public means-tested supplements.[15]

Key issues that must be dealt with in designing a well-functioning social assistance program are: How large should the program be relative to other social programs? How does the availability of noncontributory assistance affect the fiscal sustainability of the contributory program and, conversely, how does the structure of a contributory program affect the demands upon social assistance? How can moral hazard problems be avoided? How is eligibility for assistance determined? Should these criteria be different for the old and the young? And primarily, how can the program be structured to maximize the probability that assistance will reach the targeted groups, with a minimum of leakage to others?

Tradeoff between Social Assistance and Human Capital Creation

In setting up their social assistance programs for the old, governments face a tradeoff with other public programs, such as education and health services for the young, that may help people build human capital and diminish reliance on social assistance in the long run. How much should be spent on social assistance for the old versus job creation for the young and other public goods? In the face of severe budget constraints in developing countries, there is no easy answer and no one right answer for all. But the question must be asked in all cases.

Interaction between Contributory Programs and Social Assistance: Moral Hazard

Social assistance is paid to mitigate hardships on the noninsured old, but it also creates incentives to become noninsured—the moral hazard problem. Low-income workers may fail to participate in the contributory scheme, which may eventually lead to its collapse, if they think that in this way they will qualify for social assistance. Despite this disincentive, society may feel it must offer social assistance to the truly needy. The end result may be both inadequate social assistance and unsustainable social insurance.

Partly in response to this problem, many contributory programs include a redistributive component—for example, the first pillar in multipillar systems pro-

---

[15] Johnson (1998); Whitehouse (1998).

vides a safety net for contributors. This arrangement recognizes that low earners really belong in a different risk category than high earners because of their lower life expectancy. It also encourages compliance by giving them better terms. Access to a safety net within the contributory scheme helps to overcome the moral hazard problem by making participation for low earners more attractive. The impact on evasion and fiscal sustainability depends on the generosity of the social assistance program relative to the redistribution in the contributory program. The latter should be greater than the former to encourage contributions. So society faces a dilemma because of the moral hazard problem: if social assistance benefits are generous, they make the contributory program less sustainable; if they are miserly, they leave the uninsured in poverty, even those who had no opportunity to get a covered job.

This negative impact of social assistance on the contributory program is heightened if it is financed out of the social security budget, as in Brazil and Uruguay prior to their recent reforms, where the social security system was charged for beneficiaries who had only five or 10 years of contributions. While reducing the benefits from contributing, this simultaneously increases the tax burden on contributors, hence their incentive to participate in the contributory program is cut from both directions, and the program ultimately becomes unsustainable. General revenue finance, which has a broader base, is preferable, both on efficiency and equity grounds, for universal means-tested programs.

How to Target Benefits: Keeping Official and Unofficial Transactions Costs Low

The essence of means-tested social assistance is that it is targeted to low-income groups. Depending on data availability and country standards, "means" may be defined in terms of income (commonly), assets (as in Australia), or the presence or absence of scarce consumer goods such as water, electricity, and motorcycles in the households (appropriate in developing countries). Chile offers a small social assistance benefit, about 12 percent of the average wage, to the poorest of the noninsured groups over age 65, using traditional means-testing techniques. The size of the total social assistance budget is predetermined, as is the benefit level. This automatically constrains the number of beneficiaries—below the current number of eligible households. Thus, many localities have waiting lists of qualified individuals without access to benefits. Not surprisingly, most recipients are women who did not have an opportunity to participate in the labor market for enough years to qualify for the contributory guaranteed benefit.

But targeting incurs transactions costs. In cases where beneficiaries are poor, this may lead to a large leakage of funds to the middle-class bureaucrats who administer the system. Besides the official salaries that they receive, there is ample opportunity for unofficial side payments to induce rapid and favorable treatment. For example, in several Indian states, old people complain about patronage and the side payments they must make to get their applications processed.[16]

Traditional means-testing may also lead to take-up problems as some people do not apply because of ignorance or stigma, and criteria may not be applied uniformly. In Thailand, village elders identify the rural poor, mostly widows without children. This system may work well in some villages, but one can imagine personal favoritism playing a role in others.[17] Finally, means- and asset-testing create a moral hazard problem: people may be discouraged from saving for their own old age.

Realizing these disadvantages of traditional means-tested programs, countries have begun experimenting with nontraditional approaches and with proxies for need, which reduce these transactions costs. Such methods may not target precisely, but the savings from reduced leakage may more than compensate. For example, in the *Progresa* program in Mexico, a computerized model that aggregates several socioeconomic variables is used to identify poor communities, especially those in rural villages, and their residents. The econometric model is structured to give heavy weight to families with children and to provide an incentive for these children to attend school. But old people also benefit—and the relative weights given to school-attending children versus the old become a political issue.

A categorical approach is also used to reduce transactions costs: very old age may be a proxy for need. The very old who are women are often among the poorest groups, so this is an even narrower proxy for need. Argentina targets the "very old" in its social assistance program. All people whose age exceeds 70 and who have contributed for 10 years qualify. Presumably the transactions costs of this program are lower than in Chile. But given the correlation between income level and longevity, many poor people die before they ever collect, while many of those who collect are well above the poverty line. Benefits in Argentina are 19 percent of the average wage.[18] This contrasts with Brazil and Uruguay, where 15 years of contributions are required for the age-based social assistance pension but benefits are

[16] Van Ginneken (1999) and fieldwork by the author.
[17] Van Ginneken (1999).
[18] Ley de Seguridad 24.241; Vittas (1997).

higher, and Chile, where benefits are lower but can be received at an earlier age and contributions are not required. In general, we observe a tradeoff between tightness of eligibility criteria and size of benefits.[19]

Still another approach to means-testing involves self-selection: to offer assistance in a form for which mainly low-income people will apply. Self-selection can be achieved by requiring queues for receipt of small cash benefits, a cost that high-income people are less likely to be willing to incur, or by offering in-kind benefits such as free lunches that only low-income people would accept. NGOs may provide the service at lower cost and in a less bureaucratic way than the government, particularly when small-scale ventures are involved. In some countries the poorest old are accommodated by soup kitchens or dormitories run by NGOs but financed by governments. The advantage of self-selection is that it avoids the transactions costs and possible misidentification of an application process. The disadvantage is that the benefit and quality levels may not be optimal, and many needy old people may end up not participating.

At this stage, we do not really know which of these methods entails higher transactions costs and other leakages and which is more effective at targeting needy old people. This should be a high priority topic for further research.

Old versus Young Candidates for Social Assistance

Should different criteria apply to old versus young candidates for social assistance, and how much priority should be given to poor families with children versus the poor old? These two questions are interrelated.

On the one hand, some analysts argue that eligibility criteria should be more stringent for the young, since they can work and should be encouraged to seek work, while the presumption is that the old cannot work or have low productivity when they work. The old, therefore, can be offered social assistance without the labor disincentive effects that would be incurred by the young.

Of course, the expectation of receiving assistance when old may discourage saving when young, a different type of disincentive problem. In effect, means- and asset-tested social assistance impose a high marginal tax rate on savings. In Australia, the young who are unemployed and the old without adequate income and assets are guaranteed the same level of benefits, but with different eligibility crite-

---

[19] For a discussion of these tradeoffs in the contributory program as well, see James (1998).

ria regarding efforts to find employment, since the presumption is that the young can work (hence work incentives should be retained) while the old cannot. But the government in Australia feared that saving when young might be discouraged by its means- and asset-tested age pension, so it recently established a contributory mandatory saving plan for workers. This will eventually reduce the moral hazard problem regarding saving, leaving different work requirements for the old and the young.

On the other hand, one can argue that priority for social assistance should be given to young families with children, who have their entire lives ahead of them. According to this line of thought, children should not be penalized for the failure of their parents to obtain a well-paying job. Helping the children may be a better long-term investment for society. Of course, money given to families may not better the condition of the children—this depends on how the marginal income is spent. The Mexican *Progresa* program is interesting in this regard because it makes school attendance one of the criteria for aid, and the money is given directly to the mothers, who have been shown to be more likely to spend it to enhance the welfare of the children.

The Role of the Extended Family in Social Assistance Programs

The family is the oldest form of social insurance system.[20] If the old and the young live together in multigenerational households, the tradeoff between them in the allocation of social assistance is less critical. To illustrate: in South Africa a means-tested pension is paid to most older blacks who are living in rural areas. This pension originated in apartheid days and was intended for the small number of urban whites who had failed to accumulate their own private occupational pensions. A much smaller stipend was paid to blacks. But with the elimination of apartheid, the entire black population became eligible for the larger stipend, which has cut-off points and benefit amounts that are very high relative to rural black incomes. Often, family income goes up substantially when a member reaches the eligible age. Since old and young live together in multigenerational households, both groups benefit from the age stipend. But the tradeoff is not completely eliminated. The program is very costly and other uses for the money may be more targeted toward the young and may have a greater social payoff, such as increased spending on education. This is a controversial issue in South Africa today.

---

[20] See Kotlikoff and Spivak (1981) on risk sharing through the family.

When the family support system is strong, it is necessary to determine whether the income and assets of the entire family should count in applying the means test, or only those of the old person. In Western industrial societies, the move toward individual responsibility has meant that the government replaces the family as the social safety net and only the individual's means are counted. In contrast, in several Asian societies, such as Hong Kong and Singapore, children have a legal responsibility to take care of their parents, and old people can enforce this legally, albeit at great personal price. In Hong Kong, before the means-tested benefit is paid, children must testify that they are unable to support their parents. China is thinking of adopting a similar system. Indeed, in multigenerational households it is difficult to separate out the means of the parent and the child, since both share common living arrangements. But the share of total household consumption that accrues to different age groups is unknown to outsiders. Giving the older member a small stipend may increase his or her bargaining power to receive a pro rata share and in this sense may improve the welfare of the old beyond the stipend cost.

This leads to a broader question: how can governments offer social assistance while encouraging the continuation of family responsibility? How can penalties and incentives be structured to complement and crowd in, rather than crowd out, family care? Earlier work has shown that every dollar of social security benefits partially displaces private family transfers.[21] Incentives that governments have put in place to counteract this effect are tax rebates for children who care for their parents in Malaysia and for children who expand their homes to accommodate parents in Japan, Sweden, and Norway; and day care centers or respite care to give caregivers temporary relief in Hong Kong, Singapore, France, Germany, and the United Kingdom.[22] But in developing countries, where family support is strong and intergenerational households are the norm, it seems likely that such public subsidies might have only a small marginal impact, mainly constituting a financial relief for families who would have provided the services anyway. I am not aware of any careful research evaluating the efficacy of these measures. Such research would be worth doing, to inform other countries that might be considering these policies.

---

[21] Cox and Jiménez (1990).
[22] World Bank (1994).

CONCLUSIONS

The growth of formal coverage will accompany the process of economic development. Until that happens, a large proportion of the population will be uninsured or partially insured. The recent pension reforms tying benefits more closely to contributions are a step in the right direction for the contributory systems and are a necessary precondition for fiscally sound coverage expansion, but they cannot be expected to increase coverage in the short run and may even have the opposite effect. This chapter has surveyed the issues that policymakers need to address as they consider how to provide old age protection for the uninsured. While economic growth is the key to higher coverage, good policies also help.

Coverage expansion in contributory programs may be marginally encouraged by policies such as putting the social security system on a financially sustainable basis to enhance its credibility, choosing a modest target replacement rate that requires a relatively low contribution rate, allowing workers to receive a high (competitive) rate of return on their long-term retirement savings, and offering low-income workers access to safe saving instruments and partial benefits such as survivors' insurance (term life insurance), on a voluntary basis. These policies may reduce the number of "uninsured," but I would expect the impact to be small. Nonparticipation in formal old age security programs is a rational response among low-income workers, given their short expected lifetimes, high discount rates, and strong liquidity needs. For these reasons, forcing low earners to contribute to a formal program may not be optimal or feasible. But it leaves society with the problem of how to deal with the uninsured who survive to old age, are poor, and are unable to work.

This chapter has suggested two subgroups and courses of action that respond to their needs in an affordable way. First, for spouses of covered employees, who worked in the home rather than the market as part of the household division of labor, specific measures (such as the requirement to purchase survivors' benefits and joint annuities) might ensure that the implicit family contract is institutionalized and continued into old age. Second, for workers who participated in the labor market in noncovered jobs, earning enough to support themselves when young but with no surplus to save for old age, social assistance is essential. Social assistance should be financed out of general revenues and should offer less than the redistribution given to the low-income groups who have contributed, to reduce moral hazard problems.

Table 8–7. Financing and Administration of Social Assistance Pensions in Latin America and the Caribbean, 1997–98

Country	Percentage of payroll	Source of revenue				Administered by	
		Transfers from		Social insurance and assistance pension funds			
		State	Social insurance	Common	Separated	Social insurance	State
Argentina		x			x		x
Bahamas[a]	x	x	x	x		x	
Barbados[a]	x		x	x		x	
Brazil	x[b]	x[b]	x[b]	x[b]	x[b]	x[c]	x[c]
Chile	x	x			x		x
Costa Rica	x		x		x	x	
Cuba		x		d	d		e
Uruguay[f]		x	x	x		x	

a. Data are for 1987.

b. Contributions to social insurance (transfers) were used to finance the old system, hence, there is a common fund; the new system is entirely financed by the state and the social insurance fund should not be touched, but in practice it might be.

c. Social insurance manages the old system. The new system is administered by the Ministry of Social Insurance and Social Assistance, decentralized, with participation of local organizations.

d. There are no pension funds.

e. State designs policy, and administration is by organizations of people's power.

f. Data are for 1990.

Source: See table 8–4.

tance pension system was funded (and still is for those currently under that system) by payroll contributions to social insurance (transfers, in reality), but the new assistance system is financed by the state mainly by a tax on the gross turnover of private enterprises.[24] Barbados has a separate payroll contribution for social assistance pensions, but it is insufficient, and transfers are made from social insurance. In the Bahamas and Uruguay social assistance pensions are to be financed by the state, but the amount assigned is insufficient, thus leading to transfers from social insurance; the proportion of assistance pensions financed by the state in the Bahamas declined in the 1980s, while transfers from social insurance increased.[25]

In general, it is better to finance social assistance pensions from fiscal resources, particularly if the major state revenue is the income tax, because the impact on

[24] IPEA (1998a).

[25] Mesa-Lago (1988, 1994a).

distribution would be progressive. The risk is that the state controls the budget for those pensions and can cut them. A payroll contribution earmarked for social assistance could avoid that problem but create others noted above. A valuable lesson learned from past experience is that social insurance and social assistance pensions should not be mixed but must have clear and separate sources of revenue, accounts, and funds.

Financial Aid to Incorporate Special Labor Groups

Financial aid is needed to make possible the extension of health care and pensions to other groups of the population with low income and special labor conditions. When discussing the low percentage of self-employed workers who are covered by social insurance, it was argued that the financial burden imposed on them is one important cause. In the overwhelming majority of countries, the law imposes on the self-employed a percentage of contribution equal to the sum of the percentages that the salaried worker and his or her employer pay, the reason being that the self-employed lacks an employer. As a result, the percentage paid by the self-employed is two or three times that paid by a salaried worker; because most of the self-employed have an income below the minimum wage, establishing the latter as the tax base does not solve the problem. It was shown that in Costa Rica, the self-employed have a very high coverage by the social insurance health care program but a very low coverage by the pension program. Apart from the issue of priorities of the insured (health care being more urgent than long-run income security), a crucial explanation for the difference is that the percentage contribution of the self-employed to health care is slightly lower than that paid by the salaried worker but the contibution is three times higher for pensions.[26] One of the reviewers of this chapter rejected my point that the self-employed have a heavier tax burden than the salaried worker arguing that "there is no meaningful distinction between the portion of an employment tax [social security contribution] paid by the employer and the employee. The employer is not going to pay a gross wage that exceeds the worker's marginal productivity." And yet there is a long debate on whether the employer actually pays that contribution or transfers it to the worker or to prices; in the first and third possibilities the employee does not have the burden of such a contribution.

---

[26] FCN (1998a, 1998b).

To cope with the problem discussed above and avoid paying an assistance pension to the low-income elderly self-employed, three alternatives could be considered: establishing a lower level of income as the tax base, reducing that contribution and adjusting the pension accordingly (making it actuarially fair), or subsidizing the self-employed contribution for pensions. Probably, a combination of the first and second options would be the best, because they do not require a fiscal subsidy that could encourage a reclassification of work from wage to self-employed. And yet, if the amount of the pension were excessively low, some type of subsidy would be needed to effectively incorporate this group. Concerning health care, national health systems or integrated social insurance systems, as in Costa Rica, are adequate solutions for incorporating the low-income self-employed and similar groups mentioned below.

Coverage of domestic servants tends to be somewhat higher than that of the self-employed because they do have an employer (mandatory affiliation appears to be an important explanatory factor here also), but the special nature of this contractual relationship and the obstacles that impede the state's enforcement of the law are factors that contribute to low coverage.[27] Peasants are also difficult to incorporate into a pension program for several reasons: income that is below the minimum wage and that may be unstable; lack or frequent changes of employer; isolation and dispersion that make it very arduous to register, collect contributions from, and pay benefits to them (more so than the urban self-employed); extremely hard work and poor living conditions that reduce their life expectancy (the worker may be dismissed when his or her ability to work declines with age); complex and long bureaucratic procedures to prove their years of work and process a pension; and the prevailing culture that their children will take care of them in old age, although such informal protection is rapidly disappearing.[28] In Brazil, workers in the rural sector receive a pension financed by a tax on agricultural production.[29] Special social insurance schemes and methods should be designed, tailored to the peculiarities of these occupations, in order to facilitate affiliation, collection of contributions, and incentives to join.

---

[27] Mesa-Lago (1990).
[28] Mesa-Lago (1994b; 1998).
[29] Schwarzer (1999).

Impact on Income Distribution

It has been amply documented that state subsidies to social security in LA normally are not targeted to social assistance for the poor and extension of coverage to low-income strata but are mainly assigned to social insurance and middle-income strata that are already covered and often receive relatively good benefits. Such regressive effects are illustrated by the following examples.

Studies conducted in the 1980s on the distributive impact of health care in several countries of LAC indicate that public programs administered by the Ministry of Health (especially prevention and primary care), social assistance programs for the poor, and special programs for rural areas were those with the most progressive effects, while social insurance health programs and those for privileged groups (for example, the armed forces) had the most regressive effects. A reallocation of state subsidies toward public health, prevention, and primary care, social assistance, and rural areas, as well as extension of effective coverage to the poor and low-income groups would considerably improve the progressive impact on redistribution and help those in need.[30]

For pensions, in Brazil most social security expenditures and fiscal subsidies are concentrated on private employees and civil servants living in cities and developed areas, who are earning relatively high salaries and are entitled to costly seniority pensions that result in a significant regressive effect. At the end of 1997, the average seniority pension of private employees was about five times the average social assistance pension; the average seniority pension for federal civil servants was 2.5 times that of private employees, and that of federal judicial and parliamentary servants was 7.5 times higher. Pensions in the new social assistance system appear to have a progressive effect on regional distribution as they are concentrated in poor regions such as the Northeast, but their share of fiscal subsidies is so small that it cannot compensate for the regressive effect of seniority pensions.[31]

Costa Rica has one of the fairest income distributions and one of the most developed social security systems in LAC, and yet until very recently, fiscal subsidies were focused on 19 independent pension programs for civil servants, congressmen, judges, teachers, and so forth, who are among the best paid in the country; they accounted for 20 percent of the total number of pensioners but received 42 percent of the total amount of benefits; part of those pensions was fully financed by

---

[30] Mesa-Lago (1992a); World Bank (1993).
[31] IPEA (1998a, 1998b).

the state, and the rest received substantial fiscal subsidies. Reforms implemented in the 1990s are reducing such inequalities by gradually incorporating all those privileged groups (except the judiciary) into the general social insurance system, and eventually their entitlement conditions should become standardized.[32] In Chile, although a good many of the inequalities of the old social insurance pension system were eradicated, in 1997 at least 3.7 percent of GDP was spent by the state to finance the pension deficit from the old system and subsidize the new fully funded pension system, but less than 0.1 percent of GDP went to social assistance pensions, which, as already noted, are insufficient to meet essential needs.[33] All over LA (except in Costa Rica), members of the armed forces enjoy the most generous pensions and liberal entitlement conditions, and in most countries, also the best hospitals; the state heavily subsidizes those programs. Reassigning state subsidies away from middle-income and some high-income groups and directing them toward the poor and low-income strata would help to extend coverage of pensions, reduce poverty, and reverse the current regressive impact on distribution.[34]

ADMINISTRATION

There is an important need throughout LAC for the coordination of social assistance with social insurance, as well as other antipoverty programs, such as social safety nets, the health policy, and so forth. Different agencies are in charge of the administration of social assistance in the region.

Health Care

The Ministry of Health manages integrated national health systems. In only one country (Costa Rica), does the social insurance institute administer the noncontributory health program through an integrated system (which unifies all preventive and curative care), while the ministry sets policy, oversees the system, and provides some minor services. The advantage of these two approaches is that their services are integrated, and the poor tend to receive similar care as the rest of the population (I have confirmed such equality of treatment in Costa Rica). When the health system is dual or multiple, stratification results: the middle-income group is

---

[32] Mesa-Lago (1994a, 1998).
[33] Bustamante (1998); SSS (1998).
[34] Mesa-Lago (1983, 1990, 1992a); World Bank (1994).

covered by social insurance, the poor and low-income groups are legally left to the care of the ministry, and the high-income and some of the upper-middle-income groups are covered by the private sector (in Chile health maintenance organizations covered 27 percent of the total population in 1997). The best services are those of the private sector and, normally, the armed forces, followed by those of social insurance, and the worst services are those of the ministry. In about half of the countries in LA, a minority of the population is affiliated to social insurance but receives the large majority of the health care revenue; conversely the majority of the population is legally assigned to the public program of the Ministry of Health, which receives a small share of the budget.

With few exceptions, efforts to unify the services of the ministry and social insurance and decentralize the provision of services have failed, in spite of numerous reform attempts and recommendations of diverse international agencies (ILO, PAHO, World Bank). In the early 1980s Chile implemented a thorough health care reform, and a few other countries are doing the same in the second half of the 1990s (Argentina, Colombia, Peru); it is too soon to evaluate the results of this second round of reforms.[35]

Pensions

The administration of social assistance pensions is normally centralized. It is in the charge of the social insurance institute in five countries: the Bahamas, Barbados, Brazil (old system), Costa Rica, and Uruguay; and directly by the state in the other four countries: Argentina, Brazil (new system), Chile, and Cuba (table 8–7). In the Bahamas and Barbados, the management of social assistance was shifted from the state to the social insurance institute in 1974 and 1982, respectively, while the opposite has been occurring in Brazil since 1995–96. At least in two countries, there is some degree of decentralization and input from below.

Brazil's old social assistance system was fully administered (and still is for those already covered by it in 1996) by the social insurance institute. The new system began with a complete reorganization of social assistance and is based on principles of decentralization, but the social insurance institute on behalf of the state still pays pensions, although this function is expected to be eventually transferred to municipalities; popular participation is secured through local representative coun-

---

[35] Mesa-Lago (1992a); Cruz-Saco and Mesa-Lago (1999).

cils of social assistance, municipal services, and private institutions.[36] In Cuba the Ministry of Labor and Social Security designs the social assistance policy and supervises the system, while local organizations of people's power (OPP) grant the pensions; more information is needed on the OPP functions and whether they actually identify who are the poor, administer means tests, make suggestions on how to improve the system, and so forth.

It is not rare to find abuse and free riders in social assistance programs: pensions paid to those who are not poor, through political patronage or bureaucratic connections. Recent reports on pensions in Brazil and Costa Rica assert that there are irregularities such as the simulation of poverty (indigence), underdeclaration of age, false witnesses' statements, clientelism, and political interference in the selection of the beneficiaries.[37]

Some countries (for example, Costa Rica, Mexico) have tried to facilitate the incorporation of and collection of contributions from peasants and self-employed workers (an obstacle mentioned already) by using their cooperatives and associations to register and collect from them, but, although positive, the results have been small, owing to the scarce managerial ability of such intermediaries and lack of incentives offered by the social insurance institute for their effort.[38] Social insurance institutes should help to train their associations or cooperatives as efficient intermediaries and pay a commission based on the number of affiliations and amount of contributions collected. A question of administrative arrangement that has significant financial implications is whether the social assistance and social insurance pensions have separate funds or they are together in a common fund (table 8–7). In the Bahamas, Barbados, and Uruguay there is a common fund for both programs, thus facilitating the transfers from insurance to assistance. In Cuba, there are no pension funds at all, and the state pays both types of pensions out of general revenue. In Costa Rica, the two funds are separated, but due to FODESAF's incomplete or complete but insufficient transfers to social insurance, the latter ends up absorbing the difference (in the past, state debts have usually been negotiated in and paid with government bonds, but resulted in losses for social insurance). In Brazil, the old system had and still has a common fund (a minimum of 12 monthly contributions to social insurance is required to qualify for the old assistance pensions), while the new system is financed by the newly created state Fund for Na-

---

[36] IPEA (1998a).
[37] IPEA (1998b); FCN (1998b).
[38] Mesa-Lago (1998).

tional Social Assistance (FNAS). Technically, the social insurance fund is separate now and cannot be used to finance social assistance pensions but, in practice, the FNAS delays the transfer to the social insurance institute to pay such pensions, resulting in a bitter fight between the two institutions. Finally, Argentina and Chile have a separate social insurance fund that cannot be touched for social assistance pensions, which are directly paid by the state.

In view of the negative experience of several countries in LAC, it would be better if the social insurance institute is not put in charge of the administration of social assistance pensions. Even if the social insurance institute directly receives the revenue of a special tax or payroll contribution, it would be responsible for paying assistance pensions if that tax/contribution is insufficient to cover costs. The same would happen if the owed state subsidy or transfer fails to materialize or is insufficient to cover all costs. It could be argued that transfers from social insurance to social assistance have a progressive redistribution effect, but it is more transparent and less complex to achieve that end by reassigning fiscal subsidies in order to target the poor.

TWO RECENT TYPES OF REFORM: BRAZIL AND COSTA RICA

This chapter has argued that a national health system or a universal, integrated health care system is the best way to protect the poor and low-income groups, and several countries of the NLC and Costa Rica should be models for LA. The same is not true of adequate models for social assistance pensions, and this section provides two examples of them: the recent reform of Brazil (1991–96), and the proposal for such reform in Costa Rica (1998). These two countries are also important for the peculiarities of their systems: the two have the highest coverage of social assistance pensions of the population above 65 years in the region, and they have different types of administration. Costa Rica's system is managed by social insurance, while Brazil's is managed by the state. Brazil's new system is decentralized, with participation from below; and Costa Rica's proposed reform was the outcome of a process of national consensus and advocates the universalization of the old age assistance pension and the extension of coverage among self-employed with low income.

Brazil

The Organic Law of Social Assistance, widely discussed in Brazil since 1989, enacted in 1993, and regulated in 1995, established in 1996 a new national social assistance scheme.[39] It has integrated several previous institutions and programs, is decentralized, institutionalizes the participation of representative organizations, and claims to have abolished the old vices of the past: fragmentation and lack of coordination, clientelism, and corruption.[40] Three agencies that dealt with social assistance were integrated into the Secretary of Social Assistance, which is one of the two main branches of the Ministry of Social Insurance and Social Assistance (MPAS); the ministry elaborates the budget proposal and coordinates and supervises the social assistance policy at the national level. A newly created National Council of Social Assistance approves the national policy and assistance budget, registers the various institutions devoted to social assistance policy, and designs the criteria for transfer of resources to such institutions. The federal district, states, and municipalities have funds that receive the resources from the Union, contribute their own share, and manage the funds according to previous agreements signed with the MPAS. The implementation of the programs is done at the local level by Councils of Social Assistance; trade unions, municipalities, and NGOs cooperate with the councils. Norms for the social assistance policy, approved at the end of 1997, proclaim the principles of universalization, equality in access to services, efficiency, and transparency.

In 1998 an internal evaluation of the reform process reported that 67 percent of the municipalities have organized their councils, 57 percent have established the funds, and 32 percent have developed their plans. Some difficulties are noted in the report such as the need to develop managerial capacity at the local level to manage the projects in order to secure an effective decentralization process. The importance of coordinating social assistance activities at the three levels—national, state, and local—is also noted. In addition, the evaluation focused on quantities of services provided instead of their quality and targeting efficiency. Several municipalities are under severe financial stress and cannot provide their needed share for social assistance.

The system includes five programs: social assistance pensions for the poor who are old or disabled; lump sums for birth and death for poor families; assistance services; other social assistance programs; and projects to fight poverty. The key features and results of the first three programs are summarized as follows. Social assistance pensions are totally financed by the Union budget and paid through the social

---

[39] Lei Orgânica de Assistência Social (1993).
[40] This section is based on IPEA (1998a, 1998b).

insurance institute. Entitlement conditions and benefits have been described already; the number of these pensions increased twofold in 1996–97 and reached 38 percent of the total number of assistance pensions being paid in the nation (it should be recalled that the old system is closed but still is paying pensions, although the number is declining as the beneficiaries die). There are no social assistance survivor pensions in Brazil, but the new system grants lump sums for birth and death to families with a monthly per capita income below one-fourth of the minimum wage. Finally, assistance services (preventive, curative, and promotion of health) are currently provided to 15 percent of the elderly poor, as well as services of rehabilitation and promotion to 4 percent of the poor who are disabled. With the exception of pensions, other benefits are still modest, but the system has been in operation for only three years and the evaluation covered only the first two.

Attractive features of the Brazilian reform that should be followed are the integration of the social assistance system, its decentralization, and participation from below. An outside evaluation would be useful to assess the impact of the new system on poverty, whether pensions are sufficient to cover basic needs, the financial shares contributed at the three levels, effective implementation at the local level, managerial efficiency, and so forth.

Costa Rica

A Forum for National Consensus was held in Costa Rica in 1998 with wide representation from most pertinent sectors of the population (workers, employers, cooperatives, peasants, women, minorities, political parties, the Executive, NGOs) to discuss several crucial issues, one of them being pension reform. At the end of September, a document with recommendations had been elaborated by the forum and sent to the government; reportedly, a legal draft had been finished at the end of 1998 and submitted to congress for its consideration in 1999 (it was approved in 2000). The document includes two important reforms: the universalization of a social assistance pension and the extension of social insurance pension coverage among low-income groups.[41]

Principles of the document are the right of all people to a pension sufficient to cover basic needs, the extension of coverage of the social security system to the uninsured, especially among the poorest, the universalization of a noncontributory pension for the poor based on solidarity, and the state obligation to guarantee

---

[41] This section is based on FCN (1998a, 1998b); Mesa-Lago (1998).

such a pension. A noncontributory basic pension would be granted to all the population more than 70 years old and not covered by current pension schemes, starting with the least developed counties and gradually extending to the entire nation in five years. A new permanent Solidarity Fund for that purpose would be established, separate from the insurance pension fund, with the current resources provided by FODASEF (guaranteed by the government) and others from government agencies, municipalities, and communities. The new pension, it is estimated, will cost from 0.16 percent to 0.26 percent of GDP in the next twenty years. Costa Rica already has a noncontributory pension for the poor older than 65, but it has a ceiling, and a significant part of the target population does not receive such a pension. Apparently, the new program would not eliminate the current one but would be added to it. It is not clear, however, whether the new pension would be universal regardless of income or based on need and submitted to a means test. The amount of the new pension would be 50 percent of the minimum insurance pension, which suggests it might be higher than the current average assistance pension (equal to one-fifth of the average insurance pension) and close somewhat the existing gap between insurance and assistance pensions.

The power to extend coverage to low-income self-employed workers, who are not voluntarily affiliated to the insurance program, is left to the social insurance institute, which will decide to establish mandatory coverage for various sectors according to their characteristics, based on a public timetable. To facilitate the incorporation of these workers, the state will subsidize the portion of the percentage contribution assigned to employers, totally or partially depending on the worker's income. The pension will be at least equal to the minimum pension in the insurance pension program, a controversial aspect because, combined with the explained subsidy, it could encourage salaried workers (in combination with their employers) to report that they are self-employed. No estimates have been released on the cost of this program. The proposal does not mention other groups in the labor force that are difficult to incorporate into the contributory pension program (for example, peasants), but says that the social insurance institute should evaluate its agreements with associations or cooperatives of such groups and promote and help their affiliation. A special program is proposed to encourage voluntary affiliation by housewives to the contributory pension program.

The Forum document is generally positive, and most of its recommendations appear to be feasible. The proposed universalization of the social assistance pension follows most of the recommendations of this chapter, but two of its features are not clear: the type of the assistance pension and its relationship with the average insurance pension. The estimated cost of this program, as a percentage of GDP, is small, but details on the calculation are lacking. If accurate, the program should be financially viable in Costa Rica. The proposal to extend coverage to the self-employed also follows this chapter's recommendations, except, perhaps, for the determination of the level of the pension for the self-employed. The process of building a national consensus to design the crucial elements of a pension reform in Costa Rica is so far unique in the region and should be a model to follow.

CURRENT AND FUTURE PROBLEMS AND RECOMMENDATIONS

This section summarizes the major problems currently faced by social assistance and the recommendations of this chapter (organized by the four sections of the study) and explores potential future difficulties in this field.

Coverage

Problems

LAC countries with national health systems provide their services to all residents, and hence appear to cover virtually all of the population, including the poor and low-income groups; this is also true of at least the four most developed countries with social insurance systems in LA, through a combination of social insurance and assistance. In the rest of the countries with social insurance systems, total population coverage combining all programs ranges from 75 percent to 34 percent and, therefore, leaves out most or all the poor and low-income strata. Those legally entitled to protection by the public health system managed by the Ministry of Health do not have effective access to care, or the quality of the services they receive is very poor. Only one country with a social insurance system (Costa Rica) has integrated all health services and provides coverage to the poor (under social assistance) as well as low-income groups (who receive subsidies), and their treatment is equal to that of the insured. Health care coverage in rural areas (where poverty incidence is higher) is lower and poorer in quality than in urban areas; indigenous populations are usually poor, concentrated in rural areas, and largely unprotected by health care. Informal workers in urban areas, most of whom are poor, also lack effective health coverage.

Coverage of the economically active population by social insurance pensions tends to be lower than that by health care and excludes the poor with very few exceptions: in the four most developed LA countries and two NLC countries, such coverage ranges from 73 to 97 percent and, in some of them, a proportion of the poor might be covered by social assistance. Legal and statistical coverage of the self-employed, domestic servants, rural workers, and other low-income groups is considerably smaller than that by health care too. In about eleven countries, social assistance pensions are legally established for the poor, but the scarce data available suggest that they do not cover the majority of them.

Recommendations

National health care systems or integrated social insurance health systems that cover all the population with primary health care should be established in order to protect the poor; ex ante coverage by social assistance of health (prevention, health education, potable water, and waste disposal) is better and cheaper than ex post curative care; where resources are very scarce to expand coverage, priorities should be given to health care over assistance pensions; the least developed countries should also target rural areas (and indigenous populations where they exist) over urban areas; facilities should be given to middle- and high-income strata to buy additional coverage or better protection through different providers, including social insurance and the private sector but without any fiscal subsidy; social assistance pensions should be expanded to the poorest population after universal coverage in primary health care has been achieved; and the incorporation into social insurance of low-income groups, such as the self-employed, domestic servants, and employees of microenterprises could be facilitated by establishing mandatory programs for some of them or creating ad hoc schemes with lower financing burden and benefits (subsidized contributory programs ex ante are cheaper than and avoid the stigma of social assistance ex post).

Entitlement Conditions and Benefits

Problems

Although comprehensive and accurate data are not available, it appears that about one-third of the countries of LAC have social assistance pension programs in operation. All of them are based on need, and all, with the possible exception of one, are means tested. No country offers a universal, flat pension regardless of income, which is more appropriate to developed countries. Assistance pensions are granted to the poor in old age and disability; only three countries legally provide pensions to survivors (the Bahamas, Costa Rica, and Cuba), hence, poor widows and minor orphans are left without protection. Minimum ages for old age assistance pensions are higher than those required for contributory programs and range from 65 to 70 years; certain workers whose labor conditions are very harsh cannot in practice gain access to the contributory pensions and must wait a longer period to qualify for the assistance pension. We lack comparative data on how the medical test for disability is administered. In at least two countries (the Bahamas and Barbados), the levels of the social insurance and social assistance pensions are very close, hence creating disincentives for affiliation to the contributory program and encouraging free riders. Three countries (Argentina, Brazil, and Uruguay) provide minimum assistance pensions that appear sufficient to cover basic needs (in Brazil, to avoid indigence), but in other countries (Chile, Costa Rica, and Cuba) those minimums seem to be insufficient. Cuba used to provide low minimum pensions, combined with a social safety net that protected the poor, but the crisis of the 1990s has drastically reduced that minimum in real terms and virtually destroyed the additional social safety net.

Recommendations

The social assistance pension based on needs and means tested is recommended for most of LAC because of the region's scarcity of resources, high poverty incidence, and income inequality; poor widows with minor children and single mothers with a large number of children should be protected by social assistance (workfare, nutrition, health care, childcare, and training programs should be preferable to cash transfers when feasible); there must be a sufficient difference between the pension paid by social insurance and social assistance, but the reduction of the latter may result in a sum grossly insufficient to cover basic needs (changes in social assistance, therefore, should be coordinated with a reform of social insurance pensions); and ad hoc pension programs should be designed for groups of the labor force working under very harsh conditions.

Financing

Problems

The available data on social assistance expenditures are scarce and plagued by improper definitions. Such data indicate, nevertheless, that only a small proportion of social security is devoted to social assistance, and most of that goes to social insurance, despite the fact that, in half of LA, two-thirds of the population and labor force are not covered. As a percentage of GDP, assistance expenditures are usually lower than 0.5 percent, suggesting that a more significant effort is needed and could be financially feasible in many countries, particularly the most developed, if there is the political will. Ceilings are normally set to the overall sum assigned to assistance pensions, without clear priorities, which leads to a struggle for the scarce resources available. Very high percentage contributions imposed on the self-employed worker (due to the lack of an employer) are triple the percentage contribution assigned to the salaried worker, making very difficult the incorporation of the self-employed and increasing the chances that they will eventually become assistance cases. Evidence from several countries (Brazil, Chile, Costa Rica) shows that the bulk of fiscal subsidies is allocated to social insurance pensions for privileged groups (for example, congressmen, the judiciary, other civil servants, members of the armed forces), and very little is assigned to social assistance for pensions and health care, with a regressive impact on income distribution.

Recommendations

A higher proportion of social security expenditures and GDP could be devoted to social assistance programs (an increase in the proportion of GDP must be preceded by a careful feasibility evaluation); when ceilings on the amount of assistance pensions are set, clear priorities should be established to select the beneficiaries. One of the following three alternatives or a combination of them should be considered to facilitate the incorporation of the low-income self-employed into social insurance: establish a lower level of income as the tax base, reduce the contribution and adjust the pensions accordingly, or subsidize the contribution. Assistance programs for health care and pensions for the poor and low-income groups should receive fiscal subsidies currently assigned to the social insurance that covers middle-income groups and generous pensions for privileged groups.

Administration

Problems

A major obstacle for the study, evaluation, and policy design of social assistance programs in LAC is the very scarce data available on them; only the ILO provides some financial statistics (incomplete and mostly outdated), and the remaining international and regional organizations do not publish any data. There is a lack of coordination among antipoverty programs, including social assistance, and between this scheme and social insurance. The administration of health care in LA is normally under numerous institutions that provide unequal treatment to various segments of the population, generating stratification and inequalities. The administration of social assistance pensions is highly centralized, without input from local levels and beneficiaries (the poor). In a good number of countries, the pension funds for social insurance and social assistance are not separated or the state does not fulfill its financial social assistance obligations, thus resulting in transfers from social insurance to assistance, which erode the financial and actuarial stability of the former. Enforcement of the means test is not always efficient, and there are cases of fraud, political interference, and corruption.

Recommendations

An effort should be made to coordinate all antipoverty programs (social assistance, social safety nets, emergency employment), as well as other related programs such as primary health care, and those targeting vulnerable groups (children, women, ethnic groups); the current stratification in the administration of health care should be eliminated through an integrated but decentralized system capable of securing at least primary care for the poor and low-income groups, as well as facilitating their participation; the administration of social assistance pensions should also be integrated and decentralized, stimulating active participation from local levels and beneficiaries; social insurance and assistance pension schemes should be coordinated, but their funds must be separated and the state should fulfill its financial obligations to avoid transfers from and destabilization of the insurance scheme; associations or cooperatives of low-income groups should be stimulated and helped (training personnel, paying commissions) to become intermediaries that affiliate and collect contributions from them; the means test must be applied periodically (to check changing poverty conditions) in a simple and efficient manner (relying

more heavily on the information provided by local communities than on centralized bureaucratic procedures, and without political interference and fraud); and
statistical data and information on social assistance programs should be gathered
and published by countries and international organizations to better understand
and evaluate those schemes and design adequate policies.

The Inter-American Development Bank has considerable resources and a well-
designed poverty reduction policy but little experience in direct transfers to the
poor and social protection of informal sector workers.[42] The Bank could help in this
important policy area by providing financial and technical aid on the following
aspects, among others: developing information and statistics on social assistance
programs; assessing the financial feasibility of establishing these programs in LAC
countries or reforming those in existence; targeting the poor and designing simple
but efficient means tests; studying effective mechanisms for incorporation of the
informal sector in both health care and pension noncontributory programs; and
promoting administrative decentralization and participation.

Lessons from the Experience of Brazil and Costa Rica

Brazil and Costa Rica have recently introduced systems of universal social assistance pensions and, because these countries already have the highest regional coverage of social insurance pensions for those above 65 years, they should reach all
the elderly population including the poor. The Brazilian system has the following
features: it is managed by the state and totally financed by the Union, it integrates
all previous social assistance programs, it is decentralized at the local level and
procures participation from representative organizations. An outside evaluation of
the system is needed to assess its impact on poverty, whether pensions are sufficient to cover basic needs, its effective implementation at the local level, and its
managerial efficiency. The result of a process of national consensus, the Costa Rican
system will universalize social assistance pensions for all of the population 70 years
and older and extend social insurance pensions for low-income self-employed with
a state subsidy that will totally or partially substitute for the employer's contribution. It is important to clarify whether the assistance pension will be universal regardless of income or submitted to an income test, the calculation of the cost of this
program requires more precision, and the administration appears to be centralized

---

[42] Lustig and Deutsch (1998).

without representation. Features of both systems that should be emulated are the provision of a universal social assistance pension for the elderly poor (in Costa Rica, also a subsidized social insurance pension for low-income self-employed), the full financing of such pensions out of fiscal revenue, and the separation of finances for social insurance and assistance pensions. Administrative decentralization and representation from below in Brazil and the process of building national consensus in Costa Rica are additional commendable features.

CONCLUSION

Several potential future problems can be envisioned. The number of poor has been growing in LA since the beginning of the 1980s and reached between 150 million and 196 million in the 1990s. The poverty incidence of the total population rose from 41 percent to 46 percent in 1980–90, while such incidence among households increased from 31 percent to 41 percent in that period but declined to 39 percent in 1994. Although the incidence of poverty has decreased in the majority of countries, it has risen at least in Argentina, Mexico, and Venezuela.[43] The crisis of 1998–99 (particularly in Brazil) may result in an increase in the number of poor and incidence of poverty in the region, thus making it more difficult and costly to protect them. The least developed countries have the highest poverty incidence and the lowest resources to help the poor. Hence, their problem is the gravest. Poverty incidence in rural areas is much higher than in urban areas: among the total population it was 61 and 39 percent in rural and urban areas, respectively, in 1990, while among households it was 55 and 34 percent, respectively, in 1994. As the poor are concentrated in rural areas, dispersed, and often isolated, it is more expensive to provide health care to them. Yet the rural population is declining in LAC, hence, this problem should be reduced in the long run, but that does not exonerate the leadership from its current responsibility to help the rural poor.

The urban informal sector is also affected by poverty, but access to health care is relatively easier there than it is in rural areas, and yet this is not the case with pensions. Low-income groups in the urban sector, such as self-employed and unpaid family workers, employees of microenterprises, and domestic servants, constitute the bulk of the informal sector that has been expanding since the 1980s. These people either lack an employer or have one who often evades registration

---

[43] CEPAL (1992, 1996); Lustig and Deutsch (1998).

and payment of contributions. The immense majority of them are not covered by social insurance and in many cases do not meet the requirements to qualify for social assistance, particularly in pensions. As their numbers expand, this problem worsens, and the focus of public social policy should change.

The poor are uneducated, receive the lowest income, and are not organized. Hence, they lack political power to press for government help. Conversely, the most powerful groups of insured are well educated, have relatively high income, and are strongly organized (for example, civil servants, teachers). Hence, they exercise effective pressure to improve their coverage and benefits, as well as obtain fiscal support. In some countries, like Argentina and Uruguay, pensioners are organized into very powerful groups, which successfully lobby for the protection of their pensions. The risk of political-economic destabilization will increase in the future unless the poor are organized and exercise pressure on the state to provide essential services (or elect political leaders willing to do that job) or the state takes the initiative to socially protect the poor.[44]

A few LA countries have gone through the demographic transition and have aging populations and the oldest pension programs in the Americas (Argentina, Cuba, Uruguay), which means that expenditures on pensions and health care for the old will continue to expand. The majority of countries of LA are entering the demographic transition and still have relatively young populations, but that situation will change soon and fast. In 1990 the proportion of the population 60 years and older was 16.4 percent in Uruguay, 13.1 percent in Argentina, and 11.8 percent in Cuba. Those proportions will jump in 2030 to 22.5, 19.3, and 27.2 percent, respectively. However, the proportions of the youngest countries (the least developed: Bolivia, Guatemala, Honduras, Nicaragua) in 1990 were 4.2 to 5.4 percent, but in 2030 will increase to 9 to 10 percent, still lower than the 1990 figures of the oldest countries.[45] The combination of aging with increasing poverty (the "aging of poverty") could become a grave problem, hence the need to tackle now the protection of the poor and low-income groups.[46]

---

[44] Lustig and Deutsch (1998).
[45] World Bank (1994).
[46] Lustig and Deutsch (1998).

References

Banco de Previsión Social (BPS). 1998a. *La seguridad social en Uruguay*. Montevideo: Asesoría Económica y Actuarial.

———. 1998b. *Boletín estadístico 1998*. No. 53. Montevideo.

Bertranou. 1999. Personal communication.

Bustamante, Julio. 1998. "17 años del sistema chileno de pensiones." In Alejandro Bonilla and Alfredo Conte-Rand, eds., *Pensiones en América Latina: dos décadas de reforma*. Lima, Peru: OIT.

Caja Costarricense del Seguro Social (CCSS). 1995. *Reglamento del régimen no contributivo de pensiones por monto básico*. San José, Costa Rica.

———. 1997. *Anuario estadístico 1997*. San José, Costa Rica.

Comisión Económica de América Latina y el Caribe (CEPAL). 1992. *El perfil de la pobreza en América Latina*. Santiago, Chile.

———. 1996. *Statistical Yearbook for Latin America and the Caribbean 1996*. Santiago, Chile.

———. 1997. *Panorama social de América Latina 1997*. Santiago, Chile.

Cruz-Saco, María Amparo, and Carmelo Mesa-Lago, eds. 1999. *Do Options Exist? The Reform of Pension and Health Care Systems in Latin America*. Pittsburgh: University of Pittsburgh Press.

Foro de Concertación Nacional (FCN). 1998a. *La reforma del sistema nacional de pensiones: una propuesta*. San José, Costa Rica.

———. 1998b. *Informe final*. San José, Costa Rica.

Instituto de Pesquisa Econômica Aplicada (IPEA), Diretoria de Política Social. 1998a. *Assistência Social 1995-1998: Quatro Anos de Transformações*. (Background paper for the report.) Brasília, Brazil.

———. 1998b. *Previdência Social*. Brasília, Brazil.

Lei Orgânica de Assistência Social. 1993. Brasília, Brazil.

Inter-American Development Bank (IDB). 1999. Presentation at IDB conference by an official of Trinidad and Tobago (February).

International Labour Office (ILO). 1996. *The Cost of Social Security 1987-1989*. Geneva, Switzerland.

———. 1999. http://www.ilo.org/public/english/110secso/cssinder.htm.

Lustig, Nora, and Ruthanne Deutsch. 1998. *The Inter-American Development Bank and Poverty Reduction: An Overview*. Working Paper Series POV-101-R. Inter-American Development Bank, Washington, D.C.

Mesa-Lago, Carmelo. 1983. "Social Security and Extreme Poverty in Latin America." *Journal of Development Economics* 12: 83–110.

———. 1988. "Social Insurance: The Experience of Three Countries in the English-Speaking Caribbean." *International Labour Review* 127: 479–96.

———. 1990. *La seguridad social y el sector informal*. No. 32. Organización Internacional del Trabajo, PREALC, e Investigaciones sobre Empleo, Santiago, Chile.

———. 1992a. *Health Care for the Poor in Latin America and the Caribbean*. PAHO Scientific Publication no. 539. Pan American Health Organization and Inter-American Foundation, Washington, D.C.

————. 1992b. "Protection of the Informal Sector in Latin America and the Caribbean by Social Security or Alternative Means." In Víctor Tokman, ed., *Beyond Regulation: The Informal Economy in Latin America*. Boulder, CO: Lynne Rienner Publishers.

————. 1994a. *Changing Social Security in Latin America: Towards the Alleviation of Social Costs of Economic Reform*. Boulder, CO: Lynne Rienner.

————. 1994b. "Expansion of Social Protection to the Rural Population in Latin America." *Social Security in Developing Countries*. New Delhi, India: Har-Anand Publications.

————. 1997. "La seguridad social y la pobreza en Cuba." *La seguridad social en América Latina: seis casos diferentes*. Buenos Aires, Argentina: CEDLA-Konrad Adenauer Stiftung.

————. 1998. "Análisis y recomendaciones sobre la propuesta del gobierno en el foro de concertación nacional sobre el sistema de pensiones de Costa Rica" y "Evaluación del Acuerdo de la Comisión de Pensiones del FCN en Costa Rica." San José, Costa Rica: Friedrich Ebert Stiftung (August and September).

————. 2000a. "Achieving and Sustaining Social Development with Limited Resources: The Experience of Costa Rica." In Dharam Ghai, ed., *Social Development and Public Policy: Some Lessons from Successful Experiences*. London, UK: Macmillan.

————. 2000b. *Market, Socialist and Mixed Economies: Comparative Policy and Performance–Chile, Cuba and Costa Rica*. Baltimore, MD: Johns Hopkins University Press.

Mesa-Lago, Carmelo, and Sergio Roca. 1992. "Cuba." In John Dixon and David Macarov, eds., *Social Welfare in Socialist Countries*. London, UK: Routledge.

Mesa-Lago, Carmelo, and Fabio Bertranou. 1998. *Manual de economía de la seguridad social en América Latina*. Montevideo, Uruguay: CLAEH.

Ministério da Previdência e Assistência Social (MPAS). 1998. *Anuário Estatístico da Previdência Social 1997*. Brasília, Brazil.

————. 1998. *Boletín Estatístico da Previdência Social* 3 (December).

Oficina Nacional de Estadística. 1998 *Annuario Estadístico de Cuba 1996*. Havana, Cuba.

Rivero, Raúl. 1999. "La penuria acusa a cientos de jubilados cubanos [Report from Havana]." *El Nuevo Herald*. Miami, FL, January 17.

Schulthess, Walter E. 1995. "Efectos sobre la distribución del ingreso de las prestaciones no contributivas." *Previsión Social* 19: 3–30.

Schwarzer, Helmut. 1999. *Impactos Socio-Econômicos do Sistema de Aposentadorias Rurais no Brasil*. Brasília, Brazil: IPEA.

Superintendencia de Seguridad Social (SSS). 1997, 1998. *Estadísticas mensuales de seguridad social*. Santiago, Chile. (January-June).

————. 1999. *Information on Social Assistance and Social Insurance*. Santiago, Chile (January).

United Nations Development Programme (UNDP). 1997. *Investigación sobre el desarrollo humano en Cuba 1996*. Havana, Cuba: Caguayo S.A.

————. 1998. *Human Development Report 1998*. Oxford: Oxford University Press.

U.S. Social Security Administration (SSA). 1997. *Social Security Programs throughout the World 1997*. Washington, D.C.: Government Printing Office.

World Bank. 1993. *World Development Report: Investing in Health*. Oxford: Oxford University Press.

————. 1994. *Averting the Old-Age Crisis: Policies to Protect the Old and Promote Growth*. Oxford: Oxford University Press.

————. 1999. *World Development Report 1998/99*. Oxford: Oxford University Press.

CHAPTER NINE

The Safety Net Role
of Microfinance for Income
and Consumption Smoothing

Manfred Zeller

This chapter explores the role of microfinance for income and consumption smoothing. In a nutshell, improved access to financial services can have two principal effects on household outcomes. First, it can raise the expected value of income and, therefore, of consumption and future investment and asset accumulation. This is the traditional and often sole argument for provision of services by microfinance institutions (MFIs). Second, it can decrease the downward semivariances of income or consumption. It is the second effect that is relevant for the subject of this chapter.[1]

For the food-insecure, it is particularly important to reduce the downward risk of falling below some minimum threshold levels for consumption of food and other basic needs. Therefore, the poor tend to value financial services that address the risk-coping motive more whereas the wealthy can afford to demand more of financial services that generate income and accumulate assets. For example, while the rich and well-cushioned in developed countries buy stocks, middle- and lower-income families prefer to hold more certificates of deposit, and the poor keep their money in a checking account or under the pillow. Similar behavior, albeit using different financial products, including myriad informal financial substitutes, can be observed among the wealthy and poor in developing countries.

This chapter seeks to assess the role of microfinance for income and consumption smoothing by the poor.[2] The principal policy implication is that the role of

---

[1] I note that it can sometimes be more efficient to reduce the downward risk in consumption by increasing the mean income, for example, through adoption of technology.

[2] For the definition of these terms, see Morduch (1995).

microfinance for risk-coping mechanisms is not well recognized and therefore underutilized in policy and microfinance practice. Although it is admittedly more difficult to offer savings and insurance services than credit, recent product innovations by a few microfinance institutions suggest that there is room to exploit this potential more efficiently.

Generating extra income (or growth) is the traditional argument for the provision of credit and savings services.[3] Financial services that potentially raise the income of households are microenterprise credit, seasonal agricultural credit, medium- and long-term investment credit, and term deposits and savings accounts that earn interest income. For this type of service I use the term *financial services for income generation*. These services are fairly common among MFIs and constitute most often the only type of financial services they offer.

Credit, savings, and insurance services that address the demand for reducing ex ante the variance of income, or ex post the variance of consumption, are rarely offered by MFIs. Such services include insurance, the provision of savings services that are liquid and can be withdrawn at short notice, and the provision of consumption credit, or less controversially expressed, the provision of general household credit for maintaining family labor and the household's human and social capital. These services provide a shield against future risks and can thereby enable households to bear more risks. Since technology adoption and the level of production and investment increases with risk-bearing capacity, the provision of financial services for consumption smoothing (FCs) can have an indirect and positive effect on ex ante income generation.[4] FCs can potentially reduce the cost of income and consumption smoothing by, for example, substituting for some higher-cost informal savings or higher-cost informal sources of consumption credit. FCs are particularly demanded in environments of considerable interannual and seasonal income fluctuations and are, therefore, particularly relevant for rural households depending mainly on agriculture for their livelihood. Moreover, FCs gain in relative importance over MFIs for disadvantaged clientele groups such as women and wage laborers. Labor, their major production factor, is exposed to a number of health risks that can jeopardize earnings income at any time.

Policy may be well advised to recognize not only the microfinance nexus for poverty alleviation through growth but also its potential for providing social protection that can complement other measures for public and informal safety nets.

---

[3] See Zeller and others (1997).

[4] See Eswaran and Kotwal (1990).

COPING WITH COVARIANT AND IDIOSYNCRATIC RISKS THROUGH MICROFINANCE SERVICES

In this section I attempt to systematize the risks that poor households in developing countries face and that motivate the households' demand for financial services for income and consumption smoothing. I contrast this demand with the type of services commonly supplied by microfinance institutions. The gap between current supply and demand by the poor defines areas for potential policy action as well as further research.

Tables 9–1, 9–2, and 9–3 list various categories of risk that affect the process of income generation or consumption by households. These risks cause income to fluctuate and may create additional unexpected expenses that need to be met by ex post consumption smoothing measures. The second column in the three tables lists examples of typical informal responses to these risks, whereas the last column indicates the relevance of microfinance policy for addressing these risks.

When considering the risks listed in the tables, it is important to distinguish between idiosyncratic and covariant risks, that is, risks that affect only individuals or larger groups of people in the same locality, respectively. This is because the informal responses to risk that are differentiated in the second column of the tables are less effective in covering covariant risks than in protecting households against idiosyncratic risks. In general, informal responses are of a localized nature, mostly based on actions by individual household members or by informal institutions at the local community level. Mark Rosenzweig and Kenneth I. Wolpin find that sales of bullocks in India are motivated by the need to smooth consumption. Yet the effectiveness of traditional forms of savings can be severely hampered by covariant risk such as drought. Czukas and others explore the role of livestock as a form of precautionary savings in Burkina Faso.[5] Their results show that livestock transactions play less of a role in consumption smoothing than is often assumed. This phenomenon suggests that drought as a covariant risk can equally threaten the effectiveness of specific forms of precautionary savings. This is particularly true if poorly integrated markets for the assets lead to drastic declines in prices exactly at a time when a large part of households seeks to sell.

Table 9–1 systematizes the risks related to the generation of income and distinguishes between income from self-employment in farm and nonfarm microenterprises as well as wage labor income. While the latter covers the risk of

---

[5] Rosenzweig and Wolpin (1993); Czukas, Fafchamps, and Udry (1995).

Table 9–1. Risks Affecting Income Generation of Households and Their Members

Risks related to	Examples of informal responses to risk	Relevance for microfinance policy
Input markets (availability and quality of production inputs, including shortages of family labor due to ill health)	Diversifying income sources (nonfarm, on-farm, wage labor, temporary or permanent migration of household members) Establishing reliable input sources through formal contracts or through investment in social relations with input dealers Entering into bonded patron-client relationships by poor entrepreneurs with wealthy input suppliers (for example, tenant-landlord) Holding costly reserves of inputs (for example, seeds or raw material for microenterprises) Investing in social capital (informal groups that provide labor)	If input markets do not function well, credit for inputs (in cash) to microentrepreneurs may not create much benefit Organization of MFI clients to reap economies of scale, scope, and risk in purchasing inputs
Production function (for example, covariant weather risks or idiosyncratic risks affecting business, crop, or livestock enterprise)	Diversifying income (that is, foregoing profits from specialization) Risk-reducing inputs (for example, irrigation, pesticides, vaccination of animals) Postponing decisions (for example, sowing later) Diversifying operations spatially (for example, plot diversification) Choosing low-return enterprises that have lower risks	Credit and savings services for diversification in new enterprises Provision of production insurance (crop, livestock insurance)
Output markets (risks in finding a buyer and price risks)	Diversifying income Establishing contracts/informal relationships with output buyers (including bonded patron-client relationships) Producing more for home consumption than for the market (emphasizing autarky and foregoing gains from trade)	Addressing bottlenecks in marketing (again, lack of access to financial services may not be the primary cause of income fluctuation)

Table 9-2. Risks Affecting Consumption with Chronic, Permanent Effects on the Ability to Earn Income

Risk related to	Examples of informal responses to risk	Relevance for microfinance policy
Sliding into chronic poverty in its worst form (loss of all productive assets, including ability to work), for example, often caused by covariant risks, such as natural disasters, war, political upheaval and major economic crises, HIV/AIDS	Informal social welfare (for example neighborhood help, giving to beggars, raising children in foster homes, remittances by extended family) Informal precautionary savings and investment in human capital (having more children) and social capital (having access to networks that provide help)	No role for credit as there is no viable project to be financed and no repayment capacity Provision of precautionary savings services Other safety net measures are more relevant (public transfers to replenish assets, such as disaster relief or social security) Very limited role for insurance, except if coupled with international reinsurance
Permanent inability to work	Same as above	Disability insurance and precautionary savings services
Old age or death of family member	Informal precautionary savings (long-term investments in physical, human, and social capital that can provide income in old age)	Precautionary savings services Life insurance

Table 9–3. Risks Affecting Consumption with Usually Transitory Effects on the Ability to Earn Income

Risk related to	Examples of informal responses to risk	Relevance for microfinance policy
Health (temporarily affecting ability to work)		
1. Covariant health risks (for example, malaria, flu)	Reducing exposure to health risk if causes are known Holding precautionary savings Investing in social capital that provides labor, food, and care (but capacity of network for service provision may be weakened, too, because of covariance)	Public health policy (including health insurance) is most relevant MF policy can complement by providing - precautionary savings services with emphasis on low transaction costs for withdrawal and liquidity rather than return - consumption credit
2. Idiosyncratic health risks (for example, many human diseases, accident, pregnancy)	Like with covariant risks, but investment in social capital is much more likely to be effective	In addition to the above, member-based MFIs can self-finance the demand for consumption credit out of internal savings or can retail specific insurance services
Claims of social network (for example, financing social events, helping out friends and relatives in need) and communal conflicts that undermine access to essential resources for production and human welfare	Holding precautionary savings, as above	Provision of liquid savings services for unexpected claims and term deposits for anticipated claims
Divorce, domestic violence, and other causes of household disintegration	Maintaining ownership/control over assets brought into/accumulated during marriage Investing in social networks accessible by the individual household member	Promoting savings accounts and credit lines for individuals, in particular for women

unemployment, the former are specific risks related to the availability of inputs (with respect to quantity, quality, and price risks), the stochastic production function of the enterprise, and the availability of markets where products of the household and its enterprises can be sold. For brevity, I chose not to differentiate the risks affecting income generation in idiosyncratic and covariant risks. It should be noted, however, that many of these risks are covariant. For example, risks related to the conduct and performance of input, output, and labor markets have similar effects on households that engage in the same enterprises. The less diversified the local economy, the larger the share of the population that is potentially affected by the same source of risk. In other words, the resilience and ability of informal networks to deal with these types of covariant risk factors diminish with greater specialization of the local economy. Negative effects on income are of course exacerbated by poorly integrated labor, financial, and commodity markets. The proper functioning of these markets often critically depends on infrastructure.

Table 9–1 highlights the potential of microfinance policy to partially address these risks. The principal remedy to address these risks may not necessarily lie in improving financial markets but in investing in road infrastructure, technology development and transfer, or improving the performance of commodity markets. The extent to which microfinance matters ultimately depends on the specific circumstances. With respect to risks occurring in the availability and quality of inputs, credit disbursed in cash may be of little use, and addressing the underlying bottlenecks and imperfections in input markets is likely to be more relevant in many circumstances. Yet, member-based financial institutions can exploit economies of scale, scope, and risk by collective acquisition of inputs.

The role of microfinance tends to increase when one considers risks related to the production function itself. Access to credit can help households to adopt risk-reducing inputs, such as investment in irrigation or use of disease-resistant crop varieties and pesticides. It can further assist to diversify risks by entering into new enterprises for which profits are weakly correlated with the traditional income portfolio of the household. For certain types of production risks that can be easily monitored and therefore insured, sustainable provision of insurance is possible.[6] However, as far as farm enterprises are concerned, the provision of crop and livestock

---

[6] Hazell (1992) distinguishes three characteristics that make a risk insurable. First, the likelihood of the event must be readily quantifiable. Second, the damage it causes must be easy to attribute and evaluate. Third, neither the occurrence of the event nor the damage it causes should be affected by the insured's behavior (that is, absence of moral hazard).

insurance is riddled with many difficulties, although a number of crop insurance schemes exist that are linked with credit.[7] Yet, research points out that these schemes are heavily subsidized and tend to benefit larger farmers over smaller ones.[8]

The principal difficulties in crop insurance increase further when one considers the conditions of small-scale farming in developing countries. New information technology and satellite imaging that can decrease the cost of monitoring may change the future prospects for sustainable insurance of risks in smallholder agriculture. However, at present, the role of financial sector policy in addressing these risks appears fairly limited. Sensible loan repayment schedules, especially the flexibility to reschedule loans in case of crop failure, can mitigate the borrowers' risk but may also introduce the problem of moral hazard. Last, for risks related to output markets, reasoning similar to that for input markets holds. Insofar as access to finance can enable households to diversify their portfolio of enterprises to smooth income risks, microfinance could possibly make a contribution. However, for most circumstances, lack of road infrastructure and communications and policy distortions in output markets are likely to play a greater role in volatility of household incomes.

The discussion of risks related to income volatility points to a somewhat limited role of savings, credit, and insurance services related to income smoothing. The principal direct role that can be identified is that savings and credit services can enable households to acquire the necessary start-up capital for establishing new enterprises for which profits are weakly correlated with their existing portfolio. Moreover, access to credit and savings services can facilitate household investment in risk-reducing inputs such as irrigation or pesticides.

As is discussed next, access to financial services can have a far greater role for smoothing consumption and thereby increasing the risk-bearing capacity of households for increasing future income. Table 9–2 refers to rather infrequent but very large risks that can wipe out the productive capacity of a household, whereas table 9–3 lists risks that frequently occur and cause transitory shocks to consumption.[9]

---

[7] See Hazell, Pomareda, and Valdes (1983).

[8] Hazell, Pomareda, and Valdes (1983).

[9] Insofar as these risks concern the productive capacity of the household by affecting the ability of household members to work and generate income, these risks could also be viewed as affecting income generation and be listed under labor inputs in table 9–1. However, I chose to list these risks as ex post shocks as they create additional potential demand for unanticipated consumption expenditures (such as the treatment of human diseases).

The household's ability to deal with large, infrequent risks—such as war, political upheaval, successive major droughts, and other natural disasters—through informal responses is quite weak (see first row in table 9–2). This vulnerability is caused by the covariant nature of these risks (and the related weakness of informal responses to deal with such risks) or by the large impact of the risk on the household. Regarding these covariant and large risks, the role of insurance and credit is fairly limited. Insofar as these sources of risk are covariant, the provision of sustainable insurance schemes appears quite impossible under the conditions of most low-income countries unless the insurance company is well diversified at the national level and can possibly benefit from reinsurance services so that it can spread the risks over a large client base. In most cases, it is the state that is called upon to be the implicit insurer by providing social assistance. This assistance can take the form of permanent income transfers to secure a minimum standard of living, for example, in the case of permanent disability that impedes earning an income, or temporary transfers to replenish productive assets of households and to treat conditions of workers' disability. Once the ability to earn an income is restored through private or public assistance so that the capacity to repay a loan and to save is regained, savings and credit services can assist households to expand the productive capital in successive periods. However, moral hazard problems may emerge once the government is relied upon as the insurer of last resort.[10]

One may argue that temporary transfers by the state to replenish assets could be given on a loan instead of a grant basis. If the administrative network to properly administer such loans is in place and can be used with low transaction costs to the government and the target groups, it could be justified to choose a loan over a grant system. Yet, if governments use—as often is the case—local-level employees of certain line ministries who are inexperienced in the handling of credit, the repayment rates for disaster loans—such as after droughts or floods—are often extremely low. Repayment rates that hover in the teens and twenties, combined with additional administrative costs of loan provision and recovery, may well lead to total costs of service provision that are far higher for loans than for grants. Moreover, loosely monitored and ill-targeted disaster credit schemes by the state run the risk of destroying repayment motivation.

For all three types of risks listed in table 9–3, precautionary savings services could be important. A particularly large potential appears to exist for cushioning

---

[10] See Besley (1995).

the risk of permanent disability and for the case of old age and the death of family members. However, in the case of old age or permanent disability that is caused by idiosyncratic risk such as an accident, insurance services can play an important role, too. For these risks, however, there appears to be no role for credit simply because the risk under consideration wipes out the capacity to earn an income and, therefore, to repay the loan. However, if the disabled person possesses assets that provide a source of income (such as a rental house) or are good collateral to the bank, consumption credit can in principle be offered.

Table 9–3 lists risks that usually have transitory effects on the ability to earn an income. They therefore cause transitory shortfalls in consumption if informal responses are inadequate. A major source of risk for the poor is ill health caused by covariant diseases, such as malaria and flu, or by many idiosyncratic diseases. The impact of health risks increases with the level of poverty because labor is the major production factor the poor have. The rich may substitute for their own family labor by acquiring hired labor in case of temporary illness. Just as in the case of imperfect commodity markets, if the public health system does not function well, so that proper medical care and medicines are not available, access to financial services may not do much good. It appears, therefore, generally more appropriate to invest in health infrastructure and in access to safe water and sanitation that can directly tackle these health risks. Only if a health infrastructure is in place and is accessible by the poor can financial services make a difference. In studies by the International Food Policy Research Institute, the short-term impact of access to financial services on nutrition was found insignificant in all cases.[11] In the long term, however, access to financial services may increase the income of households and thereby enable communal action to use part of that income to invest in health infrastructure by, for example, funding a communal water borehole. If health services can be purchased locally, access to precautionary savings services and to credit are expected to have a considerable potential for assisting the poor in dealing with transitory health risks. The role of financial services is equally important for financing consumption goods during illness.

Other sources of transitory risks causing volatility in the poor's consumption include the manifold claims that the social network can voice. These claims include the need to advance or reciprocate help to the extended family, friends, and neighbors, and requirements for financing social events to satisfy cultural norms, such as

---

[11] See Zeller and Sharma (1998); Sharma and Schrieder (2000).

marriage and burial. For these types of transitory events, the provision of precautionary savings appears very appropriate. Since these shocks can frequently occur, and some are hard to anticipate, a range of precautionary savings services that differ with respect to liquidity and return could be offered. For example, long-term savings products are more appropriate for predictable events such as marriage, whereas frequent and unanticipated claims by the social network could be dealt with by means of current accounts and highly liquid savings services. Another source of social risk that arises from the networks at the community level is that of communal conflict regarding access to and use of resources by different socioeconomic groups, such as drinking water, land, and other natural resources that are essential for income generation or for human welfare.

The above discussion pointed to several specific risks, mostly related to consumption smoothing, that potentially can be addressed by MFIs. These risks are mainly of an idiosyncratic nature, and the dominant financial service that appears most feasible to be implemented by microfinance institutions as a response to these risks is precautionary savings and credit. The willingness of the poor to pay for financial services for income and consumption smoothing depends of course on the effectiveness and costs of informal responses, including informal forms of precautionary savings, consumption credit, and insurance.[12] Importantly, formal financial services responding to these safety net aspects of finance can crowd out informal responses, implying a smaller net benefit of formal services. If formal services are subsidized by the state, they can create social costs that exceed social benefits. Having said that, the evidence shows that informal responses are far from adequate.

To find the right mix between publicly and privately provided safety nets is, then, the true challenge. In a nutshell, some form of public assistance is necessary to alleviate poverty and protect the poor from major shocks. The main question is which policy, or even better, which bundle of policies addresses this problem in the most efficient manner. Moreover, informal responses are greatly weakened in their effectiveness if risks are correlated over time. They are also less effective for the vulnerable and socially excluded in society, that is, those who lack sufficient access to informal self-help networks. Thus, informal responses are likely to provide adequate cushioning for some, but not for others, particularly the poor. Secular trends, such as the break-up of the extended family through migration and

---

[12] On informal responses see also Alderman and Paxson (1992); Cox and Jiménez (1992); Townsend (1995); Walker and Jodha (1983); Udry (1990).

urbanization, and demographic shifts, such as fertility decline and extended life expectancy, tend to reduce over time the efficiency of informal responses, particularly regarding old age and disability insurance. Because of this weakening of informal networks over time, the demand for publicly provided safety nets as well as the demand for financial services for consumption smoothing that is provided by microfinance institutions is likely to increase in low-income countries.

RECENT INNOVATIONS OF MICROFINANCE INSTITUTIONS

In the following, I mainly focus on idiosyncratic risks, for which the implementation potential of microfinance appears to be largest and for which product innovations have already been introduced by microfinance institutions.

Since most MFIs in developing countries at present are too small in terms of size of clientele and geographical coverage, they are often unable to effectively cover covariant risks, either by direct insurance services or by pooling emergency funds financed by clients. However, as MFIs grow over time and reach operational scales like those achieved by the Bank Rakyat Indonesia (BRI), BRAC, or the Grameen Bank, there is also considerable potential for sustainable coverage of covariant risks. For example, the Grameen Bank and BRI both have rescheduled loans to clients in areas of natural disasters. BRI can do this without assistance from the state because of its high profits and business conviction that losing a good borrower is also a loss to BRI. The Grameen Bank has also rescheduled loans in the past for clients affected by flood. The Grameen Bank obligates members to deposit small amounts of savings in a so-called emergency fund. The pooling of such funds over larger areas can in principle address covariant types of risks.

The major sources of idiosyncratic risk that cause consumption to fluctuate are listed in table 9–4 and summarized in the first column: health risks, including pregnancy and temporary or permanent disability caused by accident or disease; old age and death of family members (again, as far as death is not caused by covariant risks such as war and AIDS); claims by the social network or expenses for social events that need to be met by the household; and social risks such as the break-up of families because of divorce and other reasons that leave vulnerable household members at risk, especially children, women, and the elderly. The second column in table 9–4 describes innovations in financial products that specifically address these risks. The third column gives examples of MFIs that provide such services to their clients.

The provision of health insurance for low-income people in developing countries faces a number of great challenges that are not discussed in this chapter. In developed countries, and in the case of formal sector employees in developing countries, health insurance is usually provided by specialized nonbanking institutions. Therefore, I view the role of microfinance institutions in providing health insurance as quite limited. Yet microfinance institutions can provide precautionary savings services and consumption credit that can indirectly address health risks. For example, village banks that follow the FINCA model or the model developed by the French NGO Centre International de Développement et de Recherche (CIDR) raise funds for internal lending to their members.[13]

The village bank model allows the members to decide on interest rates for savings deposits and for internal loans. For example, the village banks supported by CIDR in Madagascar set savings rates between 24 and 36 percent a year, and on-lending rates at 36 to 48 percent a year, although the formal lending rate of the agricultural bank was only 14 percent. The lending rate decided by the village banks was found to be much higher than the one for loans from friends and relatives, but less than the lending rate of about 60 percent that socially distant moneylenders charge on seasonal consumption loans.[14] In many village banks, the members explicitly allowed for consumption loans financed by internal funds. Some of the village banks even provided interest "subsidies" to members in need of such loans. Other examples of MFIs that explicitly provide consumption credit include Caja Social in Mexico and BRAC in Bangladesh. BRAC members can borrow up to 75 percent of their savings deposit for emergency purposes. SEWA in India targets microloans to very poor women and allows its borrowers to stop loan repayment during pregnancy.

Health risks can also be addressed by the provision of precautionary savings services. This type of service is useful for all types of risk listed in table 9–4, provided that the maturity of the deposit, the interest rate, and the transaction costs for depositing and withdrawing funds at short notice are adjusted accordingly. For health risks that occur relatively frequently and demand immediate response, the costs and time for withdrawal must be minimal. A current account at a village bank or a nearby bank branch offers such features, as does a term deposit that can be withdrawn at short notice with a penalty. To protect savings deposits, banking laws

---

[13] Chao-Béroff (1996); Nelson and others (1996).
[14] Zeller (1998).

Table 9–4. Innovations in Savings, Credit, and Insurance Services by Microfinance Institutions

Risk related to	Product innovations by MFIs	Examples of MFIs that have implemented innovations
Health (temporarily affecting the ability to work, such as an accident, many diseases, and pregnancy, and that usually lead to higher consumption expenditures and to shortfalls in income)	Consumption credit lines that provide cash loans at short notice to clients Frequent condition for loan eligibility: borrower must already be client of MFI (but exceptions in case of lending funds accumulated by members themselves) Loan rescheduling in case of pregnancy Precautionary savings services, such as current accounts earning no interest, or term deposits with varying maturities, interest rates and penalties for early withdrawal	Caja Social, Mexico BRAC, Bangladesh (up to a certain amount of savings deposit) Village banks following the FINCA model (in many countries in Latin America and Africa consumption loans are funded with internal savings of members, and often given with interest rebates that are decided by members) Cooperative credit and savings institutions (such as in Cameroon and Madagascar) SEWA, India BancoSol (Bolivia), a commercial bank catering to the poor
Permanent disability	Disability insurance	Village banks following the FINCA model in Kenya. FINCA assists the village banks with buying group disability insurance for their members from an insurance company
Old age or death of family member	Life insurance Precautionary savings (as above, but long-term deposits with higher interest rates)	Bank Rakyat Indonesia: the life insurance only covers debt of borrower; in case of death of borrower, the insurance pays for any outstanding debt of borrower Bangladesh Rural Advancement Committee (BRAC): the life insurance is paid out to the

		person designated by BRAC member in case of death; the lump-sum payment to the heir provides an implicit incentive to take care of the BRAC member during old age
		Mostly microfinance institutions that are registered as banks
Claims by social network	Consumption credit lines	Author does not know of any MFI that explicitly provides loans for financing social events such as marriage or burial
	Holding precautionary savings, as above	
Divorce and other causes of household disintegration	Targeting of financial services to women	Most but not all MFIs: savings accounts and credit lines are registered under individual names (husband does not co-sign)
	Promotion of social change, gender equality, women's empowerment	

Sources: Rashid and Townsend (1993); Zeller and others (1997); Wisniwski and Hannig (2000); Nelson and others (1996); Goetz and Sen Gupta (1996).

often hinder semiformal MFIs (such as village banks and group-based savings and credit schemes) from offering and diversifying their savings products in response to customer demands.[15] Yet those MFIs that are registered under the banking or cooperative law often have a variety of savings products that respond to the demand for precautionary savings to cover risks of health, disability, social claims, or old age. Examples of banks that successfully offer savings services to a diverse clientele, including the urban and rural poor, are BancoSol in Bolivia and BRI in Indonesia.

Poor households may accept nominal interest rates for savings deposits that are below the inflation rate if the costs and time of withdrawal of savings are minimal compared with alternative informal sources of savings. Nonetheless, diverse savings products that provide different forms of tradeoffs between liquidity and return are required to address the full range of savings needs of the poor. The optimal choice of savings products can be conditioned by the clients' access to labor, food, and commodity markets. For example, if food markets during the hungry season are segmented and food prices are highly volatile, households may continue to save in the form of food, even if formal savings options with high liquidity and low transaction costs are accessible. Often such conditions are found in remote areas with poor infrastructure. For example, in the rice market of Madagascar, regional and seasonal price differences reach up to 300 and 100 percent, respectively.[16]

The imperfections in the food marketing system explain why the growth and performance of member-managed rice "banks" in Madagascar, linked with a cash credit program, were quite successful during the 1990s. The rice bank scheme offers groups of smallholders the option to store their rice after harvest when output prices are low and to take out cash loans to finance consumption and to invest in off-farm enterprises during the dry season. The rice serves as collateral. Four to six months after the harvest when rice prices are high, the farmers sell their rice and repay their consumption loans. This credit with an in-kind savings scheme is attractive to farmers who face volatile food markets as it allows households to more effectively smooth their consumption during the hungry season.

Another important type of risk for the poor is a disability that hinders or prevents working. Village banks in Kenya that are promoted by FINCA provide an innovative example. The members of the village banks can purchase group disability insurance from a specialized insurance company. FINCA assists in retailing these services to the members of the village banks.

---

[15] Wisniwski and Hannig (2000).
[16] Minten (1998).

A number of MFIs offer life insurance services to cover risks of death or lack of care during old age (table 9–3). Most often, however, the insurance contract only covers the outstanding debt of the borrower in case of his or her death. This is the case, for example, for BRI in Indonesia or ASA in Bangladesh. BRAC, however, offers a life insurance contract to its members that pays a predetermined sum in case of death of the member.[17] The insurance contract can respond to two principal motives. First, in the case of women in particular, in rural Bangladesh the death of a husband usually results in the woman's loss of access to all the major assets of the household. The widow is then completely dependent on her children, brothers, parents, and father- or brothers-in-law. By buying life insurance and designating a beneficiary in her family, the woman can gain increased bargaining power to obtain care during old age. Second, women in single-parent households can provide some security to their children by buying life insurance.

Because of sociocultural constraints, women often cannot get a loan unless they are married and their husband is a cosigner on the loan application. Microfinance institutions ought to insist that such discrimination is not practiced for their loan and savings products. By providing women with individual credit lines and savings accounts, their bargaining power during marriage could increase (although this effect may not materialize).[18] Moreover, individual accounts for women would enable them to have a much stronger economic position in case of separation from the family, for example, because of divorce or the death of the husband.

CONCLUSIONS

Access to microfinance has the potential not only to assist the poor in earning income from microenterprises but also to smooth their income and consumption. The first potential effect is the traditional argument for microfinance, which one may call the growth argument for microfinance. It is presently the primary motivation for the microfinance movement. Yet the second effect gains relative importance with the increasing poverty level of MFI clients. This is the safety net argument for public support of microfinance institutions.

---

[17] When I visited Bangladesh in 1995, a BRAC member showed me her insurance certificate. In case of her death, the contract would pay 5,000 taka (about U.S.$110) to her son. When asked for her motive for buying this insurance, she replied that the insurance gives her children more security in case she dies early and gives her more security during old age, when she has to depend on her children.
[18] See Goetz and Sen Gupta (1996).

This chapter sought to distinguish these two principal effects of, and arguments for, public support of microfinance institutions. Microfinance can address aspects of growth as well as safety net policy. I entirely focused in this chapter on the safety net role and discussed the types of risks that cause fluctuations in income as well as in consumption. The largest potential for microfinance is seen in addressing idiosyncratic risks such as risks related to ill health, disability, old age, and divorce. When microfinance institutions grow in scale and reach out to diverse client groups, they also increase their potential to address covariant risks of their clientele.

Several innovative microfinance institutions offer financial products that respond to these risks. Most commonly found are precautionary savings services that provide clients with various products that offer choices concerning the transaction costs of withdrawal and the return earned on the deposit. Some MFIs offer explicit lines of consumption credit, especially the member-based financial institutions that give their members the flexibility to raise savings deposits for lending to members at terms freely decided by the members. Many village banks in Latin America and Sub-Saharan Africa offer consumption credit that is financed by internal savings collected from the banks' members. Some MFIs have ventured into insurance and developed their own insurance products, mainly life insurance. Other experiences suggest that MFIs have a potential for retailing insurance products from the formal insurance sector to their clients.

The poorer the declared target group of an MFI, the more important it is that the MFI offer financial services for income and consumption smoothing. By improving its product mix as recommended in this chapter, an MFI's costs of targeting to the poor may decrease, as the poor will have a greater incentive to become clients. However, when MFIs choose to broaden their outreach of financial services with safety net characteristics, they must be aware of the potentially greater portfolio and liquidity risks that such a strategy entails. I argued in the chapter that the MFIs will not need to worry much about idiosyncratic risks, but they need to do so for covariant risks. Prudent behavior would therefore suggest that MFIs first target areas with low covariant risks and only gradually expand client outreach in higher risk areas. Higher liquidity reserves and larger equity capital also appear to be adequate responses to covariant risks. Client-funded emergency funds that are pooled over large areas have the potential to spread these risks at sustainable levels.

The poor's willingness to pay for financial services for income and consumption smoothing will of course depend on the effectiveness and costs of informal responses, including informal forms of precautionary savings, consumption, and

insurance. Thus the provision of financial services may crowd out informal responses. To the extent that services by MFIs are indirectly subsidized by the state—
for example, by grants for product innovation, staff training, and institutional expansion—formal financial services can create social costs that exceed social benefits. Yet the evidence from recent research suggests that the informal responses are
far from adequate and that publicly supported institutional innovations in
microfinance can offer in many circumstances a viable policy instrument that generates net social benefits.

To find the right mix between publicly and privately provided safety nets
remains, therefore, the true challenge. Under many conditions, it appears that MFIs
could offer safety net-type services that are largely or exclusively financed by the
clients. Alternative forms of safety net provision supported or directly implemented
by the state, such as ex post income transfers or public works, can carry high
administrative costs for delivery and targeting and may require considerable
response times after the shock has already occurred. In comparison, precautionary
savings, insurance, and consumption credit are demand driven. And by using
local information, MFIs can adapt their services to the specific demand patterns of
various clientele groups. Depending on the subsidy level of the MFI, the costs of
service provision can be financed to a large extent or to a full extent by the clients
themselves. MFIs that are already established can offer financial products for income and consumption smoothing at relatively low variable costs as the core business is already supported by growth-oriented financial services.

For these reasons, MFIs that want to increase their relevance for the poor are
well advised to innovate financial services for income and consumption smoothing. Public action could further promote this strategy by supporting pilot projects
and related action research. The latter is especially needed to evaluate the potential
crowding-out effects on other formal and informal services and the net financial
and economic benefit of the introduction of new financial products. Nonetheless,
evaluations of MFIs that receive support from the government or donors so as to
make a contribution to the alleviation of poverty ought to include checks on whether
the MFI provides financial products for income and consumption smoothing such
as precautionary savings services, emergency credit, insurance services, or implicit
insurance substitutes. Such checks can be undertaken rapidly and at low cost by
simply looking at the terms of the financial products currently offered, and they
can identify further poverty-oriented product innovation that could easily be implemented and could increase the business volume and profitability of the MFI.

References

Alderman, H., and C. H. Paxson. 1992. *Do the Poor Insure? A Synthesis of the Literature on Risk and Consumption in Developing Countries.* Discussion Paper no. 169. Woodrow Wilson School of Public and International Affairs, Princeton University, Princeton, N.J.

Besley, T. 1995. "Credit, Savings, and Insurance." In J. Behrman and T. N. Srinivasan, eds., *Handbook of Development Economics,* vol. IIIA. Amsterdam, Netherlands: Elsevier.

Chao-Béroff, R. 1996. *Village Banks in Pays Dogon: A Successful Home-Grown Approach.* CGAP Newsletter no. 2. CGAP Secretariat, Washington, D.C.

Cox, D., and E. Jiménez. 1992. "Social Security and Private Transfers in Developing Countries: The Case of Peru." *World Bank Economic Review* 6 (January): 155–69.

Czukas, K., M. Fafchamps, and C. Udry. 1995. "Drought and Saving in West Africa: Are Livestock Really a Buffer Stock?" Northwestern University and Stanford University. Unpublished.

Eswaran, M., and A. Kotwal. 1990. "Implications of Credit Constraints for Risk Behavior in Less-Developed Countries." *Oxford Economic Papers* 42.

Goetz, A. M., and R. Sen Gupta. 1996. "Who Takes the Credit? Gender, Power and Control over Loan Use in Rural Credit Programs in Bangladesh." *World Development* 24 (January): 45–63.

Hazell, P. B. R. 1992. "The Appropriate Role of Agricultural Insurance in Developing Countries." *Journal of International Development* 4 (April): 567–81.

Hazell, P. B. R., C. Pomareda, and A. Valdes, eds. 1983. *Crop Insurance for Agricultural Development: Issues and Experience.* Baltimore, MD: Johns Hopkins University Press.

Minten, B. 1998. *Accessibilité au marché des produits agricoles et prix aux producteurs dans les villages ruraux à Madagascar.* IFPRI/FOFIFA Working Paper no. 17. Ministry of Scientific Research and FOFIFA, Antananarivo, Madagascar, and IFPRI, Washington, D.C.

Morduch, J. 1995. "Income Smoothing and Consumption Smoothing." *Journal of Economic Perspectives* 9 (3): 103–14.

Nelson, C., and others. 1996. *Village Banking—The State of Practice.* New York: SEEP Network and UNIFEM.

Rashid, M., and R. M. Townsend. 1993. "Targeting Credit and Insurance: Efficiency, Mechanism Design, and Program Evaluation." World Bank and University of Chicago. Unpublished.

Rosenzweig, M., and K. I. Wolpin. 1993. "Credit Market Constraints, Consumption Smoothing, and the Accumulation of Durable Production Assets in Low-Income Countries: Investments in Bullocks in India." *Journal of Political Economy* 101 (February): 213–24.

Sharma, M., and G. Schrieder. 2000. "Impact of Access to Credit on Household Income, Food Security and Nutrition: A Review of Empirical Evidence." In M. Zeller and others, eds., *Innovations in Microfinance for the Rural Poor: Exchange of Knowledge and Implications for Policy.* Proceedings of a workshop organized by the German Foundation for Development (DSE), the International Food Policy Research Institute (IFPRI), the International Fund for Agricultural Development (IFAD), and the Bank of Ghana, held in Accra, Ghana, 1998. DSE, Feldafing, Germany.

Townsend, R. M. 1995. "Financial Systems in Northern Thai Villages." *Quarterly Journal of Economics* 110 (November): 1011–46.

Udry, C. 1990. "Credit Markets in Northern Nigeria: Credit as Insurance in a Rural Economy." *World Bank Economic Review* (November): 251–59.

Walker, T. S., and N. S. Jodha. 1983. "How Small Farm Households Adapt to Risk." In P. B. R. Hazell, C. Pomareda, and A. Valdes, eds., *Crop Insurance for Agricultural Development: Issues and Experience.* Baltimore, MD: Johns Hopkins University Press.

Wisniwski, S., and A. Hannig. 2000. "Successful Mobilization of Small and Micro-savings: Experiences from Seven Deposit-Taking Institutions." In M. Zeller and others, eds., *Innovations in Microfinance for the Rural Poor: Exchange of Knowledge and Implications for Policy.* Proceedings of a workshop organized by the German Foundation for Development (DSE), the International Food Policy Research Institute (IFPRI), the International Fund for Agricultural Development (IFAD), and the Bank of Ghana, Ghana, November. DSE, Feldafing, Germany.

Zeller, M. 1998. "Determinants of Repayment Performance in Credit Groups: The Role of Program Design, Intragroup Risk Pooling, and Social Cohesion." *Economic Development and Cultural Change* 46 (April): 599–620.

Zeller, M., and M. Sharma. 1998. "Rural Finance and Poverty Alleviation." *Food Policy Report.* Washington: International Food Policy Research Institute (IFPRI).

Zeller, M., and others. 1997. "Rural Finance for Food Security of the Poor: Implications for Research and Policy." *Food Policy Review* 4. International Food Policy Research Institute (IFPRI), Washington, D.C.

CHAPTER TEN

Consumption Smoothing and Extended Families: The Role of Government-Sponsored Insurance

Orazio Attanasio and José-Víctor Ríos-Rull

The main aim of this chapter is to provide a conceptual framework to evaluate the provision of aggregate insurance schemes within environments characterized by both aggregate and idiosyncratic risk. Obviously the results we provide cannot be fully general, as they will depend on the particular institutional features that we discuss in our model. Our framework, however, stresses that to evaluate the desirability and the design of various insurance schemes, one has to pay attention to the way in which such schemes interact with existing private (and often informal) insurance mechanisms.

We focus on a situation in which individuals facing idiosyncratic risk can partly diversify it by entering a contractual agreement with another agent. The contract we study, however, cannot fully achieve the best possible allocation within the pair because of the presence of enforceability problems. In equilibrium, some agents will enter into pairwise relationships from which they have no incentives to deviate. We characterize the equilibrium and show that the amount of idiosyncratic risk that can be insured away depends, among other things, on the difference between the individual's intertemporal welfare and the amount she would achieve under "autarky."[1]

José-Víctor Ríos-Rull thanks the National Science Foundation for Grant SBR-9309514 and the University of Pennsylvania Research Foundation for their support. The authors are also grateful to Fabrizio Perri for his comments and for his help with the code and to Ethan Ligon and Robert Holzmann.
[1] This result has been proved in a number of studies, such as those by Thomas and Worrall (1988); Ligon, Thomas, and Worrall (1997); and Kocherlakota (1996).

In our model, we show what the effect is of reducing aggregate uncertainty for the functioning of the private insurance mechanism.[2] As we interpret the reduction in aggregate uncertainty as the provision of a "safety net" on the part of some external agent, such as an international organization or the central government, we can view our exercise as an attempt to quantify the extent to which such mechanisms might possibly crowd out private insurance mechanisms at the risk of worsening individual welfare.

The intuition behind our results is quite simple. If the provision of a "safety net" is equivalent to the elimination of the left tail of the distribution of aggregate shocks, it is possible that it reduces the amount of idiosyncratic risk insurance achieved by an enforceability compatible private contract. In other words, the provision of aggregate insurance, as it makes "autarky" outcomes less unattractive, might make the enforceability constraint more severe. The overall effect on welfare will depend on the ratio of aggregate to idiosyncratic variance and a variety of other model parameters.

The welfare computations to evaluate a proposed safety net involve a variety of components. First of all, one has to evaluate the direct effect of the transfers involved with the scheme. Obviously, by transferring resources to individuals we are increasing their welfare. To control for this effect we consider only actuarially fair schemes: that is, in "good times" we subtract a fair insurance premium from the flow of income of the individual involved in the scheme. Second, one has to evaluate the effect on aggregate welfare of the reduction in aggregate variance and compare it to the effect of the possible increase in idiosyncratic variance caused by the worsening of the enforceability constraint. The overall effect depends on the curvature of the utility function and, once again, on the relative variance of aggregate and idiosyncratic risks.

In a related but independent paper the properties of progressive taxation are explored.[3] These taxes are not distortionary. However, they change the relevant individual endowment and therefore the value of autarky. They show that the per-

---

[2] There is a slight abuse of language here. As will become clear below, for all pairs of individuals the uncertainty is aggregate. This is because the shocks to each member of the pair are not perfectly negatively correlated as in Kocherlakota (1996). Some of the uncertainty that they face is aggregate for the pair but not for the economy as a whole. The purely aggregate uncertainty is the one that the government might attempt to insure away. Therefore, when we refer to aggregate insurance, we will be referring to the villagewide aggregates, while when we refer to idiosyncratic, we mean idiosyncratic to the pair but not to the village as a whole.

[3] Krueger and Perri (1999).

verse effect that we study in this chapter may be very pervasive. Their model is different, and they study partial insurance mechanisms that involve all agents.

The considerations above suggest that the simple provision of aggregate insurance, which just shrinks the variance of aggregate shocks without considering the possible crowding out of private insurance, is not necessarily optimum. And even when such a scheme is welfare improving, it might be worth thinking about the possibility of alternative designs for safety nets that minimize the crowding out of private arrangements to insure idiosyncratic shocks. In particular, we consider the possibility that the provider of aggregate insurance requires the joint participation of the partners in the private insurance mechanism for the aggregate insurance. The ideas proposed here are somewhat similar to those behind the "peer monitoring" proposed to overcome adverse selection problems in credit markets with asymmetric information.[4]

The design of aggregate insurance mechanisms that satisfy the condition that they not interfere with existing private insurance arrangements are by no means easy. The main problem is likely to be the identification of the particular kind of mechanisms at play in a specific situation and the number of partners involved in it.

From what we have said so far, it is clear that the empirical relevance of our results depends on a variety of characteristics that can potentially be measured. For this reason, in the last part of the chapter, we discuss the implications of our result for the design of microeconomic surveys that could eventually be used for evaluating alternative safety nets. In particular, we discuss the necessity of measuring the relative importance of aggregate and idiosyncratic variance and of identifying the existence and the operation of private insurance mechanisms.

THE MODEL

We consider a stochastic endowment economy with only one good per period, which cannot be stored. There are a large number of identical separate islands that do not communicate with each other. Except when we talk about the government budget constraint, we look only at what happens on a generic island. Each island is populated by a large number of agents, normalized to be of measure one. Some of these agents are *paired* with another agent; by this we mean that they are enabled to enter a long-term relationship that will provide partial insurance. We think of these pairs

---

[4] See Armendariz and Grollier (1997); Armendariz (1998); Banerjee, Besley, and Guinnane (1994).

of agents as "extended families." We assume that these pairings are given exogenously and are immutable in the sense that they cannot be created or destroyed, and that not all agents are paired. A fraction $2\mu < 1$ of the agents is paired with one and only one other agent. The measure of such pairings is then $\mu < 1/2$. This measure may vary across islands. We think of islands where μ is large as being socially very cohesive in the sense that private institutions, the extended family, provide a mechanism to partially insure their members. On the other hand, we could think of islands with low μ as being ones where private social arrangements are weaker. We think of μ as a quantity that could potentially be measured and that is prone to vary substantially across environments.

There are different kinds of shocks in this economy. Let z denote an aggregate shock with finite support in Z. Furthermore, the shock z is Markov, with transition matrix $\Gamma_{z,z'} = \text{Prob}(z_{t+1} = z' | z_t = z)$. Let $s \in S$ denote an idiosyncratic Markov shock to each household that may be multivalued, so that it can incorporate both temporary and permanent elements. This shock also has finite support. The aggregate shock z is common to all agents on the same island. Given the large number of islands, there is no aggregate uncertainty in the economy as a whole. Conditional on two consecutive realizations of the aggregate shock, we write the stochastic process for s as having transition $\Gamma_{s,z,z',s'} = \text{Prob}(s_{t+1} = s' | z_{t+1} = z', z_t = z, s_t = s)$. In each state $\{s, z\}$ agents get endowment $e(z, s)$. We write compactly $\varepsilon \equiv \{z, s\}$ and its transition $\Gamma_{\varepsilon,\varepsilon'}$.

In general, agents can observe the aggregate shock and their own idiosyncratic shock, but not other individual agents' shocks. An important exception arises in members of a pair. These agents observe each other's endowment. Perhaps the best way of thinking of membership in a pair is that members have the ability to contact each other (and remember their past actions).[5] For paired agents, we use $y_{i,j} = (z, s_i, s_j)$, with the convention that the agent with the lowest name ($i < j$) is referred to as agent 1, and the highest name as agent 2. When this is understood, we use the compact notation y and we refer to its components as $\{z(y), s_1(y), s_2(y)\}$. We also write compactly the transition matrix of the pair as $\Gamma_{y,y'}$. We denote by $\gamma^*(y)$ the stationary distribution of the shocks.[6] Moreover, the history of shocks relevant to the pair up to t is denoted by $y^t = \{y_0, y_1, \ldots, y_t\}$. We use $\pi(y^t | y_{-1})$ to denote the probability of history y^t conditional on the initial state of the economy y_{-1}.

---

[5] This assumption about the observability and record-keeping properties of the shocks prevents the endogenous formation of pairs in the economy.

[6] We make sufficient assumptions on the Γ terms to ensure that there is a unique stationary distribution and there are no cyclically moving subsets.

There is a government in this model economy. The government does not observe the idiosyncratic components of household shocks, but it does observe the island specific shock z. For now, we assume that the government does not observe whether individual agents belong to a pair or not. However, the government knows the number of individuals that are paired, that is, it knows μ. The government can raise taxes across islands and uses the receipts to make transfers. In the process, it keeps a balanced budget. Given the lack of storage, these taxes and transfers, which are in effect a form of compulsive insurance, can be no better than actuarially fair. We denote these taxes (net of transfer) by $-\tau(z)$, or $-\tau(\varepsilon)$, or $-\tau(y)$, depending on the context. However, it is understood that the tax only depends on the aggregate state. This is the only role of the large number of islands that exist in the model, to simplify the characterization of government policies.

We assume that the agents of our model maximize the expectations of a standard intertemporally separable, strictly concave and differentiable utility function, in which future expected utility is discounted at a rate $\beta < 1$:

$$(10\text{-}1) \qquad E_0\left\{\sum_t \beta^t u(c_t)\right\}.$$

For any given unpaired individual agent, we assume that there are no trading opportunities except for those involved by the government transfer. Therefore the consumption of an unpaired agent is $c(\varepsilon) = e(\varepsilon) + \tau(\varepsilon)$. We write the value of the autarkic agent recursively as

$$(10\text{-}2) \qquad \Omega(\varepsilon) = u[e(\varepsilon) + \tau(\varepsilon)] + \sum_{\varepsilon'} \Gamma_{\varepsilon,\varepsilon'}\,\Omega(\varepsilon').$$

Paired agents are affected by each other's idiosyncratic shocks and their joint consumption is restricted by the pairwise feasibility constraint that now takes the form

$$(10\text{-}3) \qquad c_1(y) + c_2(y) = e_1(y) + e_2(y) + 2\tau(y).$$

In the absence of enforceability problems, agents would equate their marginal utilities in all states of the world, taking into account the transfers from the government:

$$(10\text{-}4) \qquad \frac{u'[c_1(y)]}{u'[c_2(y)]} = \text{a constant independent of } y.$$

While it is trivial to show that any optimal allocation has to satisfy equation 10-4,[7] theory is silent on how the surplus is split. Replication arguments and equality between the agents imply that a competitive equilibrium allocation within the pair would be symmetric. In any case, we denote with $W(y, 1)$ the value of the first best that treats both types symmetrically, starting from each of the possible states y.

Notice that in such a situation an actuarially fair aggregate insurance scheme would be welfare improving, as it would diversify island risk across all the islands. From the point of view of individual agents such a scheme would be equivalent to a reduction of the variance of aggregate shocks. Both paired and unpaired agents would gain from such a scheme, given the concavity of the utility function.

We characterize the degree of enforceability of contracts between the two members of a pair by a function $P(y)$. This function denotes the cost for an individual of breaking the agreed arrangement. When $P(y) = \infty$ we are in the standard perfect enforcement case. When $P(y) = 0$ (no commitment) there are no external means to enforce those contracts and it is the typical case studied in the literature. This function can be used to study special institutions, such as the family, where certain social activities can be used to increase the costs of breaking the agreement. We further assume that if an individual breaks a contract, she will not be able to enter any similar contract in the future and will be in a state of autarky that is equivalent to the disappearance of the pair to which the agent belongs. We could think of this as the most severe subgame-perfect punishment.[8]

Besides incurring cost $P(y)$, upon breaking the contract agents get utility $\Omega[\varepsilon(y)]$. This means, among other things, that we assume that the government cannot observe who broke a contract and who did not in order to select the transfer. If this were possible, the government could use the transfer to enhance the set of privately achievable allocations by reducing the value of autarky.

The paired agents can engage in a mutually advantageous relationship that may allow them to smooth consumption even without commitment.[9] Any allocation for the pair should satisfy enforcement constraints. That means that at each

---

[7] It just follows from strict concavity and the possibility of transferring resources across dates and states.

[8] See Abreu (1988).

[9] To describe how this is done we draw from Kehoe and Perri (1997), who in turn follow the recursive approach of Marcet and Marimon (1992, 1995). The characterization of the optimal contracts in a model with imperfect enforceability is stated in different terms in Ligon, Thomas, and Worrall (1997, 2000) and Alvarez and Jermann (1997). We find the approach that keeps track of the current ratio of utility weights both more transparent and computationally easier.

point in time and in every state of the world, y^t, the members of the pair prefer the allocation they receive to autarky (after incurring in the cost $P(y_t)$ of breaking away). These enforcement constraints, therefore, take the form

(10-5) $$\sum_{r=t}^{\infty}\sum_{y^r} \beta^{r-t}\, \pi(y^r|y^t)\; u[c_i(y^r)] \geq \Omega[\varepsilon(y_r)] + P(y_t) = \hat{\Omega}[\varepsilon(y_t)].$$

Let us consider the problem of maximizing a weighted sum of utilities subject to the resource constraints and the enforcement constraints, that is, the problem of choosing allocations $\{c_1(y^t), c_2(y^t)\}$ for all y^t to solve

(10-6) $$\max_{\{c_i(y^t)\}} \lambda_1 \sum_{t=0}^{\infty}\sum_{y^t} \beta^t\, \pi(y^t)\; u[c_1(y^t)] + \lambda_2 \sum_{t=0}^{\infty}\sum_{y^t} \beta^t\, \pi(y^t)\; u[c_2(y^t)],$$

subject to equations 10-3 and 10-5, where λ_1 and λ_2 are nonnegative initial weights. We can write the Lagrangian as

(10-7)
$$\sum_{t=0}^{\infty}\sum_{y^t} \beta^t\, \pi(y^t) \left\{ \sum_{i=1}^{2} \lambda_i\, u[c_i(y^t)] \right.$$
$$\left. + \sum_{i} \mu_i(y^t) \left[\sum_{r=t}^{\infty}\sum_{y^r} \beta^{r-t}\, \pi(y^r|y^t) u[c_i(y^r)] - \hat{\Omega}_i[\varepsilon(y_r)] \right] \right\}$$

plus the standard terms that relate to the resource constraints.

Noting that $\pi(y^r|y^t)$ can be rewritten as $\pi(y^r) = \pi(y^r|y^t)\pi(y^t)$, we can rewrite the Lagrangian as

(10-8) $$\sum_{t=0}^{\infty}\sum_{y^t}\sum_{i} \beta^t\, \pi(y^t)\, \{M_i(y^{t-1})\, u[c_i(y^t)] + \mu_i(y^t)\, [u[c_i(y^t)] - \Omega_i[\varepsilon(y_r)]]\}$$

plus the terms that refer to the feasibility constraint. The newly introduced variable, $M_i(y^{t-1})$, is defined recursively as $M_i(y_{-1}) = \lambda_i$ and

(10-9) $$M_i(y^t) = M_i(y^{t-1}) + \mu_i(y^t).$$

Note that at time t, the $M_i(y^t)$ terms are equal to the original weights plus the cumulative sum of the Lagrange multipliers on the enforcement constraint at all periods from 1 to t. The first-order conditions that can be derived from this modified Lagrangian include

(10-10)
$$\frac{u'[c_1(y^t)]}{u'[c_2(y^t)]} = \frac{M_2(y^{t-1}) + \mu_2(y^t)}{M_1(y^{t-1}) + \mu_1(y^t)}$$

in addition to the complementary slackness conditions. The next step consists of renormalizing the enforceability multipliers by defining

(10-11)
$$\varphi_i(y^t) = \frac{\mu_i(y^t)}{M_i(y^t)} \quad \text{and} \quad x(y^t) = \frac{M_2(y^t)}{M_1(y^t)}.$$

The virtue of this normalization is that it allows us to keep track only of the relative weight x. Its transition law can be written as

(10-12)
$$x(y^t) = \frac{[1 - \varphi_1(y^t)]}{[1 - \varphi_2(y^t)]} x(y^{t-1})$$

by noting that $[1 - \varphi_1(y^t)] M(y^t) = M(y^{t-1})$.

We are now in a position to write this problem recursively. To do so we define a mapping from values into values, to a fixed point at which the value functions characterize the solution to our problem. To solve our model numerically, as we do in the next section, we actually follow this procedure, that is, we iterate from a certain initial set of value functions. Successive approximations have yielded in every case the desired fixed point. The state variables are the current value of the shocks y (recall that, due to the fact that the shocks are Markov, their current value is sufficient to evaluate conditional expectations) and the current value of the relative weights x. We use three value functions, one for the planner, denote it $V(y, x)$; and one each for the agents, denote them $V_i(y, x)$. These functions satisfy the following property:

(10-13)
$$V(y, x) = V_1(y, x) + x V_2(y, x).$$

To update the value functions, that is, to obtain $T(V)$, $T(V_1)$, and $T(V_2)$, we first solve the following auxiliary problem, where no incentive constraints are taken into account:

(10-14)
$$\Phi(y,x) = \max_{c_1,c_2} u(c_1) + x\, u(c_2) + \beta \sum_{y'} \Gamma_{y,y'}\, V(y',x),$$

subject to the feasibility constraint (10-3), with solution c_i^{Φ}. Note that in this problem the relative weight x is constant. Next, we verify the enforceability of the solution to equation 10-14. This means verifying whether

(10-15)
$$u[c_i^{\Phi}(y,x)] + \beta \sum_{y'} \Gamma_{y,y'}\, V_i\,(y',x) \geq \hat{\Omega}[\varepsilon(y)] \quad \text{for } i = 1,2\,.$$

If equation 10-15 is satisfied, then $T(V) = \Phi(y,x)$, and $T(V_1)$ and $T(V_2)$ are given by its left-hand side. It is easy to see that equation 10-15 cannot be violated for both agents at the same time (just note that autarky is a feasible allocation). The only remaining problem is to update the value functions when the constraint is binding for one of the agents, say agent 1. In this case, we solve the following system of equations in $\{c_1, c_2, x'\}$:

(10-16)
$$\hat{\Omega}[\varepsilon(y)] = u(c_1) + \beta \sum_{y'} \Gamma_{y,y'}\, V_1(y',x')$$

(10-17)
$$x' = \frac{u'(c_1)}{u'(c_2)}$$

(10-18)
$$c_1 + c_2 = e_1(y) + e_2(y) + 2\tau(y)$$

with solution $\{c_1^*, c_2^*, x^{*'}\}$.[10] To update the value functions we let

(10-19)
$$T(V_1)(y,x) = u(c_1^*) + \beta \sum_{y'} \Gamma_{y,y'}\, V_1(y',x^{*'})$$

(10-20)
$$T(V_2)(y,x) = u(c_2^*) + \beta \sum_{y'} \Gamma_{y,y'}\, V_2(y',x^{*'})$$

---

[10] There will typically be only one solution, given the monotonicity of all the functions involved.

(10-21) $$T(V)(y,x) = V_1(y,x) + x\, V_2(y,x).$$

A fixed point of operator T gives us the value for the problem of maximizing a weighted sum of utilities.[11] Moreover, it also gives us a way to completely characterize the properties of such a solution by numerical methods. This means that for any parameterization we can tell whether the enforceable allocation is autarky, the first best, or anything in between. We can also study how the enforceable allocations are affected by changes in the environment.

One question that remains is how this allocation is actually implemented. Like in the first best, the theory is silent about how to split the surplus initially. Let's assume a symmetric split. This means that the starting value for x is 1. From there a contract can be implemented by a state-contingent transfer, say $\theta(y, x)$, that specifies what agent 1 gives to agent 2 (it can be negative) when the state is given by the pair $\{y, x\}$. This transfer is just the difference between the endowment and the solution to the problem above. The law of motion for the state variable x is also given by the procedure described above.

This completes our description of the model and its solution. The steps between equation 10-13 and equation 10-19 reflect the steps of the simulation program we use below to characterize the quantitative properties of some examples.

GOVERNMENT-PROVIDED INSURANCE

In the model above, we considered a particular form of government insurance. In particular, we assumed an actuarially fair insurance that depends only on aggregate shocks and that is distributed uniformly across individuals. In this section we evaluate this type of scheme and show that it can crowd out private insurance and, potentially, lead to a decrease in aggregate welfare. Obviously, the one we consider is not the only possible insurance scheme. On the one hand, it can be argued that it might be important to consider transfers that simply provide relief in exceptional circumstances, such as natural disasters. If these transfers were financed by international organizations, it would not be necessary to consider the premium that an actuarially fair insurance would imply in good times. Furthermore, a naive and careless insurance scheme in some circumstances might bring about a reduction in

---

[11] See Marcet and Marimon (1992, 1995) for details.

welfare by simply overinsuring the agents in the economy. On the other hand, one might argue that the government could devise more complicated insurance schemes to avoid or minimize possible interference by an aggregate scheme with the functioning of private insurance mechanisms.

As far as the first objection is concerned, it should be stressed that a simple transfer is very likely, especially if large in size, to increase the welfare of the agents who receive it. By focusing on an actuarially fair scheme, we want to consider not just the possible benefits of a proposed scheme but also its costs. Moreover, stressing the possible crowding out effects that an aggregate insurance scheme might have allows us to focus on its inefficiencies and possible ways to improve it. That is, regardless of whether a proposed insurance scheme increases or decreases welfare, the presence of crowding-out effects stresses that such a scheme might be suboptimal and, subject to some caveats, could be improved.

These considerations lead us to the second objection, the subject of the next two subsections. Under "A More Sophisticated Scheme," we consider more complex schemes that attempt to avoid the problems considered under "Simple Aggregate Insurance." It should be stressed, however, that in this respect the assumptions made about the information held by the government are crucial. Obviously, if the government were able to observe idiosyncratic shocks, or even observe who deviated from private insurance arrangements, it would be trivial to construct schemes that would avoid crowding out. Under "A More Sophisticated Scheme" we only consider situations in which the government does not observe idiosyncratic shocks or is unable to identify the individual responsible for the breaking up of an extended family. Indeed, we consider a situation in which the government does not even observe membership of an extended family. We assume only that the government has information on the nature of the various shocks and on the extent to which private arrangements are able to diversify idiosyncratic risk.

Simple Aggregate Insurance

In this subsection we describe the effects of a simple aggregate insurance scheme of the kind discussed above. The effect that simple aggregate insurance schemes might have on welfare and on the performance of the economy described by our model is complex and depends on a variety of factors. In particular, in addition to preferences, the effects depend crucially on the properties of the aggregate shocks and how they interact with individual shocks, on the amount of individual risk that can be diversified in equilibrium, and on the relative importance of aggregate and idiosyncratic shocks. The full characterization of the effects of the introduction of a government-sponsored insurance policy can only be done, within our model, with numerical simulations.

We are mainly interested in the long-term properties of the policies and not necessarily in those of the transition, that is, we define the properties of a policy in terms of the long-term averages that it implies. As the stationary distribution of the equilibrium values is hard to compute analytically, to compute these long-run averages we simulate the model economy for long periods of time. Different policies are valued by starting the economy at the same initial condition and letting it run for a long time. We plan to investigate the issues involved with the introduction of the policy in future work.[12]

Before presenting the numerical results, it is possible and useful to discuss the intuition behind them and describe the effects of aggregate insurance in some special cases. As we discussed above, the presence of enforceability constraints has the effect of limiting the amount of idiosyncratic risk that individuals can diversify by entering the private arrangements available to them in our model. The main reason for this is that the contracts individuals enter have to satisfy the constraint that each individual will never have the incentive to default and walk away from the arrangement.

The amount of risk sharing that can be achieved by these types of contracts depends on a variety of parameters, such as the discount factor, the variance and persistence of idiosyncratic and aggregate risk, and the cost of default (over and above the loss from being excluded from future contracts). In particular, we can construct scenarios in which either the full insurance outcome is reached or no private contract is possible. This is done in a very simple way by varying the dis-

---

[12] This means asking what the effects of a switch of policies are (for the introduction of a policy, we think of the previous one as being $\tau(y) = 0$ for all y). Doing this means taking into account that the economy is in some state at the time of the introduction of the new policy. In terms of our model, this implies that at a point of time, the island economy is characterized by an aggregate shock z, a distribution of unpaired individuals over their idiosyncratic shocks s with total measure $1 - \mu$, and a distribution of paired individuals over the pairs of idiosyncratic shocks and the current state of their relative weights x. This state is stochastic and depends on the history of shocks. To analyze policy switches, we will then generate a large number of possible initial states by simulation.

This is an important question, since there is no unique solution to the problem of which allocation gets picked by each paired household. We will follow the principle of maintaining the relative weight that households have. The problem shows up because the new policy will have changed the relevant range where x lies. We will assume that the share of the newly defined surplus is the one that obtains from keeping the relative weights x between the agents.

the form of occupational pensions, have a large role in reducing poverty, especially in the Netherlands, but also in the United Kingdom, Canada, Germany, and the United States. Social retirement still plays the largest role, but in Sweden, the United Kingdom, Canada, France, and Spain, social assistance also plays a not-insignificant role among the elderly.

Education and Income Sources

Our final breakdowns of poverty are by education status of the head of the household. Cross-national levels of education are not coded in a comparable way in any data set. In some, for example, the United Kingdom data set used by LIS, age of leaving school is the only variable that is present. However, two recent LIS papers have re-coded education into low, medium, and high levels and have assessed the robustness of these results.[16] We use these classifications in table 11–3.[17]

There is a clear and pronounced relationship between poverty status and head's educational attainment. The largest differences across education groups show up in the first column. Higher levels of education produce lower household poverty rates in every nation and this effect is most pronounced in the high-poverty nations like the United States, where there is a more than sixfold difference between the MI-based poverty status of the least educated compared with the highest educated. In every country smaller but similar differences occur, with single-digit MI-based poverty rates appearing in Germany and Spain as well. Tax and transfer policy reduces MI poverty in all nations and with similar "percentage change" has an impact across education categories in most nations. But the largest drops in the absolute numbers of the poor owing to tax and transfer policy take place among the least educated in most nations. Only in the United States do we find the lowest educated receiving the least antipoverty effect for social protection systems relative to other groups.

The net effect of education on MI plus taxes and transfers reduces poverty to 7 percent or less for the highly educated in all nations studied here. The least educated reach single-digit poverty rates only in Sweden. In every other nation, those with the least education have poverty rates of 10.8 percent or more, with rates of 25

---

[16] O'Connor (1994); Sullivan and Smeeding (1997).

[17] The actual re-codes of LIS education variables into these categories are available on the LIS website (http://www.lis.ceps.lu) or from Sullivan and Smeeding (1997), which is also available online from this same source.

Table 11–3. Household Poverty Rates by Income Source and Education Level of Household Head

Percentage of household heads 25 to 64 years old

Country, year, education level	Market income (A)	Column (A) + private income transfers (B)	Column (B) + universal and social transfers (C)	Column (C) − taxes (D)	Column (D) + social assistance transfers (E)	Percent change in columns A to E (F)
Australia, 1994						
Low	31.6	30.9	30.9	32.0	20.3	−35.8
Medium	15.9	14.9	14.9	16.7	10.4	−34.6
High	12.6	11.0	11.0	11.5	7.0	−44.4
Overall	23.2	22.2	22.2	22.8	14.8	−36.2
Canada, 1994						
Low	40.2	36.5	27.0	28.7	24.9	−38.1
Medium	20.7	18.1	12.9	14.2	12.3	−40.6
High	11.1	8.7	7.0	7.6	6.9	−37.8
Overall	23.9	21.1	15.4	16.6	14.5	−39.3
Germany, 1994						
Low	32.4	30.5	20.1	22.5	18.5	−42.9
Medium	18.2	17.3	9.5	11.1	8.3	−53.3
High	8.3	5.5	3.5	5.9	5.5	−33.7
Overall	19.0	17.7	10.3	12.1	9.4	−50.5
The Netherlands, 1991						
Low	39.4	32.4	15.9	19.6	10.8	−72.6
Medium	18.7	14.0	7.3	8.9	5.2	−72.2
High	12.8	10.6	6.5	8.7	4.5	−64.8
Overall	24.1	19.1	9.8	12.2	6.9	−71.4
Spain, 1990[a]						
Low	28.3	27.4	13.9	—	13.2	−53.4
Medium	10.0	8.8	4.6	—	4.5	−55.0
High	5.3	4.2	2.2	—	2.2	−58.5
Overall	23.1	22.1	11.3	—	10.8	−53.2

Sweden, 1992						
Low	26.4	26.1	5.3	10.4	5.1	−80.7
Medium	19.5	18.7	4.0	6.7	3.2	−83.6
High	11.8	11.5	5.1	6.2	2.5	−78.8
Overall	20.7	20.1	5.0	8.5	3.8	−81.6
United States, 1994						
Low	52.5	50.9	46.4	49.8	46.0	−12.4
Medium	23.0	20.5	17.6	19.9	18.2	−20.9
High	8.1	6.3	5.5	6.6	6.2	−23.5
Overall	23.2	21.0	18.4	20.5	18.9	−18.5

— Not available.

a. Tax information is not available for Spain, 1990.

Note: Poverty is measured at 50 percent of median-adjusted household disposable income. The three education levels are low, medium, and high attainment. For the United States, the break between low and medium is completion of high school, and between medium and high, the completion of a bachelor's degree in college. This conceptual definition transfers to Canada and Australia fairly well but less so to European countries. For example, a liberal definition of high, when applied to the Swedish and Dutch data, includes some persons with something similar to the American two-year associate's degree. At the same time, the German system relies more heavily on vocational education, and many German workers without a university degree possess job skills comparable to American college graduates of the same age. For details, see Sullivan and Smeeding (1997) and O'Connor (1994). See table 11A–1 in the appendix to this chapter for definitions of income categories and poverty rates. All households are headed by an adult, 25 to 64 years old.

Source: Authors' calculations.

percent in Canada and 46 percent in the United States. Clearly the better educated are the least poor, often by a wide margin, in every nation studied here.

Summary

The LIS data reveal a rich and varied pattern of social protection among the nations examined. Self-protection, in the form of low MI or pre-tax and transfer poverty rates, produces the best results for the highly educated and for childless couples, extended families, and households with at least one full-time earner. While they may not always be classified as a social protection, the labor market and the extended family are clearly strong antipoverty devices in all rich nations. Full employment policies and extended family have definite measurable economic benefits.

   Private transfers and taxes largely offset one another for most nonelderly groups. Social assistance plays a large and often significant role in many nations (for example, Australia, the United Kingdom) and for some specific groups (for example, single parents, elderly). But two factors seem to hold the most promise for poverty reduction: the education system, which directly produces lower MI-based poverty in every country; and the overall expense, extent, and generosity of the social insurance system, which provides the bulk of antipoverty effect for working-age adults (including those who are not at all employed) and for the elderly in all nations (with the singular exception of Australia). While many nations have responded well to the "traditional" needs for social protection, for example, old age, extended unemployment, and disability, not all have done so. And only Sweden, and to a far lesser extent France, Spain, and the Netherlands, appear to have dealt at all well with social protection against the "new risk" of single parenthood.[18]

DISCUSSION AND CONCLUSION

The ultimate question posed for this chapter seems to be, what, if any, lessons can social protection policy for the poor in the developing world take from the social protection policies and results in the developed world? The short answer is, that

---

[18] Overbye (1997).

depends. Here we assess the findings above in light of the institutional, demographic, and economic situation of the developing world.

Expansive social insurance systems are a double-edged sword. On the one hand, large amounts of social protection have strong antipoverty effects as demonstrated above. While extensive social insurance systems prevent widespread poverty for most groups, without the problems of stigma or take-up found in social assistance schemes, three negative factors associated with these programs need also be taken into account: their aggregate expense; their effect on labor markets; and the current nonsustainability of social insurance for the aged in pay-as-you-go pension schemes. We will deal with each in turn.

As seen in figure 11–2, the more that a nation spends on social protection, the better the antipoverty effects for working-age adults and for the elderly and near elderly. But social protection is expensive: more than 12 percent of GDP for cash programs for the nonelderly alone in the Netherlands and Sweden; 18 to 21 percent of GDP or more in overall elderly and nonelderly cash outlays in the United Kingdom, France, and Germany; and 25 percent or more in Sweden and the Netherlands. And this does not count public expenditure for health care or public education. These large outlays have significant effects on labor markets in three ways.

First and foremost, large social retirement systems, complete with early retirement (at 55 or over) in the guise of disability transfers or unemployment insurance (or clearly stated as "early retirement" or "unemployment retirement" benefits), have reduced labor force participation for men at relatively young ages throughout Europe and Scandinavia. One striking statistic: only 16 percent of Dutch men 61 or over participate in the labor force. In the Netherlands, France, Germany, and many other European nations, the fraction of men who work is now less than 35 percent for 62-year-olds.[19] The extension of early retirement benefits leads to work stoppage in every nation studied, but especially in the high-unemployment nations of northern and central Europe. Here "joblessness" is passively fought by finance ministers and social ministers with social insurance programs, which effectively remove most older workers from the labor market. In the face of ever-expanding life expectancy in old age, these policies suggest the strong possibility of near future fiscal catastrophe as suggested below.

Second, extended unemployment benefits are notorious for their negative effects on work and labor supply behavior in such diverse nations as Poland and

---

[19] See Gruber and Wise (1998); Smeeding and Quinn (1998).

Canada.[20] Another rule of thumb is that the more recent the study, the greater the negative effects of social insurance on labor markets. Disability insurance at younger ages has similar impacts in every rich nation.[21]

Finally, income-tested (or means-tested) social assistance has negative effects on work in most nations, though these are probably of a lesser magnitude than is popularly believed. Some nations, for example, Sweden and France, have found good ways to mix work and income support for low-income single parents (or couples). Canada has found ways to phase out universal and social insurance policies such as child allowances and extended unemployment insurance at higher income levels.[22] Most nations, however, for example, the United Kingdom, have not done well on this front, creating social assistance systems with severe work disincentives or so-called poverty traps. Whether U.S.-style "welfare reform" will work in these nations is open to question.

Hence, the costs of reduced labor supply must be counted in when assessing such programs. Unfortunately, the negative effects of income transfers on work effort are not well studied in any of these nations. Robert Moffitt finds modest negative effects in the United States, where the tax and transfer system is the smallest of the nations studied.[23] An early comparative study of the United States and the Netherlands found large negative effects of the Dutch tax and transfer system on work effort compared to the United States.[24] But we know of no later similar studies for the overall transfer systems of other nations covered, much less for developing countries.

Most of the "classic" studies of the work-reducing effects of social transfers are largely out of date.[25] Many focus to a large extent on the third type of problem mentioned above—that is, social assistance—at the expense of studying extended unemployment or retirement income. The work-reducing effects of early retirement are also largely ignored in several studies.[26] The third major shortcoming of expansive pay-as-you-go social insurance systems for the elderly is their economic and demographic nonsustainability. The United States publicly worries about a

---

[20] Schmidt and Gora (1998); Lemieux and MacLeod (1998).
[21] Aarts, Burkhauser, and de Jong (1996).
[22] Banting (1997).
[23] Moffitt (1992).
[24] Haveman (1985).
[25] Danziger, Haveman, and Plotnick (1981).
[26] For example, Atkinson and Mogenson (1993); Burtless and Haveman (1987); and Moffitt (1992).

projected 2 percent of GDP shortfall between revenues and expenses for social retirement in the year 2030. The Germans, French, Canadians, and Dutch only wish
their situation were so favorable. Early retirement and generous benefits mix with
ever-growing life expectancy at older ages and declining birthrates to produce revenue shortfalls of 4 to 6 percent of GDP for social retirement schemes over this
same horizon in these nations.[27] Even at this time, attempts to raise retirement ages,
cut pensions, or build in added tiers for occupational retirement are meeting increased resistance.

Finally, we should mention measures to address the "new risks" of rich societies: social protection for single parents and work-enabling policies for mothers,
married and unmarried.[28] Few Western nations have met this challenge in a meaningful way. Child support by absent parents is either largely unpaid (United States,
Canada) or subsumed by "advance maintenance" social insurance benefits, which
provide for guarantees in the absence of payment by absent parents while more or
less ignoring the parental obligation.[29] The problem of adequate levels of support
for single parents is an issue that is unsolved by most rich societies.[30]

In summary, Western-style tax and transfer systems are not currently
budgetarily affordable by developing nations, and they are liable to have large economic costs in any case. While classic tax and transfer social protection systems are
liable to have large automatic stability effects on consumption levels, they are also
liable to retard economic growth in the developing world. Fortunately a more modest
set of policies also offers promises of universal social protection at lower costs.

---

[27] Smeeding and Sullivan (1998).
[28] Overbye (1997).
[29] Skévik (1997).
[30] For example, Smeeding and others (1998).

APPENDIX. DIFFERENCES IN CONCEPTS OF WELL-BEING AND POVERTY BETWEEN RICH AND POOR NATIONS

The measurement of economic poverty in all nations, rich or poor, involves the calculation of economic well-being or resources relative to needs. Economic well-being refers to the material resources available to households. (We use the terms *household* and *family* interchangeably. Our formal unit of aggregation is the household—all persons living together and sharing the same housing facilities—in almost all nations. Only in Sweden does "household" refer to a more narrow definition of the "family" unit.) The concern with these resources is not with material consumption itself but rather with the capabilities they give household members to participate in their societies.[31] These capabilities are inputs to social activities, and participation in these activities produces a particular level of well-being.[32] Measurement of these capabilities differs according to the context in which one chooses to measure them, particularly within rich nations compared with poor ones.

All advanced or rich societies are highly stratified socially. Some individuals have more resources than others. The opportunities for social participation are vitally affected by the resources at the disposal of the family, particularly in nations like the United States, where there is heavy reliance on the market to purchase such social goods as health care, education, and child care services.[33] Money income is the central resource in these societies. But there are still other important kinds of resources, such as social capital, noncash benefits, education, and access to basic health care, all of which add to human capabilities.[34] There are also many forces in rich societies that reduce well-being by limiting capabilities to participate fully in society, such as violent geographically and socially isolated neighborhoods and poor quality public education. Earnings and job instability also increase economic insecurity in many rich countries.

In poor nations, where poverty is more basic—often the difference between life and death—real consumption of food and shelter is the preferred measure of well-being. Economic poverty emerges and is measured by having too few resources for survival or living on life's edge. Here life expectancy, mortality rates at young ages, lack of access to public health, illiteracy, and other basic measures of poverty

---

[31] Sen (1992).
[32] Rainwater (1990); Coleman, Rainwater, and McClelland (1978).
[33] Rainwater (1974).
[34] Coleman (1988).

and social exclusion are much more common and much more easily measured than is income. And social capital in the form of family support may be the major form of social protection in developing countries, particularly in rural communities.

In rich societies, lower life expectancy and higher infant mortality are also correlated with poverty, though to a lesser extent than in developing countries.[35] But in rich countries, consumption—or the ability to consume—is the key measure of economic resources and the ability to avoid poverty, while income—consumption plus change in net worth—brings with it more complicated issues of period of measurement and life cycle considerations. However, income is a much more appropriate and, we would argue, more easily measured index of well-being for rich nations than is consumption.[36] Further, an emphasis on income, in addition to consumption, allows researchers to focus not only on today's consumption but also on ability to protect future consumption, that is, savings and access to credit markets.

In rich nations, one measures poverty based on annual disposable money income. Detailed comparable information exists on money income by source, taxes paid, and certain kinds of transfers that have a cashlike character, such as housing allowances, fuel assistance, and food stamps. We do not take into account the major in-kind benefits that are available in most countries, such as health care, education, day care and preschool, and general subsidies to housing. To the extent that the level and distribution of these resources are different in different countries, our analysis of money income must be treated with some caution. But since we are interested in the effects of safety nets on poverty, we prefer instead a measure of poverty that focuses on the short-term responsiveness of governments and other agencies in providing social protection to the poor.

Equivalence Scales and Economies of Scale

Households differ not only in terms of resources but also in terms of their needs. We take differing needs, owing to differences in household size and other factors (for example, urban-rural differences), into account by adjusting income for family size using an equivalence scale. The adjustment for household size is designed to account for the different requirements families of different sizes and different circumstances have for participating in society at a given level. Different equivalence scales will yield different distributions of well-being. Several studies in Europe, the

---

[35] Jung and Smeeding (1999).
[36] See Johnson and Smeeding (1998) on this topic.

United States, and Australia point to an equivalence scale that implies fairly large economies of scale in the conversion of money incomes to social participation among families with children and also among the aged.[37] Because choice of equivalence scale may favor small versus large families, depending on which scale is selected, we aim to find a middle ground value that is appropriate for measuring vulnerability for both large families (for example, those with two or more children) and smaller units (for example, single elderly women living alone).

Buhmann and others have proposed that disposable income be adjusted for family size in the following way:[38]

$$\text{Adjusted income} = \text{disposable income}/\text{size}^E.$$

The equivalence elasticity, or "equivalence factor," E, varies between 0 and 1; the larger is E, the smaller are the economies of scale assumed by the equivalence scale. The various studies reviewed in the survey make use of equivalence scales for analyses of per capita income ranging from E = 0 (or no adjustment for size) to E = 1 (which ignores all economies of scale).[39] Between these extremes, the range of possible values is evenly covered. The reader should keep in mind that all money income estimates in this chapter are based on adjusted or equivalent income calculated according to the above formula.

The obvious question is which measure of E to use for this study. Following Anthony Atkinson, Lee Rainwater, and Timothy Smeeding, we have selected an E value of 0.5, similar to that used by the OECD and Eurostat. For the most part, national rankings by *overall* poverty rates are not sensitive to the measure of E selected.[40]

However, subgroup poverty rates are very sensitive to the choice of equivalence scale. As demonstrated in appendix figure 11A–1 for Spain, poverty rates among the elderly (usually small families in rich nations) and children (larger families, particularly in developing nations and in richer Catholic nations) vary systematically according to the level of the equivalence factor. When E = 0, there are complete economies of scale and smaller households have higher poverty rates

---

[37] Buhmann and others (1988); Bradbury (1989); Rainwater (1990). For the aged see Burkhauser, Smeeding, and Merz (1996).

[38] Buhmann and others (1988).

[39] Buhmann and others (1988); Atkinson, Rainwater, and Smeeding (1995).

[40] Atkinson, Rainwater, and Smeeding (1995, especially chapters 2, 3, and 7). For OECD see Förster (1993), and for Eurostat see Hagenaars, De Vos, and Zaidi (1994). See also Burkhauser, Smeeding, and Merz (1996).

(owing to the correlation between income and household size) than do larger ones. The opposite result is obtained at higher levels of the equivalence factor, all the way to E = 1, where there are no economies of scale and each additional person needs as much as the first person to be nonpoor. Two important notes can be added. First of all, this same relationship obtains for every rich nation; the crossing of the lines in figure 11A–1 is not unique to Spain. Second, there is far too little research on the appropriate measure of E in developing nations. Simplistic measures of poverty such as "$1.50 per person per day" imply E = 1 equivalence scales and hence the likelihood of family size biases apparent in figure 11A–1.[41]

Having defined equivalent income in this way, we determine the equivalent income of all households and all individuals in each country. We then examine the distribution of equivalent incomes of households and of persons in households in relation to the selected poverty line. That is, we tabulate the percentage of persons who have given characteristics and the percentage of households with given characteristics. In technical terms, our person calculations are weighted by the number of persons of each type (all persons including children, adults, elderly) residing in each household type.

Relative versus Absolute Poverty

Needs can be measured in two ways, an absolute definition and a relative definition. Relative poverty involves deciding on the income concept for relativity (median or mean) and on the fraction of adjusted income that signifies poverty. Absolute poverty measurement means locating the "absolute" poverty line and then converting that poverty line into national currency.

We rely here on a relative concept of poverty, the percentage of persons with incomes below half of median income. This income is in line with a well-established theoretical perspective on poverty.[42] Such a measure is now commonly calculated by the European Commission, by the OECD, and by other international groups.[43] Only the British and one other major international study use a fraction of mean income as a standard, though Cantillion and others use both mean and median income–based poverty rates in their study.[44]

---

[41] World Bank (1990); Ravallion, Datt, and van de Walle (1991).
[42] Sen (1992); Townsend (1979).
[43] Hagenaars, De Vos, and Zaidi (1994); Ramprakash (1995); Förster (1993).
[44] Cantillion, Marx, and van den Bosch (1996).

In fact, most studies use the "average," or median, household as the point of reference, as do we. Using the average, or mean, income means measuring social distance from something other than the average household. Moreover, the decision to use one measure versus the other can lead to quite different results in poverty trends when inequality is changing. In the United States from 1973 to 1994, the mean income grew 15 percent more than the median income, thus ensuring that poverty measured relative to the mean grew much more than poverty relative to the median.[45]

The determination of "absolute" poverty lines requires both the selection of an absolute poverty line in one currency and its translation into other currencies. Such translations rely on "purchasing power parties" (PPPs), such as those constructed by Robert Summers and Alan Heston or by the OECD.[46] However, PPPs are based on aggregated data and income (consumption) concepts that are not well suited for use with microdata, which are highly sensitive to the price deflator used when rapid inflation takes place (as is often the case in Latin America), and which are sensitive to the overall quality of the income data reported on the survey in question. Hence, we rely on the relative poverty–based headcount measure alone.

While we stress the half of median measure, we use one additional measure of relative poverty to test the sensitivity of our headcount measures to alternative poverty lines. Forty percent of the median is chosen for comparison because it is almost exactly the ratio of the United States poverty line to the United States median. This poverty measure is used in figure 11–1 and table 11A–3.

---

[45] Burtless (1996).
[46] Summers and Heston (1991); OECD (1986).

FIGURE 11A–1.
Poverty Rates as a Function of the Equivalence Factor, Spain, 1990

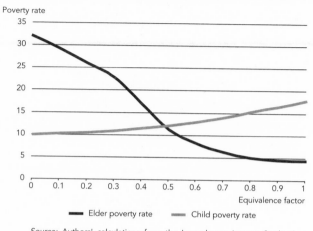

Source: Authors' calculations from the Luxembourg Income Study. See Smeeding and others (1998).

FIGURE 11A–2.
Relationship between Social Expenditure as a Percent of GDP and Poverty Reduction among Nonelderly Persons

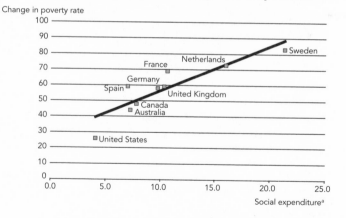

a. Social expenditure as a percent of GDP is taken from OECD (1999). The most recent year is used in cases where the exact year is not available. Social expenditure includes all public cash and near-cash expenditure for social protection. Health care is excluded. Poverty reduction is measured by the percentage reduction in poverty rates between market income and disposable income-based poverty rates (last column of table 11–2).
Source: Authors' calculations from the Luxembourg Income Study. See Smeeding and others (1998).

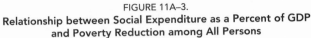

FIGURE 11A–3.
Relationship between Social Expenditure as a Percent of GDP and Poverty Reduction among All Persons

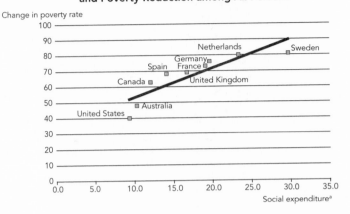

a. Social expenditure as a percent of GDP is taken from OECD (1999). The most recent year is used when the exact year is not available. Social expenditure includes all public cash and near-cash expenditure for social protection except for those received by the aged and survivors. Health care is also excluded. Poverty reduction is measured by the percentage reduction in poverty rates between market income and disposable income poverty (last column of table 11–2).
Source: Authors' calculations from the Luxembourg Income Study. See Smeeding and others (1998).

Table 11A–1. Poverty Measurement and Definitions of Categories That Affect Income

Poverty measurement

The poverty rate is the percentage of households (table 11–1), adults (tables 11–2 and 11A–4), or all persons (adults/elderly/children—figures 11–1 and 11–2 and table 11A–3) with income less than a given percent of median-adjusted disposable income for all persons. In tables 11–1 and 11–2, the poverty rate is 50 percent of the median income; in table 11A–4, it is 40 percent; in table 11A–3, rates for 50 and 40 percent of the median are shown. Incomes are adjusted by E = 0.5, where adjusted income equals actual income divided by household size to the power E. Adjusted income equals income/S^E.

Categories

All income amounts are adjusted by E = 0.5, as described above.

Market income	Earnings and cash property income.
Private transfers	Occupational pension income, alimony, child support, private interfamily transfers, and other cash income.
Universal and social transfers	Universal benefits and social insurance, including social retirement, survivors' benefits, unemployment compensation, short- and long-term disability, maternal and paternal benefits, sickness benefits, and child allowances.
Taxes	Payroll and income taxes.
Social assistance transfers	Income-tested benefits, means-tested (income- and wealth-tested) benefits, and emergency benefits, cash and near cash. The earned income tax credit in the United States and the family tax credit are counted as social assistance in these nations, not as "negative taxes."

Table 11A–2. Luxembourg Income Study Database List

Country	Historical databases	Wave I	Wave II	Wave III	Wave IV
Australia		1981	1985	1989	1994
Austria			1987		1995[a]
Belgium			1985	1988/1992	1997[a]
Canada	1971, 1975	1981	1987	1991	1994
Czech Republic				1992	1996[a]
Denmark			1987	1992	1995[b]
Finland			1987	1991	1995
France		1979/1981	1984A/1984B	1989	1994
Germany	1973, 1978	1981	1983/1984	1989	1994
Hungary				1991	1994
Ireland			1987		1995[b]
Israel		1979	1986	1992	1997[a]
Italy			1986	1991	1995
Luxembourg			1985	1991	1994
The Netherlands			1983/1986[a]/1987	1991	1994
Norway		1979	1986	1991	1995
Poland			1986	1992	1995
Portugal					1995[b]
R.O.C. Taiwan		1981	1986	1991	1995
Russia				1992	1995
Slovak Republic				1992	1996[b]
Spain		1980		1990	1995[b]
Sweden	1967, 1975	1981	1987	1992	1995
Switzerland		1982		1992	
United Kingdom	1969, 1974	1979	1986	1991	1995
United States	1969, 1974	1979	1986	1991	1994/1997[c]

a. Received; waiting to be harmonized.
b. Under negotiation.
c. State file 199567.

Table 11A–3. Poverty Rates for All Persons by Income Source

Country, year, poverty measure	Market income (A)	Column (A) + private income transfers (B)	Column (B) + universal and social transfers (C)	Column (C) – taxes (D)	Column (D) + social assistance transfers (E)	Percent change columns (A) to (E) (F)
Australia, 1994						
50 percent median income	30.3	28.6	25.6	26.1	15.7	–48.2
40 percent median income	27.8	25.8	22.8	23.0	8.0	–71.2
Canada, 1994						
50 percent median income	30.5	25.5	12.5	13.5	11.2	–63.3
40 percent median income	27.2	21.9	9.0	9.3	6.6	–75.7
France, 1989						
50 percent median income	38.1	37.1	11.9	12.5	10.2	–73.2
40 percent median income	32.9	31.7	6.8	7.3	6.0	–81.8
Germany, 1994						
50 percent median income	31.3	28.2	8.5	9.8	7.6	–75.7
40 percent median income	29.4	25.9	5.8	6.6	4.1	–86.1
The Netherlands, 1991						
50 percent median income	33.5	25.3	8.0	10.4	6.7	–80.0
40 percent median income	32.5	23.6	7.2	8.3	4.2	–87.1
Spain, 1990[a]						
50 percent median income	32.1	30.7	11.3	—	10.4	–67.6
40 percent median income	27.6	26.3	6.0	—	5.2	–81.2
Sweden, 1992						
50 percent median income	37.6	37.3	9.7	13.5	7.3	–80.6
40 percent median income	34.9	34.7	6.0	7.3	4.6	–86.8
United Kingdom, 1995						
50 percent median income	38.1	31.1	20.0	21.3	11.8	–69.0
40 percent median income	35.9	28.3	14.9	15.5	5.7	–84.1
United States, 1994						
50 percent median income	30.7	26.7	18.3	20.1	18.4	–40.1
40 percent median income	26.8	22.6	13.7	14.8	12.4	–53.7

— Not available.

a. Tax information is not available for Spain, 1990.

Note: See table 11A–1 for definitions of income categories and poverty rates.

Source: Authors' calculations.

Table 11A–4. Adult Poverty Rates by Income Source

Poverty measured at 40 percent of median-adjusted household disposable income

Country, individual category	Market income (A)	Column (A) + private income transfers (B)	Column (B) + universal and social transfers (C)	Column (C) − taxes (D)	Column (D) + social assistance transfers (E)	Percent change columns A to E (F)
Australia, 1994						
All adults (25 to 64)	19.1	17.9	17.9	18.1	6.3	-67.0
Couples with children[a]	13.0	12.6	12.6	12.9	5.7	-56.2
Single parents[b]	65.2	62.6	62.6	62.6	22.4	-65.6
Extended families[c]	16.0	15.7	15.7	15.8	3.2	-80.0
Childless adults[d]	21.0	19.3	19.3	19.5	6.3	-70.0
Elderly (65 and over)	78.0	70.1	70.1	70.1	14.4	-81.5
Canada, 1994						
All adults (25 to 64)	18.4	15.4	9.4	9.8	6.9	-62.5
Couples with children	12.8	12.2	7.0	7.3	5.3	-58.6
Single parents	56.9	54.2	46.4	46.7	29.8	-47.6
Extended families	12.0	10.8	5.9	6.3	3.5	-70.8
Childless adults	20.6	15.8	9.3	9.6	7.1	-65.5
Elderly (65 and over)	75.6	56.2	2.1	2.2	1.3	-98.3
France, 1989						
All adults (25 to 64)	21.9	21.2	5.9	6.4	5.2	-76.3
Couples with children	11.7	11.4	4.2	4.6	3.5	-70.1
Single parents	41.2	39.3	29.3	29.3	12.3	-70.1
Extended families	20.2	19.9	6.3	6.6	4.8	-76.2
Childless adults	28.9	27.9	6.1	6.8	6.2	-78.5
Elderly (65 and over)	84.2	83.8	8.9	9.5	9.1	-89.2
Germany, 1994						
All adults (25 to 64)	14.9	13.6	5.5	6.3	3.5	-76.5
Couples with children	7.2	7.0	4.3	5.3	2.7	-62.5
Single parents	57.5	53.1	45.3	49.5	32.7	-43.1

	1	2	3	4	5	6
Extended families	6.3	6.1	3.4	4.8	2.2	−65.1
Childless adults	18.5	16.5	4.8	5.3	2.9	−84.3
Elderly (65 and over)	88.6	74.8	5.1	5.1	4.4	−95.0
The Netherlands, 1991						
All adults (25 to 64)	21.1	15.6	6.5	7.7	3.6	−82.9
Couples with children	8.3	8.0	4.3	5.3	3.6	−56.6
Single parents	78.6	70.6	51.9	54.4	14.3	−81.8
Extended families	9.9	8.1	4.4	4.4	2.8	−71.7
Childless adults	28.2	19.1	6.3	7.6	3.3	−88.3
Elderly (65 and over)	91.1	61.8	3.2	3.2	3.0	−96.7
Spain, 1990[e]						
All adults (25 to 64)	19.7	18.9	5.9	—	5.4	−72.6
Couples with children	10.7	10.2	6.3	—	6.2	−42.1
Single parents	46.3	31.4	17.2	—	17.2	−62.9
Extended families	16.8	16.1	5.6	—	5.1	−69.6
Childless adults	27.7	26.7	5.5	—	4.8	−82.7
Elderly (65 and over)	68.3	64.8	6.6	—	4.6	−93.3
Sweden, 1992[f]						
All adults (25 to 64)	15.8	15.6	3.1	4.1	1.8	−88.6
Couples with children	8.5	8.4	2.4	3.2	1.4	−83.5
Single parents	34.2	31.7	6.6	8.1	1.3	−96.2
Extended families	—	—	—	—	—	—
Childless adults	19.0	19.0	3.3	4.3	2.2	−88.4
Elderly (65 and over)	89.1	89.1	1.5	2.2	1.5	−98.3
United Kingdom, 1995						
All adults (25 to 64)	25.0	20.4	14.4	15.1	5.9	−76.4
Couples with children	17.9	17.2	14.4	15.4	7.2	−59.8
Single parents	75.4	71.0	65.8	67.3	16.2	−78.5
Extended families	20.7	19.2	13.5	15.0	3.7	−82.1
Childless adults	25.6	18.2	10.3	10.6	4.4	−82.8
Elderly (65 and over)	81.1	60.3	13.5	13.8	13.8	−83.0

Table continues on next page.

Table 11A–4. Adult Poverty Rates by Income Source (continued)

Country, individual category	Market income (A)	Column (A) + private income transfers (B)	Column (B) + universal and social transfers (C)	Column (C) – taxes (D)	Column (D) + social assistance transfers (E)	Percent change in columns A to E (F)
United States, 1994						
All adults (25 to 64)	17.2	14.9	11.7	12.9	10.6	–38.4
Couples with children	9.5	9.1	7.9	9.1	6.6	–30.5
Single parents	51.8	48.3	45.1	46.9	38.3	–26.1
Extended families	21.5	20.2	17.3	18.8	14.1	–34.4
Childless adults	17.9	14.4	9.9	10.8	9.8	–45.3
Elderly (65 and over)	70.0	54.8	14.8	15.0	13.3	–81.0

— Not available.

a. Adults, 25 to 64 years old, living in households with children headed by a married or cohabiting couple with no other adults present.

b. Unmarried household heads, 25 to 64 years old, living in households with children and no other adults present.

c. Adults, 25 to 64 years old, living in households with children and adults other than the head and partner (if married or cohabiting).

d. Adults, 25 to 64 years old, living in households with no children present.

e. Tax information is not available for Spain, 1990.

f. Cannot identify extended families in Sweden, 1992.

Note: Forty percent of the median is chosen because it is almost exactly the ratio of the U.S. poverty line to the U.S. median. See table 11A–1 for definitions of income categories and poverty rates.

Source: Authors' calculations.

Table 11A–5. Estimated Population of Individuals

Country, measure	Adults, 25 to 64 years old					Elderly, 65 and over	Total
	Couples with children	Single parents	Extended families	Childless	Overall		
Australia, 1994							
Thousands	2,905	233	776	4,864	8,779	1,924	10,703
Percent of total	27.1	2.2	7.2	45.4	82.0	18.0	100.0
Canada, 1994							
Thousands	4,860	500	1,542	8,391	15,293	3,243	18,536
Percent of total	26.2	2.7	8.3	45.3	82.5	17.5	100.0
France, 1989							
Thousands	9,782	549	2,684	13,480	26,496	7,271	33,767
Percent of total	29.0	1.6	7.9	39.9	78.5	21.5	100.0
Germany, 1994							
Thousands	13,045	979	3,112	23,735	40,871	12,278	53,149
Percent of total	24.5	1.8	5.9	44.7	76.9	23.1	100.0
The Netherlands, 1991							
Thousands	2,895	191	497	4,415	7,999	1,900	9,899
Percent of total	29.2	1.9	5.0	44.6	80.8	19.2	100.0
Spain, 1990							
Thousands	5,930	110	4,676	8,040	18,755	5,321	24,077
Percent of total	24.6	0.5	19.4	33.4	77.9	22.1	100.0
Sweden, 1992							
Thousands	1,629	215	—	2,528	4,372	1,518	5,889
Percent of total	27.7	3.6	—	42.9	74.2	25.8	100.0
United Kingdom, 1995							
Thousands	9,587	1,306	1,735	15,572	28,199	8,086	36,286
Percent of total	26.4	3.6	4.8	42.9	77.7	22.3	100.0
United States, 1994							
Thousands	40,383	5,466	17,223	68,516	131,589	31,241	162,830
Percent of total	24.8	3.4	10.6	42.1	80.8	19.2	100.0

— Not available.
Source: Luxembourg Income Study. See Smeeding and others (1998).

Table 11A–6. Estimated Population of Households by Working Status

Country	Full-year, full-time	Part-time	Non-earners	Overall
Australia, 1994				
Thousands	3,219	972	793	4,985
Percent of total	64.6	19.5	15.9	100.0
Canada, 1994				
Thousands	5,629	1,771	1,099	8,499
Percent of total	66.2	20.8	12.9	100.0
Germany, 1994				
Thousands	14,802	5,534	2,639	22,975
Percent of total	64.4	24.1	11.5	100.0
The Netherlands, 1991				
Thousands	2,769	930	879	4,578
Percent of total	60.5	20.3	19.2	100.0
Sweden, 1992				
Thousands	1,642	925	253	2,820
Percent of total	58.2	32.8	9.0	100.0
United Kingdom, 1995				
Thousands	8,433	2,335	4,931	15,698
Percent of total	53.7	14.9	31.4	100.0
United States, 1994				
Thousands	53,290	15,852	8,386	77,528
Percent of total	68.7	20.4	10.8	100.0

Note: Data are not available for France or Spain.
Source: Luxembourg Income Study. See Smeeding and others (1998).

References

Aarts, Leo J. M., Richard V. Burkhauser, and Philip de Jong, eds. 1996. *Curing the Dutch Disease: An International Perspective on Disability Reform*. Aldershot, UK: Avebury Press.

Atkinson, Anthony B., and Gunnar Mogenson. 1993. *Welfare and Work Incentives: A North European Perspective*. Oxford, UK: Oxford University Press.

Atkinson, Anthony B., Lee Rainwater, and Timothy M. Smeeding. 1995. *Income Distribution in OECD Countries: The Evidence from LIS*. Paris, France: OECD.

Banting, Keith. 1997. "The Social Policy Divide: The Welfare State in Canada and the United States." In Keith Banting, George Hoberg, and Richard Simon, eds., *Degrees of Freedom: Canada and the United States in a Changing World*. Montreal and Kingston, Ontario, Canada: McGill Queens University Press.

Bradbury, Bruce. 1989. "Family Size Equivalence and Survey Evaluations of Income and Well-Being." *Journal of Social Policy* 11: 383–408.

Buhmann, B., and others. 1988. "Equivalence Scales, Well-Being, Inequality and Poverty." *Review of Income and Wealth* 34 (June): 115–42.

Burkhauser, Richard V., Timothy M. Smeeding, and Joachim Merz. 1996. "Relative Inequality and Poverty in Germany and the United States Using Alternative Equivalence Scales." *Review of Income and Wealth* 42 (December): 242–63.

Burtless, Gary. 1996. "Trends in the Level and Distribution of U.S. Living Standards: 1973–1993." *Eastern Economic Journal* 22 (Summer): 271–90.

Burtless, Gary, and Robert Haveman. 1987. "Taxes and Transfers: How Much Economic Loss?" *Challenge* (March–April): 45-51.

Cantillion, Bea, Yves Marx, and Karel van den Bosch. 1996. "Poverty in Advanced Economies: Trends and Issues." Paper presented to the Twenty-Fourth General Conference of the International Association for Research on Income and Wealth (IARIW), Norway.

Coleman, James. 1988. "Social Capital in the Creation of Human Capital." *American Journal of Sociology* 94: S95–S120.

Coleman, Richard P., Lee Rainwater, and Kent A. McClelland. 1978. *Social Standing in America: New Dimensions of Class*. New York, N.Y.: Basic Books.

Danziger, Sheldon, Robert Haveman, and Robert Plotnick. 1981. "How Income Transfer Programs Affect Work, Savings, and Income Distribution: A Critical Review." *Journal of Economic Literature* 19 (September): 975–1028.

Danziger, Sheldon, and Markus Jäntti. 2000. "Income Poverty in Advanced Countries." In Anthony B. Atkinson and François Bourguignon, eds., *Handbook on Income Distribution*. Amsterdam, Netherlands: Elsevier Science Ltd.

Danziger, Sheldon, Lee Rainwater, and Timothy M. Smeeding. 1997. "Child Well-Being in the West: Toward a More Effective Antipoverty Policy." In Giovanni Andrea Cornia and Sheldon Danziger, eds., *Child Poverty and Deprivation in the Industrialized Countries 1945–1995*. London, UK: Oxford University Press..

Förster, Michael. 1993. *Comparing Poverty in 13 OECD Countries: Traditional and Synthetic Approaches*. Studies in Social Policy Paper no. 10. OECD, Paris, France.

Gottschalk, Peter, and Timothy M. Smeeding. 2000. "Empirical Evidence on Income Inequality in Industrialized Countries." In Anthony B. Atkinson and François Bourguignon, eds., *Handbook of Income Distribution*, vol. 1. Amsterdam, Netherlands: Elsevier Science Ltd.

———. 1997. "Cross-National Comparisons of Earnings and Income Inequality." *Journal of Economic Literature* 35 (June): 633–87.

Gruber, Jonathan, and David Wise. 1998. "Social Security and Retirement: An International Review." *American Economic Review* 88 (May): 158–63.

Hagenaars, Arie, Klas De Vos, and Azghar Zaidi. 1994. "Patterns of Poverty in Europe." Paper presented to the Twenty-Third General Conference of the International Association for Research on Income and Wealth (IARIW), Canada.

Haveman, Robert. 1985. "Does the Welfare State Increase Welfare?" Inaugural Lecture, Tinbergen Chair in Economics, Department of Economics, Erasmus University, The Netherlands.

Johnson, David, and Timothy M. Smeeding. 1998. "Measuring the Trend in Inequality among Individuals and Families: Consumption or Income?" Center for Policy Research, The Maxwell School, Syracuse University, Syracuse, N.Y. Unpublished.

Jung, Kwangho, and Timothy M. Smeeding. 1999. "Income Inequality and Population Health among 18 Developed Countries." Center for Policy Research, The Maxwell School, Syracuse University, Syracuse, N.Y. Unpublished.

Kenworthy, Lane. 1998. *Do Social Welfare Policies Reduce Poverty? A Cross-National Assessment.* LIS Working Paper no. 191. Luxembourg Income Study, Differdange, Luxembourg, and Syracuse University, Syracuse, N.Y.

Lemieux, Thomas, and William MacLeod. 1998. *Supply Side Hysteresis: The Case of Canadian Unemployment Insurance.* Working Paper no. 6732. National Bureau for Economic Research, Cambridge, MA.

Moffitt, Robert. 1992. "Incentive Effects of the U.S. Welfare System: A Review." *Journal of Economic Literature* 30 (March): 1–61.

O'Connor, Inge. 1994. *A Cross-National Comparison of Education and Earnings.* LIS Working Paper no. 116. Center for Policy Research, The Maxwell School, Syracuse University, Syracuse, N.Y.

Organization for Economic Cooperation and Development (OECD). 1998. *Purchasing Power Parities.* Paris: OECD.

———. 1999. *Social Expenditures Database.* Paris: OECD.

Overbye, Einar. 1997. "Policy Responses to Household Vulnerability: The Norwegian Case in an International Context." Paper presented to the Fourth International Research Seminar on Social Security, Sigtuna, Sweden.

Rainwater, Lee. 1974. *What Money Buys: Inequality and the Social Meanings of Income.* New York, N.Y.: Basic Books.

———. 1990. *Poverty and Equivalence as Social Constructions.* LIS Working Paper no. 91. Luxembourg Income Study, Syracuse University, Syracuse, N.Y.

Ramprakash, Deo. 1995. "Poverty in Europe." *European Journal of Social Policy* 15: 161–68.

Ravallion, Martin, G. Datt, and Dominique van de Walle. 1991. "Quantifying Absolute Poverty in the Developing World." *Review of Income and Wealth* 37: 345–61.

Schmidt, Christophe, and Marek Gora. 1998. "Long-Term Unemployment, Unemployment Benefits and Social Assistance: The Polish Experience." *Empirical Economics* 23(1-2): 55–85.

Sen, Amartya. 1992. *Inequality Reexamined.* Cambridge, MA: Harvard University Press.

Skévik, Anne. 1997. "The State-Parent Relationship after Family Break-Up: Child Maintenance in Norway and Britain." Paper presented to the Fourth International Research Seminar on Social Security, Sigtuna, Sweden.

Smeeding, Timothy M. 1997a. "Poverty in Developed Countries: The Evidence from LIS." *Poverty and Human Development, 1997*. New York: United Nations.

———. 1997b. "U.S. Income Inequality in a Cross-National Perspective: Why Are We So Different?" *Looking Ahead* 19(2-3): 41–50. Reprinted in David Auerbach and Richard Belous, eds., *The Inequality Paradox: Growth of Income Disparity*. Washington, D.C.: National Policy Association.

Smeeding, Timothy M., and Joseph F. Quinn. 1998. "Cross-National Patterns of Labor Force Withdrawal." In Peter Flora, ed., *The State of Social Welfare, 1997*. London, UK: Ashgate Publishers.

Smeeding, Timothy M., and Dennis Sullivan. 1998. "Generations and the Distribution of Economic Well-Being: A Cross-National View." *American Economic Review* 88 (May): 254–58.

Smeeding, Timothy M., and others. 1998. *Poverty and Parenthood across Modern Nations: Findings from the Luxembourg Income Study*. LIS Working Paper no. 194. Differdange, Luxembourg.

Sullivan, Dennis, and Timothy M. Smeeding. 1997. "Educational Attainment and Earnings Inequality in Eight Nations." *International Journal of Education Research* 27 (6): 513–25.

Summers, Robert, and Alan Heston. 1991. "The Penn World Tables (Mark 5): An Expanded Set of International Comparisons." *Quarterly Journal of Economics* 105 (2): 327–68.

Townsend, Peter. 1979. *Poverty in the United Kingdom: A Survey of Household Resources and Standards of Living*. Berkeley, CA: University of California Press.

U.S. Bureau of the Census. 1998. *Poverty in the United States: 1997*. Current Population Reports, Series P-60, no. 201. Government Printing Office, Washington, D.C.

World Bank. 1990. *World Development Report*. New York, N.Y.: Oxford University Press.

Authors

Orazio Attanasio is a Professor of Economics at University College, London.

Alain de Janvry is a Professor in the Department of Agricultural and Resource Economics at the University of California, Berkeley.

Paul Gertler is a Professor of Economic Analysis and Policy at the Haas School of Business at the University of California, Berkeley.

Hugo A. Hopenhayn is a Professor of Economics in the Economic College at the University of Rochester.

Estelle James is a Lead Economist in the Development Economics Research Group and the World Bank Institute at the World Bank.

Steen Lau Jørgensen is a Sector Manager in the Social Protection Unit of the Human Development Network at the World Bank.

Nora Lustig is Chief of the Poverty and Inequality Advisory Unit at the Inter-American Development Bank.

Gustavo Márquez is an Economist in the Research Department at the Inter-American Development Bank.

Carmelo Mesa-Lago is a Professor of Economics at the University of Pittsburgh.

Juan Pablo Nicolini is Chairman of the Department of Economics at Universidad Torcuato di Tella, Buenos Aires.

José-Víctor Ríos-Rull is a Professor of Economics at the University of Pennsylvania.

Katherin Ross Phillips is with the Urban Institute.

Elisabeth Sadoulet is a Professor in the Department of Agricultural and Resource Economics at the University of California, Berkeley.

Timothy M. Smeeding is a Professor and Director of the Center for Policy Research at Syracuse University.

Julia Van Domelen is a Senior Economist in the Social Protection Unit of the Human Development Network at the World Bank.

Manfred Zeller is a Professor at the Institute of Rural Development at the University of Göttingen.

Index

Activities of daily living (ADLs),
Indonesia, 117–37
Administration: health care and pension
systems in Latin America and Caribbean,
199–200; of labor-intensive public works, 47
Adverse shocks: management strategies for, 6-
-10; types of, 4, 6–7. *See also* Economic
shocks; Environmental shocks;
Natural shocks; Physical shocks; Social
or political shocks
Altimir, Oscar, 23
Alvarez, Fernando, 260–61
Argentina: determinants of urban poverty in,
27–28; employment generation programs
in, 49–50, 56t; Participatory Social
Fund, 103n14; short-term training
programs, 59t; targeting in social
assistance program, 168; unemployment
insurance system, 43; wage subsidies, 48
Atkinson, Anthony B., 292
Australia, social assistance program, 169–70

Bank Rakyat Indonesia, 228
Bolivia, universal benefit system, 162
Brazil: employment generation programs in,
50, 56t; short-term training program in,
53–55, 59t; social assistance, 168–69;
social assistance reform, 202–4, 211–
12; social security system, 158;
unemployment insurance system, 43–44
Buhmann, B., 292

Chen Shaohua, 139
Chile: employment generation programs in,
51, 57t; short-term training programs
in, 53–54, 60t; social assistance
benefits, 167–68; social security
program, 157–58
China, health care services, 137–44
Cochrane, John, 115
Consumption: effect of risks on, 221–11,
224–28; household health insurance to
cover, 124–28; public subsidies as
insurance for, 135–37; risks affecting,
221–26; willingness to pay concept
related to, 114–15, 136
Consumption smoothing, 2; China's health
care system as, 140–44; financial
services for, 218; microfinance programs
for, 15–16; over periods of illness,
110; related to health insurance, 114–
15; related to illness costs in
Indonesia, 128–31; social insurance for, 110
Costa Rica: employment generation programs
in, 51, 57t; short-term training program
in, 53, 55, 60–61t; social assistance
reform, 204–6, 211–12
Credit: importance of access to, 223–26;
offered by microfinance institutions,
234; provided by microfinance
institutions, 229, 232

Data sources: analysis of China's health
care services, 139; analysis of
Indonesian health care system, 116–17;
analysis of poverty rates in nine
developed countries, 270–71; OECD
social expenditures data base, 274n9; on
poverty and inequality, 23–24, 36
Deaton, Angus, 115, 126, 129
Decentralization: as characteristic of
social funds, 101; social funds as
support for, 96
Developed countries: provision of health
insurance in, 229; social protection for
the poor in, 267–94
Developing countries: financing of old age
security, 150–53; people without social
security in, 149–50; social security
programs in, 14–15, 149–60
Dow, William, 117

Economic growth: as determinant of change
in inequality, 35–36; growth spells and

rates in Latin America *(1970-94)*, 23–
    25; sectoral composition of, 30–31
Economic shocks: effect on levels of
    poverty, 3t; employment generation
    programs to alleviate effects of, 46–
    51; types of, 4, 6–7
Education: effect on levels of urban
    poverty, 30; relation to poverty status,
    270, 283–85; social fund investment in, 102
Employment generation programs: labor-
    intensive public works, 46–48; wage
    subsidies, 48–51
Environmental shocks, 6–7

Financial services: for consumption
    smoothing, 218; effects on household
    outcomes, 217; short- and long-term
    impact of access to, 226

Gertler, Paul, 110, 113, 117, 136
Government: action to prevent adverse
    shocks, 8; employment generation
    programs of, 46–51; as insurer of last
    resort, 225; intervention for social
    protection, 1; intervention in health
    care markets, 111, 113; subsidies to
    microfinance institutions, 235
Grameen Bank, 228
Gruber, Jonathan, 110

Hazell, P. B. R., 223n6
Health care markets: government intervention
    in, 111
Health care systems: China, 137–44;
    Indonesia, 117–37; Latin America and
    Caribbean, 177–82, 185, 196–200
Health status, Indonesia, 115
Hong Kong: means-tested social assistance, 171
Hopenhayn, Hugo, 45
Household survey design, 261–63

Income: distribution in health care and
    pensions in LAC, 198–99; labor-
    intensive public works programs as
    support for, 46; risks affecting
    generation of, 219–20, 223–26; short-
    term training programs for transfer of, 53–
    54
Indonesia: analysis of health care system,
    117–37; health care delivery system,
    116; health status indicators, 115

Inequality: change related to length of
    economic regime, 35–36; determinants of
    change in, 33–35; effect of economic
    growth on, 24–26; income elasticities
    of, 36–37; initial level of urban, 28–30
Insurance, government-provided: extension of
    model, 260–61; implications of model
    for survey design, 261–63; model of,
    241–48; simple insurance crowds out
    private insurance, 248–59;
    sophisticated scheme avoiding private
    insurance, 259–60
Insurance, private: crowded out by simple
    government insurance, 249–59; offered
    by microfinance institutions, 234

Jamaica: employment generation programs in,
    57–58t; short-term training program in,
    53, 55, 61t
Jermann, Urban, 260–61

Kochar, Anjini, 110
Krueger, Dirk, 251

Labor market: wage subsidies distort, 49.
    See also Unemployment insurance
Life insurance: offered by microfinance
    institutions, 222, 233
Ligon, Ethan, 251, 260–61

Macroeconomic performance: characteristics
    of, 25–26; effect on urban and rural
    poverty, 26–27, 31; volatility in Latin
    America, 41
Market failure: causes of, 8; of private
    health insurance, 111
Mazza, Jacqueline, 44n2
Mexico: employment generation programs in,
    51, 58t; school attendance as criterion
    under *Progresa* program, 170; short-term
    training programs in, 52–53, 55, 61t;
    targeting of needy in *Progresa* program,
    168; unemployment insurance system, 43–
    44
MFIs. *See* Microfinance institutions (MFIs)
Microfinance institutions (MFIs): adaptation
    of services, 235; consumption smoothing
    role, 15–16; credit offered by, 234;
    potential for, 234; privately financed
    safety net services, 235; recent
    innovations in, 228–34; services of, 15-

-16, 217–18. *See also* Financial services
Moffitt, Robert, 288
Molyneaux, Jack, 117, 136
Moral hazard: with government as insurer of
 last resort, 225; microfinance loan
 repayment, 224; in social assistance
 programs, 166–67
Morduch, Jonathan, 129

Natural shocks, 6–7
Nicolini, Juan Pablo, 45

Optimal contract theory: optimal
 unemployment insurance contracts under,
 64, 66–77; risks of contracts under, 64

Payroll taxes: to finance social security,
 151–52; problems of collection, 154–55
Pension systems, Latin America and
 Caribbean, 182–85; administration of
 social assistance pensions, 200–202;
 financial aid to extend, 196–97; reform
 of, 45; social assistance grants for, 185–92
Perri, Fabrizio, 251
Peru: employment generation programs in, 51,
 58t; short-term training programs in, 61t
Physical shocks, 6–7
Pistaferri, L., 263n19
Poor people: nonparticipation in old age
 security, 155–58; social funds target,
 97–98; social protection in developed
 countries for, 267–94; willingness to
 pay for financial services, 234–35
Poverty: conceptual differences in rich and
 poor countries, 290–94; determinants in
 Argentina of urban, 27–28; determinants
 of change in rural, 31–33; determinants
 of change in urban, 26–30; effect of
 economic growth rates on, 24–26;
 effects of social protection on, 275–78;
 incidence in Latin America (*1980s-1990s*),
 212–13; income elasticities of, 36–37; in Latin
 American urban informal sector, 212–13;
 prevention among older women of, 163–65;
 relative and absolute, 293–94; role of initial
 level of urban, 30
Poverty rates: by education level in seven
 developed countries, 270, 283–85; of
 households in nine developed countries,
 269–72, 276–77; of individuals in
 seven developed countries, 270–77

Rainwater, Lee, 292
Ravallion, Martin, 28, 139
Recession: impact on poverty, 26–27, 37
Risk management: social funds in framework
 of, 99–104; strategies, 6–10
Risks: differences faced by unemployed
 workers, 64–73; effect on consumption,
 221–22, 224–28; effect on income
 generation, 219–20, 223–24; main
 sources of, 6–7; microfinance
 institutions responding to, 234; risk
 pooling in China, 138; using social
 funds to mitigate, 102–4
Romania, Social Development Fund, 103n14
Rosenzweig, Mark, 219
Rothschild, Michael, 111n7

Safety net, proposed, 240–41
Savings services: provided by microfinance
 institutions, 229–31
Singapore: means-tested social assistance, 171
Smeeding, Timothy, 292
Social assistance: criteria for candidates,
 169–70; effect on poverty in United
 Kingdom, 272, 299t; legal entitlement in
 Latin America and Caribbean, 183–85;
 means-tested and noncontributory, 165–
 71; role of extended family in, 170–71;
 self-selection, 169; spending for, 166
Social assistance, Latin America and
 Caribbean: benefits, 187, 190–92;
 coordination with other programs, 199–
 200; costs, 192–94; effect on income
 distribution, 198–99; entitlement
 conditions for health care and pensions,
 185–89; financial aid to low-income and
 special labor groups, 196–97; formal
 and informal, 175–77; for pensions, 185-
 -92; problems and recommendations, 206–
 11, 206–12; reform in Brazil and Costa
 Rica, 202–6, 211–12; revenue sources, 194–
 96
Social capital, 105–6
Social funds: adaptation to local
 circumstances, 92, 93, 104–6;
 contribution to local capacity, 104–6;
 countries with, 92–95; definition and
 characteristics of, 13, 91–95, 101;
 difference from public works programs,
 100; effectiveness of, 96–99, 101–2;
 financing of, 92; investment in

education, 102; investments of, 93, 97–
98, 103–4; objectives of, 95–96;
recommended design of, 104–6; in risk
management framework, 99–102; as social
protection, 94–95, 99; strategies to
consider, 103–4; trends in, 96
Social insurance: aggregate expense in
developed countries, 287–89; benefits
and premiums, 112–13; benefits in low-
income countries, 113; China's health
care insurance, 138; design to include
consumption smoothing mechanism, 110; in
developing countries, 111–12;
disability insurance to smooth
consumption resulting from illness, 132–
35; effect on labor markets of, 287–88;
effect on poverty in developed
countries, 272–73, 299t;
nonsustainability of pay-as-you-go
systems, 287–89; public medical care
insurance to smooth consumption, 135–37
Social or political shocks, 6–7
Social protection: antipoverty effects in
nine developed countries, 272–73;
defined, 1; effect on poverty of, 275–
83; pattern in nine developed
countries, 286; for the poor, 1–2;
reduction in poverty related to, 2, 274;
spending in United States for, 274. *See
also* Social funds
Social security programs: contribution
patterns, 155–58; correlation of per
capita income and coverage, 153–54;
coverage in developing countries, 14–
15, 149–60; effect of noncontributory
social assistance on, 166–67;
multipillar reforms, 157–58; people not
insured under, 152–53; policy changes
to increase coverage, 159–60; rationale
for mandatory old age, 154; uninsured
people under, 149–50; universal
benefits, 161–62; voluntary retirement
savings contributions, 161
Social security systems: financed by payroll
tax contributions, 151–52; to include
coverage of women, 163–65; policy
changes to increase coverage, 159–60;
uninsured under, 149–53; voluntary and
universal systems outside contributions,
160–62

Solon, Orville, 113
South Africa, social assistance, 170
Stiglitz, Joseph, 111n7
Subsidies: distort labor market, 49;
insurance value of public medical care,
135–37; risk reduction function, 112;
wage subsidies in Argentina, 48
Subsidies: to microfinance institutions, 235

Taxation: evasion of payroll tax, 154–55,
161; properties of progressive, 240–41.
See also Payroll taxes
Thomas, Jonathan, 251, 260–61
Townsend, Robert, 110, 115, 128, 129
Training programs, short-term, 51–55

Unemployment insurance: coverage under, 45;
financing in Latin America, 44; proposed
design to monitor employment status of
beneficiaries, 85–88; reemployment
hazard rates in, 64; in some Latin
American countries, 41–43
Unemployment insurance, optimal: related to
workers with high risk of unemployment,
85; risk exposure with cyclical
variation, 73–84; with two sources of
heterogeneity, 65–73, 83–84
United Kingdom, social assistance programs,
165–66
Uruguay: social assistance, 168–69; social
security system, 158; unemployment
insurance system, 43–44

Venezuela, unemployment insurance system, 43
Verdera, Francisco, 49

Well-being: conceptual differences between
rich and poor countries, 290–94;
defined, 290; policy interventions to
improve, 2
West, Lorraine, 140
Willingness to pay, 114–15, 136, 227, 234–35
Wolpin, Kenneth, 219
Workfare, 47
World Bank, Social Funds *2000* Impact
Evaluation Study, 98–99
Worrall, Tim, 251, 260–61